Space and Time in Epic Theater

Studies in German Literature, Linguistics, and Culture

Edited by James Hardin
(*South Carolina*)

Sarah Bryant-Bertail

SPACE AND TIME
IN EPIC THEATER

THE BRECHTIAN LEGACY

CAMDEN HOUSE

First published 2000
by Camden House

Camden House is an imprint of Boydell & Brewer Inc.
PO Box 41026, Rochester, NY 14604–4126 USA
and of Boydell & Brewer Limited
PO Box 9, Woodbridge, Suffolk IP12 3DF, UK

ISBN: 1–57113–186–8

Library of Congress Cataloging-in-Publication Data

Bryant-Bertail, Sarah.
   Space and time in epic theater : the Brechtian legacy / Sarah Bryant-Bertail.
      p. cm. – (Studies in German literature, linguistics, and culture)
   Includes bibliographical references and index.
   ISBN 1-57113-186-8 (alk. paper)
   1. European drama—20th century—History and criticism. 2. European
   drama—19th century—History and criticism. 3. Space and time in literature.
   4. Brecht, Bertolt, 1898-1956—Influence. I. Title II. Studies in German
   literature, linguistics, and culture
   (Unnumbered)

   PN1851 .B79 2000
   792.9'5—dc21

                                                                    99-058828

A catalogue record for this title is available from the British Library.

This publication is printed on acid-free paper.
Printed in the United States of America

to Georges Bertail, Jessica Bryant-Bertail,
and the memory of
Quince Phillips Bryant, 1894–1995, and
Emmett Phillips Bryant, M.D., 1918–1988

Contents

Acknowledgments

THIS BOOK HAS BEEN IN THE MAKING for several years, and I would like to acknowledge a number of agencies and people who have helped me along the way. I thank the following for providing grants to support my travel, research, and time off from teaching: the National Endowment for the Humanities, the Goethe Institute, the International Research Exchange Fund, the American Council of Learned Societies, and the Universities of Minnesota, Washington, and South Carolina.

Fellow scholars who have provided counsel, inspiration, and encouragement and read earlier versions of this study over the years are Wlad Godzich, Samuel Weber, Göran Stockenström, Dennis Kennedy, Thomas Postlewait, Terje Leiren, Cynthia Steele, Eli Rozik, Janelle Reinelt, Antony Tatlow and the late Michael Quinn. I wish to give special thanks to my editors, James Hardin and James Walker of Camden House, for their advice, patience, friendly working style, and belief in this project.

For sharing their material or helping me obtain documentation on the productions analyzed in this book I would like to thank Virginia Scott, Marvin Carlson, Mark Bly, Brian Singleton, Josette Féral, Denis Salter, Mary Angiolillo, Georges Baal, Gretchen Heath, Florian Nelle, Vessela and Michael Warner. Thanks also to indexer Grainne Farren.

For providing photos and other documentation I thank the Guthrie Theatre in Minneapolis, photographer Helga Kneidl in Berlin, the Théâtre du Soleil and photographer Michèle Laurent in Paris, and the Stadtsbibliothek, Bertolt-Brecht-Archiv, and Erwin-Piscator-Center, in Berlin.

The chapter on *Les Atrides* is a revised version of my article, "Gender, Empire, and Body Politic as Mise en Scène: Mnouchkine's *Les Atrides*," *Theatre Journal* 46 (March 1994):1–30. The chapter on *Schwejk* is an expanded version of *"The Adventures of the Good Soldier Schwejk* as Dialectical Theater," in *The Performance of Power: Theatrical Discourse and Politics,* edited by Sue-Ellen Case and Janelle Reinelt (Iowa City: University of Iowa Press, 1991).

I wish to express my gratitude to my graduate students at the University of Washington, who have been a constant source of inspiration and good cheer. Finally, this book would never have been possible without the love and support of my husband Georges Bertail and daughter Jessica Bryant-Bertail, and my sisters Katie Sparks, Phyllis Loe, and Gail Deml.

S. B.-B.
Trinity College Dublin,
May 2000

Introduction: Spatio-temporality as Sign in Epic Theater

on the question of *realism:* the usual view is that the more easily reality can be recognised in a work of art, the more realistic it is. against this i would like to set up the equation that the more recognisably reality is mastered in the work of art, the more realistic it is. straightforward recognition of reality is often impeded by a presentation which shows how to master it. . . . the artist who is a realist . . . exposes all the veils and deceptions that obscure reality and intervenes in his public's real actions.

— Bertolt Brecht[1]

What Brechtian dramaturgy postulates is that today at least, the responsibility of a dramatic art is *not so much to express reality as to signify it.*

— Roland Barthes[2]

THE FRENCH CRITIC ROLAND BARTHES had just witnessed the Berliner Ensemble's renowned touring production of *Mother Courage,* directed by Bertolt Brecht, which appeared at the Théâtre des Nations in Paris in 1954. Barthes's phrase above is from one of many essays on Brecht to appear in *Théâtre populaire,* the journal through which Barthes became France's foremost defender and interpreter of the theory and practice of epic theater. In this essay he recognizes the affinity between the principles of epic theater and those of semiotics, defined as the study of how signs communicate meaning in society. That affinity is the starting point of this book.

Jean-Paul Sartre notes that the advent of film in the early twentieth century did not destroy the theater, as had been feared, but forced it to give up naturalism and become critically self-aware of its unique ability to represent time through concrete spatial images and space through temporal ones — and thus to show how the historical consciousness of a society is produced. That is, it was realized that theater is able not only to naively *reflect* how the culture imagines its own temporal existence but also to *critique* the process of producing these images. Sartre discerned that in epic theater the whole theatrical apparatus became dialectical, with each element acting as a signifying language in its own way.[3] This book aims to show that the dynamic force of this dialectic is epic theater's representation of space and time, its *spatio-temporality.* Of all theatrical practices in this century, epic theater has seized spatio-temporality in a more theatrically, politically, and theoretically productive way than any other. Today's spectators, informed directly or indirectly by epic theater, can look at all theater and other spectacular media in a new way: as a semiotic process through which space and time are *produced.*

Barthes's wide-ranging work has inspired the investigation of three interconnecting areas that are the focus of this book: (1) the principles and practice of epic theater, (2) the representation of space and time in theater performance, and (3) a historically based semiotics that joins productively with other critical practices. These three areas will be explored in the performance of epic theater as practiced by its cofounders Brecht and the director and scene designer Erwin Piscator, and continued by contemporary artists and spectators.

Defining Epic Theater

In the 1920s Brecht and Piscator coined the term *epic theater* to distinguish their practice from what they called the *dramatic theater,* which replicated the view of a single individual at one point in time and space, a tradition that had dominated Western theater since the Renaissance. They contended that this tradition, which Brecht traced back to Aristotle, rendered theater incapable of representing larger realities beyond the illusory world of the play: the cataclysms of war, revolution, social and economic conflict and change, and new technology. As the preeminent "dramatic theater" of the late nineteenth and early twentieth centuries, the theater of naturalism, and to a lesser extreme the "poetic realism" of Ibsen and Chekhov, modeled itself on the scientific method so exalted in the nineteenth century: the stage became a kind of sociological laboratory, demonstrating a "slice of life" in order to typify and isolate particular social and economic problems so objectively that the spectators could understand and then solve them. Brecht and Piscator, however, believed that the naturalistic theater failed in this task because its seeming objectivity was still unified around the limited perspective of the single individual — a mode of representation by then so habitual that others were hard to imagine. Both collaboratively and individually Brecht and Piscator sought alternatives to this perspective, rejecting the doctrine of the three unities and drawing inspiration from popular film, cabaret, puppet theater, the music hall, the circus, Berlin Dada, Russian constructivism, and a legacy of dramatic works that will be outlined below.

Piscator and Brecht agreed that the ideological basis of epic stage practice was Marx's historical materialism. This practice called for the relating of stage events to the material situation of the spectators and characters; the theater was to demystify the operation of social, economic, and political forces by showing how certain orders of reality had developed historically and were perpetuated. This demonstration meant arming actors and spectators with *disillusionment,* not as a helpless state of mind but as an active critical practice — *a semiotics* by which to critique the theatrical apparatus. Piscator and Brecht also followed Marx in showing that political reality was often produced by flamboyantly theatrical means: Marx's *The Eighteenth Brumaire of Louis Bonaparte* chronicles the process through which the French bourgeois state was legitimized, exposing it step by step with incisive humor as a splendid *coup de théâtre.*[4] If theatrical means were used in gaining real political power, then the epic theater could reveal the working of this machinery of illusion.

The first definitive epic theater production for both Brecht and Piscator was *The Good Soldier Schwejk* in 1928 at the Piscator-Bühne in Berlin, which is the subject of Chapter 1. *Schwejk* was directed by Piscator, with Brecht helping to adapt the script from Jaroslav Hašek's great antiheroic novel set during the First World War. In collaboration with others, Piscator and Brecht dealt with the definitive problems of epic theater: how to structure epic time and space, how to represent characters as members of a class, war's effect on the economy and the social hierarchy and vice versa, the impact of technology, the roles of the church and the law, and the ideological discourses that rationalized what was happening. The 1928 *Schwejk* is the prototype of epic theater: a critical demonstration of twentieth-century human work in progress, a narrating podium that used not only the old, aristocratic-based media of actors and pictorial set but also the new media of the conveyor-belt stage, films, slides, loudspeakers, electric signs, and the radio, phonograph, and telegraph.

That Brecht's name has become synonymous with epic theater is understandable, since he has been the major force in defining it through his stage practice and theoretical writings over the past seventy years. His 1949 production of *Mother Courage* is doubtless his most influential work, not only immediately through its tours but also, over the long term, through the publication of its extensive photographic and textual documentation.[5] In this staging, discussed in Chapter 2, material objects, human bodies, and the bodies of animals are circulated as signs through both visible and invisible space, representing war as a vortex economy that swallows up every living and nonliving thing, reifies it, and "orders" it into self-destruction. Considering that a main aim in *Mother Courage* and Brecht's other works was to critique and historically frame the cherished bourgeois notions of the autonomous individual, the hero, and the monster, it is ironic that there is such a persistent tendency to think of Brecht as a giant force unto himself and either adulate or vilify him.[6] Brecht above all artists did not work in a historical vacuum but was extremely knowledgeable about the dramatic works and stage traditions preceding and contemporary with him. He and his allies thought of themselves as one generation contributing to the collective building of a theater that could address the crucial issues of its time with intelligence and artistic excellence. This task had begun long before him and would continue after him as a movable *theory-in-practice* rather than a style fixed and complete.

The Epic Legacy

In its aims of presenting history from conflicting class perspectives and exposing powerful ideologies rather than simply reproducing them, the epic theater is part of a German counter-tradition beginning with the *Sturm und Drang* dramatists of the 1770s, who emulated Shakespeare's disregard of the three unities and rebelled against neoclassic drama and its aristocratic values. The presentation of reality from contradictory class perspectives is strikingly evident in Jacob Michael Reinhold Lenz's *The Tutor* of 1774, which is why Brecht was drawn to adapt and direct it for the Berliner Ensemble in 1950. In framing Lenz's play as historical parable, Brecht warns of the need to recall the past so that the "ABCs of German Misery" will not be passed on to the future, an important message for the newly founded German Democratic Republic. This adaptation, its rehearsal process, and its performance are explored in Chapter 3.

The epic legacy in Germany leads from Lenz directly to Georg Büchner's works of the 1830s: his revolutionary essays; the plays *Woyzeck, Danton's Death,* and *Leonce and Lena;* and the novella *Lenz.* The novella is clear evidence of Büchner's admiration and empathy for his brilliant young predecessor; it is based on an eye-witness account of Lenz's descent into mental illness and isolation. JoAnne Akalaitis's 1988 adaptation *Leon and Lena (& lenz)* at the Guthrie Theatre in Minneapolis, discussed in Chapter 5, was an epic montage of two primary spatio-temporal dimensions: *Leon and Lena* was acted on a contemporary set evoking that of the television program *Dallas,* while the eighteenth-century chronicle of *Lenz* unrolled as a silent, black-and-white, expressionistic film on large screens suspended above the "live" action on stage.

Brecht himself also considered the English Restoration comedies and Strindberg's nineteenth-century history plays[7] important to the development of epic theater. As will be argued in Chapter 5, Ibsen's great poetic-satiric-historic-folkloric play *Peer Gynt* of 1867 is also epic in both the traditional and the Brechtian senses. It is an intentionally dialectical critique of the social and philosophical assumptions of the nineteenth century. Two contemporary stagings attest to *Peer Gynt*'s fundamentally epic spatio-temporal structure: Peter Stein's overtly epic, neo-Marxist production in Berlin at the Schaubühne am Hallischen Ufer in 1971, and a 1990s production in India directed by the postcolonial theater scholar Rustom Bharucha, who was drawn to the folk and epic elements of *Peer Gynt* and to its "translatability" into the Indian artistic context, where it became an effective medium of social and political critique.

At the turn of the twentieth century the plays and cabaret ballads of Frank Wedekind would also contribute to the epic legacy.[8] Wedekind was idolized by Brecht and his generation of young artists disillusioned and radicalized by the First World War, the 1917 Bolshevik Revolution, the crushing of the 1919 Spartakus Revolt in Germany, the abdication of the Kaiser, the unstable Weimar Republic that followed, and its collapse with the rise of fascism. Yet these traumatic years also saw many new artistic and intellectual movements that quickly became international in scope. Cross-cultural exchange between Asian and Western theater was an important facet of the new internationalism. Brecht and Piscator, Artaud, Meyerhold, Yeats, and many other European and American artists began to borrow from classical Asian theater at the same time that Western-style realistic "spoken drama" took hold in China, Japan, and India. Chapter 6 deals with Ariane Mnouchkine's 1991–92 tetralogy *Les Atrides,* which added Euripides' *Iphigenia at Aulis* to Aeschylus's *Oresteia* with dance, costumes, and music inspired by India's Kathakali theater. Mnouchkine, in more than thirty years as director of the Théâtre du Soleil in Paris, has remained strongly epic in her basic tenets while adapting them to new political, social, and artistic circumstances. Her aim in staging Western classics through forms adapted from Asian theater is the same as was Brecht's: to subject these canonized texts to the *Verfremdungseffekt* so that the audience may hear their *stories* anew, though unlike Brecht, Mnouchkine tries to get as near as possible to the original texts and does not add to them. In *Les Atrides* the sexual and racial violence of the founding myth of Western culture becomes apparent, and the *Oresteia* is revealed as a playing out and legitimization of power relations still in place today.

As in the past, the principles of epic theater continue to draw politically engaged artists who want to stage history as eminently changeable, a continuing human work capable of being rewritten. Through the showcase of the Berliner Ensemble and the publication of Brecht's plays and theories, these principles have been disseminated widely and, consciously or not, have been adopted and reintegrated with other practices by theater and film artists around the world who share a commitment to social and political critique.[9] The principles of epic theory-in-practice have been taken up in the work of contemporary playwrights, including socialist feminist Caryl Churchill's *Vinegar Tom, Cloud Nine, Mad Forest,* and *Fen;*[10] the "gay fantasia" of Tony Kushner's *Angels in America* and *Perestroika;* Suzan-Lori Parks' *The Death of the Last Black Man in the Whole Entire World;* Luis Valdez's *Los Vendidos;* the plays of Edward Bond and Howard Brenton; the documentary performance art of Anna Deavere Smith; and the work of feminist, minority, and gay and lesbian groups such as the Monstrous Regiment, Split Britches, and Spiderwoman. Major directors whose work has been profoundly influenced by epic theater include Ariane Mnouchkine, her compatriots Roger Planchon and the late Antoine Vitez, Giorgio Strehler of the Piccolo Teatro of Milan, Peter Stein of the Berlin Schaubühne, and, in the United States, Augusto Boal with his Theater of Oppression, Jo-Anne Akalaitis, Judith Malina, and the late Julian Beck.

Since the 1970s artists and scholars in Africa, Asia, and Latin America have also embraced the plays and stage practices of epic theater, incorporating them with indigenous performance traditions. In Latin America epic theater is by far the most widely used model for the theaters of liberation collectively called El Teatro Nuevo.[11] In Africa *Sizwe Banzi is Dead,* the collaborative work of Athol Fugard, John Kani, and Winston Ntshona, is a prime example of the effectiveness of epic spatio-temporal structure, exposing apartheid as a knot of racial, economic, political, and personal injustices — a set of arbitrary semiotic codes of color marking difference. In Asia, Africa, and Latin America directors, playwrights, performers, and scholars have often noted that the epic theater seems more compatible with their own performance traditions than with those in the West — it is already at home.[12]

Thus the epic legacy is not a matter of one formula followed by all but a set of basic principles and a tradition of texts and performances that carry on a dialogue with each other and with their audiences, a cross-historical dialogue that nonetheless focuses on the specific historical context of each work, while also allowing it to engage with new contexts as they emerge. Epic texts and performances are ultimately concerned with *critiquing their specific historical situation.* They are anything but "timeless," and herein is their strength.

Definition of Theatrical Spatio-temporality

The definition of theatrical spatio-temporality — the representation of space and time — employed in this book draws inspiration from the work of the philosophers, literary critics, and theater semioticians discussed in this essay yet differs from many in recognizing both the aesthetic and historical functions of the sign. To recognize both functions is desirable in approaching all theater, but for epic theater it is crucial, because the dialectic of these two functions is the raison d'être and critical perspective of the performance itself.

For all theater, spatio-temporality unfolds as a multi-dimensional event in each performance, concretely staging historical agency for that particular moment. This dynamic interweaving of space and time is the event of signification. Space is represented by temporal forms and time by spatial ones. Space and time are thus not preexisting containers for the dramatic event but are themselves the event — a journey toward meaning. Theatrical space is not just the set, the fictional locale, or the theater building but the way in which these present themselves through time, interrelating rhythmically with each other and with the dialogue, sound, and light to create a spatiality. Likewise, theatrical time is not just a series of connected units — minutes, hours, acts, and scenes — but the process by which temporal dimensions and rhythms are revealed through spatial images. The interweaving of the signifiers of space and time constitutes the work's spatio-temporality.

Spatio-temporality is signified through dialogue, stage directions, the unfolding scenic and lighting design, the movement and placement of actors and objects, the theater's architecture and social function, and the historical context of the performance. What distinguishes epic theater is that its signification of space and time is exposed as an apparatus at work, as the staging of historicity itself. The dramatic theater disguises its materiality, melting all the signs together into a synthesis, a *Gesamtkunstwerk* (collective work of art) that aims to envelop the spectator in an illusory world, whereas epic theater holds up semiosis for analysis: the elements of dialogue, scene design, lighting, music, costume, sound, and actors' movement are separated and set into conflict. As always in theater, spatio-temporality is the means through which ideology is codified, but epic theater relentlessly exposes the volatility of these codes: one space-time construct may encode ideological systems that are antithetical to each other. Epic theater thus draws our attention to the contradictions within and among these ideologies rather than trying to reconcile them by submerging them under one seamless aesthetic effect.

Space and Time in the Philosophical and Critical Tradition

A basic tenet of this book is that the key to epic theater's continuing usefulness for politically engaged artists is its dynamic, self-aware representation of space, time, and history. The tradition set by the Greek geometrician Euclid and the seventeenth-century physicist Isaac Newton, saw time, and especially space, as stable geometric elements divided into measurable units, the universe as a series of containers within containers, and every action as having an equal reaction. The philosopher Immanuel Kant believed that space and time are not entities in themselves but functions of the human mind. That is, we perceive our *interior* self-awareness — our soul — as time and all *exterior* to this as space, which obeys the laws of geometry. Kant's distinction between exterior and interior was absolute; only through these, he thought, can we perceive phenomena as *ordered* in space (near or far, above or below) and time (before, after, or simultaneous). Kant took space and time to be universal human forms of consciousness *prior* to all experience:

> We reach out to things and see them located in external space. . . .
> There is [also] an internal sense by which the mind is aware of itself.
> . . . This sense does not present the soul as an object to be observed.
> . . . The soul's operations pertain to the relationships of time. Time
> cannot appear as an external matter any more than space can appear to
> be something within.[13]

In *The Philosophy of History*, Hegel attempts to historicize Kant's recognition of the preeminence of space and time as forms of cognition.[14] Hegel believed that the Idea developing in space is Nature, while the Idea developing in time is Spirit. The latter process is History, which is a movement of the Idea out of the geometrical space of Nature.[15] Thus Hegel does not actually abandon Kant's valuation of space as a kind of exterior *matter* or body and time as the animate human mind, *soul,* or spirit.

To Hegel "historical man," epitomized by Napoleon, is the one in whom the potentialities of the time are concentrated. America was the absolute "land of the future" and represented the end of the world-historical process, through which "the history of the races" would unfold. In Hegel's view, Kant had tried to examine human understanding before he looked at the nature of things; Hegel characterizes Kant as "a scholar who wanted to learn to swim before going into the water" (xvi). In response to Kant's contentions that a thing can be "in itself" outside of human cognition and that God is humanly unthinkable in his essence, Hegel answered that even God is not "in himself" or beyond human thought (xvi). History to Hegel is the progressing self-determination of the Idea and of the Spirit. Yet, like Kant's *soul* or "mind aware of itself," Hegel's Spirit is free in its *inner* nature, not in its outer one, which is the world as exterior objects, including the human body as an object. With unapologetic racial chauvinism Hegel wrote: "In Oriental civilization, one was free; in Greece and Rome some were free, while in Germanic/Anglo-Saxon civilization all are free" (xxii–xxiii). Even Marx succumbed to the Hegelian temptation of universality, but Marx rejected the idea of Freedom.

To Hegel, Space is the "Idea outside itself," while Time is the time of consciousness; through Time the Spirit or consciousness empties and externalizes itself. Interestingly, Hegel sees two types of time, one as the time of Nature bound to physicality and space, and the other as the time of the Spirit, i.e., the time in which the Spirit develops. Time is to Spirit as Logical Structure is to Idea (xxii). Hegel's concept of History as the *free* progression of the Spirit through historical time would be critiqued not only by Marx, Ibsen, Brecht, and other moderns but much earlier by the playwright Georg Büchner as a myth and an illusion imposed on experience. While to Hegel time is the element wherein the Spirit of Freedom realizes itself, Büchner's characters experience time as a torture of spatial emptiness from which they cannot escape. Here, time is the physical manifestation of nothingness.

The twentieth-century phenomenologist Gaston Bachelard critiques Kant's reliance on what Bachelard calls the "myth of inside and outside" typical of the philosophical tradition that sees the cosmos as a series of *containers*, as did Euclid and Newton. Bachelard asserts that the values Kant placed on space and time are actually reversed in most people's thinking (including that of Kant himself); that is, we perceive our psyche in spatial terms as "inner" and the world in temporal ones as "outer." In fact, Bachelard notes, the relation of space and time in human cognition is not a balanced one; instead, space is the dominant mode, while time is perceived only through space. In our psychic imagination

> space is everything. . . . Memory . . . does not record concrete duration. . . . We are unable to relive duration. . . . We can only think of it, in the line of an abstract time . . . deprived of all thickness. . . All we know is a sequence of fixations in the spaces of the being's stability — a being who does not want to melt away, and who, . . . when he sets out in search of things past, wants time to "suspend" its flight. In its countless alveoli space contains compressed time.[16]

To Bachelard "the myth of inside and outside" is the unacknow-
ledged model for philosophy's concepts of being and nonbeing. Citing
the critic Jean Hippolite, Bachelard takes a presciently deconstructive
view of signification:

> You feel the full significance of this myth [of inside and outside] in
> alienation, which is founded on these two terms. Beyond what is ex-
> pressed in their formal opposition lie alienation and hostility between
> the two.[17]

"And so," says Bachelard, "simple geometrical opposition becomes
tinged with aggressivity. Formal opposition is incapable of remaining
calm." "One of these terms always weakens the other," because one is
"spoken so forcefully" that the terms of any problem are "sharply
summarized in a geometrical fixation," resulting in a *dogmatization of
philosophemes.*" He proposes instead that inside and outside are two
poles of a *dialectical metaphor,* and that human existence represents a
spiral with countless *invertible dynamisms:* "One no longer knows . . .
whether one is running toward the center or escaping. . . . Thus the
spiraled being who, from outside, appears to be a well-invested center,
will never reach his center. . . . Sometimes [too] the prison is on the
outside" (212–215).

Clearly taking up Hegel's attempt to historicize Kant's ideas of
space and time, Bachelard posits that the imagination is a moving spiral
connecting space to time; that is, the individual first rests in a sense of
the self as an interior space but then is moved by a need to connect to
the world, which is sensed as exterior time or *history.* This moving dialectic connecting time and space is exemplified for Bachelard in the image and metaphor of the *road,* and experience is seen as a kind of
mapmaking (10–11).

For Bachelard this is a "writing" and "reading" of and through
space. He did not deal with the fact that spatial and temporal perceptions are culturally specific, but he would help open the way for others
who do, such as the geographer Yi Fu Tuan,[18] the phenomenologist
Maurice Merleau-Ponty,[19] and the sociologist Michel de Certeau.[20] All
are concerned with *topographies:* modes of perceiving the physical and
social spaces in which we live.

Mikhail Bakhtin, like Bachelard, sees Einstein's theory of relativity
as a major catalyst for the shift away from thinking of space and time as
separate entities.[21] Bakhtin differentiates between his own concept of
the *chronotope* and Kant's definition of space and time as preexistent
universal forms allowing human consciousness to emerge. He defines
the chronotope as

literally, 'time space,' . . . the intrinsic connectedness of temporal and spatial relationships . . . artistically expressed in literature. . . . Time . . . thickens, takes on flesh, becomes artistically visible; likewise, space becomes charged and responsive to the movements of time, plot and history.[22]

Bakhtin's concept of the chronotope is highly applicable to theater, because the interrelation of space and time is immediate and concrete for theater as an art of performance. Likewise useful are Bakhtin's terms *dialogic* and *monologic* to describe the relationship of the artwork to its social context. The dialogic work and its context reciprocally intervene with each other, while the monologic work and its context are either static mirrors of each other or in a "melting pot" where the differences between them are dissolved. The dialogic work retains traces of its multi-voiced context, while the monologic work suppresses all under one seemingly homogeneous voice. Bakhtin agrees with Kant and Bachelard that spatio-temporal perception is a requisite of human cognition but departs from them in stressing that the *ideological values* attached to spatio-temporal signs are volatile and not at all universal but the constructs of historically specific cultures, classes, and eras. The ideological values attached to each side of a polarity are liable to reverse themselves.

One spatio-temporal structure whose volatility is seen over and over in the history of stage practice is that of *verticality versus horizontality*. This structure has been dominant in the literary and stage history of *Peer Gynt* and volatile in its ideological values. Bakhtin points out that the ideological values of the medieval era were consistently represented via a vertical hierarchy: the cosmos itself was imagined as a vertical formation, the great chain of being with every entity in its assigned position from top to bottom. The values attached to verticality were permanence, equilibrium, and immobility. Time was a repeating cycle. With the Renaissance the vertical axis began to give way to a horizontal one, to which were attached the new values of change, dynamism, and mobility. Time moved forward and developed. In the medieval era it was of course possible to travel horizontally over the land, but such movement held little *significance,* whereas to travel vertically — upward towards heaven or downward towards hell — was very significant. However, during the Renaissance outward horizontal movement beyond one's origins held much significance and was valued positively — and well rewarded financially, if one recalls the explorers who traded and colonized all over the globe.

Such spatio-temporal structures are an organizing principle in all stagings, but in epic theater it is this volatile reversibility of every structure's values that makes *dialectical contradiction* possible. Epic theater unceasingly acknowledges the volatile historicity of every sign in the text and on stage. No sign is expressed without also being *signified*, but these two functions never "fuse" as in illusionistic theater. The work of the semiotic-based sociologist Michel de Certeau allows the transition from philosophical and literary definitions of space and time to those of theater.[23]

De Certeau shares Bakhtin's insistence on a *dialogic* relation between art and its sociohistorical context. Both also view spatio-temporal forms as directly arising out of that context and both place great importance on social topography. Although he does not use this term, the *chronotope*, or time-space, is also a key concept for de Certeau. His view of the relationship between space and time, however, is less totalizing than Bakhtin's. Likewise, he faults Foucault's concept of the *panoptic* institution with denying any possibility of resistance against it.[24]

For de Certeau the strongest resistance against a *closed* unity of signs under the chronotope of the road is the simple act of *walking*. He shares with Brecht the tenet that space and time are also constructed by ordinary people as they maneuver through the great territorial structures built by those in power. His essay "Walking in the City" recognizes that *"the walker makes spatial order exist."* Like actors on a stage, pedestrians can make parts of the city disappear and exaggerate others. The "walker's city down below" is opposed to the panoptic "voyeur's city" seen from on high as an abstract geometric spatial design. This distinction also corresponds to two types of scenography: the panoptic view, which unites everything on stage under one master-concept, and the walker's view, which is "a migrational city that slips into the panoptic one."[25]

To de Certeau, walking is a *tactic* through which pedestrians survive and subvert the *strategy* of the social space as planned by those in power. Brecht and his long-time set designer Caspar Neher always began their collaboration by simply observing how the actors used the empty stage, the spatial patterns they traced out in establishing their social relationships. Only after the actors' paths, centers, and flow of movement began to cohere did Brecht and Neher design the set. In a direct parallel to de Certeau's championing of pedestrians, they allowed the actors to create their own tactical map of the stage and never imposed an *a priori* conceptual design.

Nearly a century after the revelations of quantum physics and Einstein's relativity, container time and space still pervade our thinking, even if we have lost faith that the "walls" of that container are solid and nostalgically describe it as fragmented, serialized, devalued, and infinitely reproducible. Yet container spatio-temporality is only one historical construct, made material by the perspective proscenium stage of Renaissance Europe. The medieval Europeans had a different image of the cosmos and represented time as cyclical and simultaneous, rather than linear and sequential, and space as noncontiguous. It was considered only natural that Heaven, Hell, ancient Jerusalem, and a contemporary European village shared the playing area simultaneously. These two conflicting constructs coexisted, not always peacefully, for several centuries.

For his part, Brecht recognized the difficulty of conceiving of space and time in unfamiliar ways; but far from feeling uneasy about these human limitations, he found pleasure in their confirmation:

> philosophers get irritated by Heisenberg's proposition, according to which points in space and points in time cannot be coordinated. . . . the physicists have overturned [the philosophers' proposition that nothing happens without cause.] . . . space as a quality of matter is something philosophers cannot conceive of.[26]

> i like the world of the physicists. [people] change it, and then it looks astonishing. we can appear as the gamblers we are, with our approximations, . . . our dependence on others, on the unknown, on things complete in themselves. so once again a variety of things can lead to success, more than just one path is open. oddly enough i feel more free in this world than in the old one.[27]

Epic Space and Time as Historicizing Critique

The epic theater demystifies the concept of an essential human nature living out its inevitable fate, by showing both human nature and fate as historical and thus changeable human constructs. The concept of fate is held up in contrast to that of a historical agency open to human intervention. Brecht faulted the "dramatic theater" with naturalizing these essentialist concepts and the passivity they entail. Its whole aesthetic aim was the hiding of its own constructedness — its art consisted in appearing to be artless. In other words, its semiotic apparatus was disguised. By contrast, Brecht believed that truly realistic art had to be an "anti-nature." Thus, in epic theater history does not *unroll* as a panorama of inevitable fate but is exposed as a kind of theater whose *effects* are very real. This rolling panorama had long been *contained* by the proscenium stage of the dramatic theater. While acknowledging the proscenium's power to contain the constructedness of history, Brecht nonetheless allowed other spatio-temporal dimensions to invade, and thus contradict, the illusory world on stage. He disliked "experimental" theater space and always insisted on a proscenium stage; yet he flooded stage and audience in white light, subjecting it all to the *Verfremdungseffekt*.

All theatrical spatio-temporality is the representation of space and time through the many sign systems or "languages" of the stage, including dialogue, actors' movement and placement, scenography, costumes, objects, sound, lighting, and music. It is the dynamic *process of signification* that the spectator experiences as a *journey toward meaning*. For epic theater this journey is always dialectical, with every sign pointing in two contradictory directions: *the way taken and the way not taken*.

Semiotics and Epic Theater

Barthes's distinction in the passage at the outset of this study between the semiotic and the expressive is parallel to Brecht's famous list of the qualities of epic versus dramatic theater.[28] Whereas in the dramatic theater thoughts, feelings, and characters are *expressed* as essences, in the epic theater we are shown the semiotic production of these expressions. The epic spectator and the semiotician share an attitude of analytic questioning, not asking *"What does it mean?"* but *"How does it mean?"* In the same essay with the list Brecht also observes:

> When the epic theatre's methods begin to penetrate the opera the first result is a *radical separation of the elements*. . . . So long as the expression 'Gesamtkunstwerk' (or 'integrated work of art') means that the integration is a muddle, . . . the various ['fused'] elements will all be equally degraded, and each will act as a mere 'feed' to the rest. The . . . spectator . . . gets thrown into the melting pot too and becomes a passive . . . part of the total work of art. . . . *Words, music and setting must become more independent of each other.*[29]

This "radical separation of the elements" is dialectical in Brecht's sense and also semiotic, even if the founders of epic theater did not know this term: epic theater aims to separate out and expose systems of signs as culturally and historically determined. Dramatic theater does not aim to *analyze* but to *synthesize*. Thus illusionistic theater aims to be the *expression* of an organic human nature, the flow of a mysterious creative essence out of some unseen source — which Brecht irreverently called a "fog."

Barthes's championship of both epic theater and semiotics is not an accident: as critical practices they share a history, as well as the tenet that reality is signified rather than expressed. They are not only compatible but also illuminate each other. Barthes's critical writings are exemplary of this shared history and philosophy. Theater — especially epic theater — would remain at the nexus of his thinking, as he explains: "At the crossroads of the entire *oeuvre*, perhaps the Theater: there is not a single one of his [Barthes's] texts, in fact, which fails to deal with a certain theater, and spectacle is the universal category in whose aspect the world is seen."[30] Unlike other postmodernist critics, Barthes never uses theater as a convenient metaphor based on one stereotype. The theater usually assumed by such a metaphor has a naturalistic set; histrionic acting; a linear, contrived plot; and aims to dazzle and deceive the audience with special effects. In fact, it resembles the dramatic theater, which to Brecht was the antithesis of epic theater. Barthes's experience and knowledge of theater prevented him from reducing it to an unthinking metaphor: he had studied theater at the university and acted in a student troupe that performed classical Greek drama. As a critic he always draws on a *specific* theater for each of his essays, a theater with a particular stage practice and historical and cultural context. A decade after his encounter with the Berliner Ensemble in 1954, he published the first major semiotic study of the drama, *On Racine.*[31] Here, as elsewhere, he does not employ semiotics as an isolated method of analysis but interconnects it with structuralist anthropology, sociology, linguistics, psychoanalysis, and scholarly knowledge of Racine's texts and stage practices and of the texts and staging of ancient classical Greek and Roman drama which was Racine's model. *On Racine* illuminates with great clarity and originality the representation of space and time as the basic structure of theater. As the preeminent theorist of a semiotics wherein *all* cultural signs — verbal and nonverbal — may be read as coded historical texts, Barthes was profoundly inspired by the example of Brecht, with whom he engaged in imaginary dialectical conversations. His insights as an epic spectator are woven throughout all his work.[32]

The parallel emergence of epic theater and semiotics in the 1920s and 1930s, and their convergence in the work of Barthes and others from the 1960s on, is also not a historical coincidence. In fact, the two fields are traceable to the same intellectual sources. John Willett recounts that Brecht's key concepts of *Verfremdung* and the *Verfremdungseffekt* were in all likelihood directly translated from the Russian Formalist Viktor Shklovsky's phrase *priem ostrannenija,* or "device for making strange." Accordingly, the most precise translation of Brecht's Verfremdung is "making strange" rather than "alienation."[33] To Brecht, as to the Russian Formalist critics and constructivist artists of the 1920s and 1930s, the greatest power of art lay in its ability to challenge our habitual modes of perception.[34] This does not mean simply erasing old modes and inventing new ones, but rendering even old ones newly *apparent* and thus able to reconnect with the historical present. In the 1930s Roman Jakobsen, Petr Bogatyrev, and others in the Russian Formalist group became part of the Prague School of semiotics. Prague

School scholars Jan Mukařovsky and Jiri Veltrusky worked specifically to develop a semiotics of theater, but with the rise of Stalin their work came under political attack, like that of the Formalists, constructivists, expressionists, futurists, epic theater, and anyone else who did not practice socialist realism.[35] Under Stalin, *formalist* became a pejorative term connoting an aesthetic of "empty form" — that is, empty of "the historical life of the people."[36] In the wake of Khrushchev's denunciation of Stalin in 1956 these Eastern European scholars and artists were finally exonerated and their long-suppressed works made available. From the mid-1960s through the 1970s the writings of the Prague School semioticians and structuralists, Mikhail Bakhtin, and the Russian Formalists were translated into French, English, German, and Italian. Their writings influenced the French semioticians, including Barthes, Julia Kristeva, Tadeusz Kowzan, and Patrice Pavis; Kristeva and Kowzan were themselves emigrés from Bulgaria and Poland, respectively.

In another parallel development, the 1920s and 1930s also saw the rise of nonillusionistic political theater worldwide, with Brecht, Piscator, and the Russian constructivist Vsevolod Meyerhold its foremost directors. Ironically, semiotics and epic theater are still regularly accused of being "formalistic" in a similar sense as in Stalin's time: "excessively theoretical" "empty structures," "closed systems" that ignore history and real life. Nothing could be farther from the aims of epic theater or of the semiotics practiced in this book. Far from being self-sufficient systems sealed off from historical reality, both practices aim at cultural criticism and are firmly based in historical specificity. Both practices also reject innovation as a goal in itself and conceive of themselves as holding a vigil at the crossroads of ideological discourses. What Barthes says of semiotics also applies to epic theater:

> Semiology is not a science like the others ([although it is] rigorous), and . . . it has no intention of substituting itself for the great *epistemes* which are our century's historical truth, but rather . . . it is their servant; a vigilant servant who, by representing the snares of the Sign, keeps them from falling victim to what these great new knowledges claim to denounce: dogmatism, arrogance, theology; in short, that monster: the Last Signified [Ultimate Truth].[37]

Like semiotics, epic theater is also a "vigilant servant" of great epistemological discourses — even the discourse of Marxism. It is "vigilant," too, of the theater tradition with which it is always in dialogue. Epic theater does not simply reject older artistic forms and strike out on its own; rather, it reengages these forms in a new dialectic for the new historical situation. Brecht explains in a diary entry from 1938:

3 August 38. because i am an innovator in my field, there is always somebody . . . ready to scream that i am a formalist. they miss the old forms in what i write: worse still, they find new ones; and as a result they think forms are what interest me. but . . . if anything i underrate the formal aspect . . . i have studied the old forms of poetry, the story, the drama and the theatre, and i only abandoned them when they started getting in the way of what i wanted to say.[38]

This book shares Barthes's use of semiotics as an instrument of aesthetic and cultural criticism, not as a truth claim. The *codes* at the base of all semiosis are always culturally specific and simply do not exist in a historical vacuum. Likewise, the sign is neither "freely floating" nor trapped in a closed system but always tied to a historical referent at any given moment. Therefore, semiotics cannot and does not pretend to stand alone, much less to replace other methods. In fact, its greatest strength is its ability to join with other methods, to be a versatile, watchful servant of the "great epistemes" of social and political philosophy.

Space and Time in Theater Studies

Just as traditional philosophers and historians have divided time into discrete epochs and sequential units of duration, theorists of theatrical space have often been content to invent typologies that would do as well for painting, photography, or architecture. Here theater space is viewed as a series of discrete stage *pictures,* and the critic's task is to classify these pictures as open, closed, expressionistic, neoclassical, poststructuralist, or even epic. Such typologies ignore the interrelatedness of space and time in theatrical representation and thus ignore the historicity of the theatrical sign. Marvin Carlson, in *Places of Performance: The Semiotics of Theatre Architecture* (1989), departs from this tradition, analyzing several established theaters in multiple contexts: the internal and external architecture of the theater building, its cultural and historical significations, its physical placement within the city, its function as a social and economic institution, and its past and present audiences.[39]

The pioneering Formalists, structuralists, and semioticians of the early twentieth century began to see the semiotic importance of space and time in literature, theater, and other arts, yet even today theater semioticians are rarely aware of the extent to which they still base their thinking upon the Euclidian/Newtonian concept of space and time. The Prague School theorists Jan Mukařovsky[40] and Petr Bogatyrev[41] in the 1930s and Tadeusz Kowzan in the 1960s[42] all describe theater semiosis as operating *within* space and time. That is, space and time are not considered as semiotic per se but as inert containers of semiosis.

The contemporary theater semioticians Anne Ubersfeld,[43] Michael Issacharoff,[44] and Patrice Pavis regard space as an empty expanse waiting to be defined and animated by the signifiers of the "performance text" or staging. Their work often brilliantly analyzes the process through which space, in particular, is signified in the performance and text, but echoes of Kant are detectable even here. In *Languages of the Stage* Pavis defines the performance text, using telling images of theatrical space and time:

> The performance text is . . . always an open structure, or at least "half-open. . . ." There is always "play in the structure" and the writing of this text depends [largely] on [semiotic] structures organized by the audience. . . . In this way theatre space might resemble *a gigantic score* on which the actor and the whole theatre team trace out *figures, stops and starts, arrangements* of characters, living and moving *tableaux.* . . . Writing/reading the performance text consists of structuring the *continuum* of the performance [time] into *meaning-blocks,* into *chains of episodes* and attitudes, in transitions reflecting the changes of situation or rhythm [italics mine].[45]

Pavis follows Barthes in granting that the spectators are a primary organizer of structures through their "knowledge of the ideological codes of the reality reproduced." Pavis affirms that the codes from which meaning is drawn are historically determined. His image of theater space as a "gigantic score" implies, however, that the space is a blank expanse (a page) until the artists begin filling it with animated figures and movement — "writings and drawings" for the audience to read. Time in the "performance continuum" is likewise described as "blocks of meaning" and "chains of episodes": time here is a large container filled with smaller containers inside which meaning is packed. Yet it is also imagined as a continuously moving chain whose links are the plot episodes. Interestingly, Pavis contradicts his implicit Kantian assumptions by adding that Brecht as a director was able to dialectically mobilize space and time.[46]

Spatio-temporality and the Principles of Epic Theater

Verfremdung

The dramaturgical principles of epic theater are often mistakenly reduced to a *style,* a set of familiar techniques: placards, direct addresses to the audience, songs out of character, and nonhistrionic acting. Unfortunately too, Brecht's key notion of *Verfremdung* is traditionally translated as "alienation," which in English carries negative connotations: isolation, hostility, emotional coldness, and rejection of fellow-ship and fun.[47] Verfremdung is also a "distancing," associated with po-larization and spatial separation. Epic space is, thus, conceived in Euclidian terms as two mutually exclusive areas, that of the rational spectator "outside" the performance in static opposition to that of the spectacle "inside" it. Significantly, "alienation" is also the usual transla-tion of Marx's term *Entfremdung*. But epic Verfremdung, in contrast to Entfremdung, gives a hopeful sense of active agency through its pre-fix *ver-*, which connotes *movement around* a *static central entity*. More accurate translations of Verfremdung are "making strange" or "defa-miliarization." In epic theater Verfremdung, like signification, implies an active *verb*, a dynamic *process* rather than a finished *product*.

Epic space is not static areas blocked out on stage, filled up or emp-tied of props or scenery, separated, united, stretched out, or otherwise rearranged. Rather, space becomes a dynamic *spatiality* in process, which always involves at least two ideologically coded contradictory spatial dimensions at any moment, in an ongoing juxtaposition with each other. This juxtaposition, or *contradiction,* may be simultaneous or successive or both at once. In *Mother Courage,* as in all of Brecht's works, songs are often the means by which an invisible space-time "in-vades" the visible. Courage's son Eilif dances with his saber as he sings "The Song of the Fishwife and the Soldier." The invisible "other space" is the shore and then an icy sea wherein the soldier floats, an im-age of the space of death. The saber of the Eilif on stage is linked to the knife of the dead soldier in the song in a semiotic chain joining the liv-ing to the dead. Georges Banu notes the influence of Chinese and Japanese theater and pictorial art on Brecht, especially the breaking up of the compact, centralized space of Western theater into "floating" scenes that are not contiguous and around which there is empty space. This floating allows more freedom and mobility of the gaze. Parallel lines never join at the horizon, as in Western perspective, and are thus able to indicate an immense space of water, land, or nothing, depend-ing on the observer.[48]

Space and Time Defined by Each Other

Likewise, the epic theater's critique of naturalized time is usually no-ticed only when the linear flow of the plot is interrupted by songs, printed signs, and direct address, as if the overt narrative were the only signifier of time. In fact, to call attention to spatio-temporality as a historical semiotic construct is a basic aim of epic practice. Carl Weber recalls that for Brecht "the blocking should tell the main story of the play and its contradictions by itself, so that a person watching through a glass wall, unable to hear what was being said, would be able to understand."[49] This language of movement in space was articulated through rhythm:

> After the last dress rehearsal Brecht always did an exercise . . . he called . . . "marking.". . . The actors, not in costumes, quoting the text very rapidly, without any effort at acting, but keeping the rhythm, the pauses, etc., intact. The effect . . . was . . . like an early silent movie: . . . people moving and gesturing very quickly, but you couldn't hear the words or get any . . . emotions except the most obvious. This . . . made the actors relax, helped them to memorize every physical detail and gave them a keen sense for the show's rhythmic pattern.[50]

In the overt and covert rhythms lie the performance's *Grundgestus* (fundamental Gestus), which always includes not only the main story but also its dialectical others, its *contradictions:* to use a familiar Brechtian formula, the performance must show not only the way taken but also the ways *not* taken. Louis Althusser, in *For Marx* (1969), accuses orthodox Marxist critics of clinging to a notion of time that does injustice to the work of artists such as Brecht who show that time is experiential and differentiated rather than an unchanging, universal element:

> It is not enough . . . to say . . . that *there are* different periodizations for different times, that each time has its own rhythms, some short, some long; we must also think these differences in rhythm and punctuation in their foundation, in the type of articulation, displacement, and torsion which harmonizes [them]. . . . We cannot restrict ourselves to *visible* and measurable times. . . ; we must . . . [examine] . . . *invisible* times, . . . invisible rhythms . . . concealed beneath the surface of each visible time.[51]

Althusser notes approvingly that in *Mother Courage* there are "forms of temporality that achieve no mutual integration," which Brecht placed in dynamic juxtaposition. Indeed, their non-integration is the salient characteristic of the play's spatio-temporality. In particular, the three dominant rhythms defined by human activities — Courage's maternal life, her business, and the war — do not harmonize with each other.[52] In Brecht's Berliner Ensemble production the visible rhythms and spaces of domestic life conceal — though never completely — the war in the other time and space beyond our sight. Seemingly innocent props and characters in the visible domestic space are implicated in the murders being committed in the invisible space of the war: the spectator sees Mother Courage on stage cleaning her cooking knives and learns later that this was the moment when her son was being executed by soldiers.

Gestic Music and Sound

Althusser clearly thinks of temporality in musical terms. In theater, film, and indeed in everyday life, music not only can describe the tempo of activity but also has the power to *order* and *control* it. All sound, including music, can also give space materiality: expand or contract it, give it texture and weight, warmth and coldness. In the geographer Yi-Fu Tuan's words, "sound dramatizes spatial experience."[53] Epic music is never "purely music" but points to itself as a humanly produced sound, most obviously by the musicians who are always on stage in full light. Epic music often signifies two simultaneous but contradictory spatio-temporal dimensions juxtaposed with each other: a marching song whose tune is hearty and uplifting but whose text describes a slaughter, or a gentle lullaby about a well-clothed child sung to a ragged corpse. Through his sword dance and song Eilif is already being pulled into another spatio-temporal dimension. He is joining a Dance of Death. Here we see what Althusser calls an "invisible" time and space concealed beneath the surface of the visible. Both music and sound effects can connote or denote an invisible space or time. In *Mother Courage* the flute and drums denote the march of offstage armies and by the end of the play also connote the death march of a whole civilization.

Epic music is dialectical and contradictory not only in its denotation and connation but also in the texture of its sound: it is never pure, smooth, and disembodied. Rather, it has a corporal materiality that Barthes, speaking of vocalists, calls the *grain* of the voice.[54] Epic music never signifies *only* mood, and no one mood is allowed to "wash over" the audience unimpeded; instead, it shares the stage with a contradictory mood, and the audience must think about both of them. Epic music is often taken from popular forms associated with particular classes, such as German folk music in the case of *Mother Courage* or the *Moritat* (a street ballad telling of a murder) in *The Threepenny Opera*.

Montage

The nonintegration or contradiction that characterizes the spatio-temporality of epic theater follows the same dialectical principle as in Eisenstein's cinematic montage: two opposing images, which Eisenstein parallels with the thesis and antithesis, are given to the spectator, auditor, or reader, in whose perception the images collide and "explode" dialectically into a third image — into revolutionary meaning, which Eisenstein calls the synthesis.[55] Brecht is more economical, however, because his contradictory images may be simultaneous as well as sequential; whereas in Eisenstein each sequence is a three-part narrative chain that links to the chain following it, each of Brecht's sequences is multitemporal and multispatial in itself, able to stand independently.

The Gestus

The *Gestus* is the main organizing principle of epic spatio-temporality, both as an aesthetic structure and as a sociohistorical signifier of ideology. It *materializes* the social relationships of the characters, both in the separate scenes and for the work as a whole. Every sign in epic theater, from the smallest to the largest, is *gestic,* in that it participates in defining the Gestus and is, conversely, defined by it. The Gestus condenses time in each separable scene, and, in doing so, is able to point beyond itself, to recall a past and project a future. Brecht literally writes the *Grundgestus* of each scene in one prefatory sentence that communicates the events and the social attitudes and relationships of the characters; in his own stagings these sentences often appeared as type on a banner above the set or projected onto a screen or wall. The Gestus also may be a nexus where contradictory spatio-temporal dimensions and their ideological valuations cross paths at one material object. In this function it can be compared to an intense focusing of light on one spot of material that will soon be burning. In *The Exception and the Rule,* for instance, the entire Gestus of the play is focused at the moment when the Coolie stands in the river holding out his canteen of water to offer the Merchant a drink. The canteen is a *gestic object,* the focal point of an encounter where the dichotomous worlds of rich and poor, powerful and powerless meet. "Naturally" assuming that the canteen is a rock with which the Coolie is about to murder him, the Merchant shoots and kills the Coolie. With this Gestus, the "forward flow" of the narrative in effect stops, so that the characters and spectators may analyze it, projecting "backward and forward" in time and space (the characters are crossing a desert). The illumination of the two characters' paths leading up to and away from this encounter culminates in a trial scene, by which time the whole course of the paths they did *not* take is also illuminated.

The Dialectical Object

Concrete and abstract objects also help define spatio-temporality. As semiotician Anne Ubersfeld defines them, objects encompass far more than the stage properties; they also appear in textual stage directions and in spoken or written dialogue, either through direct reference or through imagery. On stage they may include a part of the set or even part of an actor's body. They pass from character to character, connect one scene to another, mark out certain frequencies and rhythms, and appear and disappear, moving between what Michael Issacharoff calls the *mimetic* and the *diegetic* space, which he defines as the immediately visible space versus the invisible space created in the imagination through dialogue. Visible or invisible objects participate in every transformation of the scenic space. Finally, in a key function of epic theater, objects interrelate with the actors in an immediate material way and are thus often the *anchor of the Gestus.* To Brecht they were the carriers of what he called the *details:* moments of contact between people and material objects that illuminate the story of a life in one Gestus. For Barthes the social situation, attitude, past, and future of Mother Courage is revealed at the moment when she bites down to test the coin.[56] The gestic object is also the nexus of signs where the contradictions of the character's attitude and historical situation are made clear.

The Body as Sign

The spatio-temporality of the performance is also signified through culturally constructed and ideologically marked human bodies. These bodies are materially anchored in the actors on stage but touch every other element of the production. The real bodies of actors and the fictional bodies of characters belong to two discrete yet interweaving sign systems. Rather than trying to merge them seamlessly into one, epic theater strongly marks their separateness, so that the actor's body never recedes, thus also preventing the historical present from receding. Retaining their dialectical separateness, they can act as a primary nexus where signs of gender, class, race, and political power intersect — and seem to be generated. The resulting *constructed* bodies are not limited to actors or characters but are dispersed as images throughout the mise en scène, marking its boundaries, shapes, and rhythms. Thus the body-as-sign is not simply *in* the theatrical time and space of the production but helps constitute it. This phenomenon is what Ariane Mnouchkine calls *écriture corporelle,* or writing with the body: the actors "write" the story through their movements, gestures, and placements in relation to each other on stage, not as a smooth inexorable *flow* but with every moment marked off ideologically.

Spatio-temporality may also be defined by a certain image of the human body that pervades the work. This image is constructed through several signifiers: the actors' real bodies in dynamic relation to each other on stage, the characters' bodies in relation to the *Fabel,* i.e., the story as narrative and symbolic paradigm. The image of a body is created through all these signifiers and *organizes* the space and time. Such a body pervades *Mother Courage:* the dialectical image of a maternal body superimposed upon the ravaged, barren landscape of Europe during the Thirty Years War. This image of a maternal body as nurturer and destroyer functions as a nexus of the Fabel, a social and physical landscape, and an economic system; the maternal body here is akin to what Bakhtin calls the *grotesque body.*[57] In Brecht's staging of *The Tutor* the image gradually superimposed upon the stage action is that of a castrated male body, a radically *disciplined* body in Foucault's sense, trained by class-bound institutions to both represent and police the boundaries of a social order.[58] Feminist film theorist Teresa de Lauretis extends Foucault's concept to include the gendered body, which is an important signifier in *The Tutor, Peer Gynt,* and *Les Atrides,* while in *Mother Courage* it is a *supersign* that pervades the spatio-temporality of text and stage.[59] De Lauretis notes that the woman's body traditionally has provided the "mythic space" — "the boundary, matrix, blank screen, passive matter, womb, space of his movement, the stage upon which Man, the true subject, can carry out the action."[60] As feminist critic Judith Butler explains in *Gender Trouble* (1990), the human body can be made to stand for any boundaried system that feels itself under threat.[61] The female body, far more often than the male, is used as the outer boundary of such ideological systems. The Tutor's castrated body has the same function, however; it is what Butler calls an *abject body*[62] that stands for the *outside* of the class system, confirming his superiors' position as *insiders.* Thus we see that epic practice, Brechtian theory, and a historically aware semiotics engage in a productive dialogue.

Conclusion

Before turning to the analyses of individual performances to demonstrate this dialogue, it would be helpful to summarize for the reader the main issues and theoretical concepts that have been explored in the preceding pages and will be employed in the chapters to follow. Epic theater-in-practice is a semiosis that does not *synthesize* its own process but *analyzes* it. The signification of space and time in epic theater is a process, an apparatus at work, and thus is a staging of historicity. Each of the theatrical elements (stage languages) is *separated* from the others and allowed to signify, to tell the story, in its own way, creating a dialectical movement experienced by the spectator as the *theatrical event.* Epic spatio-temporality codifies ideology, as does all theater, but epic theater does not *merely* codify. Rather, it draws attention to its own process of codification, and thus to the contradictions within and among the ideologies it is signifying. It never *reconciles* these ideologies and social attitudes through its aesthetic design, but presents them to us in their irreconcilable state. The rest is up to us.

The spatio-temporal dynamic of each text and performance cannot be separate from our experience as spectators or readers; indeed, our experience helps constitute it. There is no "transcendental" spatio-temporality valid for theater in all eras and cultures. There are only spatio-temporalities, chronotopes (Bakhtin's *time-spaces)* that exist in a dialogical relationship with their cultural, social, and political contexts; that is, they are not only formed by but also help to form their contexts. Epic theater never presents a finished interwoven spatio-temporal design; rather, it stays in the process of weaving. Its spaces and times are always separable — even if one chronotope, such as the chronotope of the road, seems to cohere them, it does not reconcile them. The dialectical spatio-temporality of epic theater *signifies rather than expresses* the human experience as a pleasurable yet painful disjuncture, a juxtaposition of many perspectives and of old and new media. Epic theater is a movable theory-in-practice and not a solipsistic formalist experiment, as Stalin charged. It remains relevant to contemporary theater because it is a montage-of-separate-pieces and trusts in us to *reconstruct* from these pieces the material and ideological contradictions of our own society. It is fitting that Brecht have the last word, which will serve to introduce the coming chapters.

> a simple presentation of non-aristotelian drama should always start from the need to deal better (more practicably) with the subjects that affect our times than was possible in the old manner. 'all' that had to be eliminated from naturalism was the element of fate. this step made the whole huge reorganisation necessary. here is the poor dumb peasant, poverty and stupidity treated not as a fact of life but as things which are independent and can be eliminated — then we have non-aristotelian drama.[63]

Notes

[1] Bertolt Brecht, entry August 4, 1940, in *Bertolt Brecht Journals 1934–1955,* ed. John Willett and Ralph Manheim, trans. Hugh Rorrison (London and New York: Routledge, 1993), 84. Hereafter abbreviated as *BBJ.*

[2] Roland Barthes, "The Tasks of Brechtian Criticism," in his *Critical Essays,* trans. Richard Howard (Evanston, IL.: Northwestern UP, 1972), 74.

[3] Jean-Paul Sartre, "Myth and Reality in Theater," in *Sartre on Theater,* ed. Michel Contat and Michel Rybalka, trans. Frank Jellinek (New York: Pantheon, 1976), 135–157.

[4] Karl Marx, *The Eighteenth Brumaire of Louis Bonaparte* (1851), in *The Marx-Engels Reader,* ed. Robert C. Tucker (New York: Norton, 1979), 594–619.

[5] Bertolt Brecht et al, *Theaterarbeit: 6 Aufführungen des Berliner Ensembles* (Dresden: VVV Dresdner Verlag, 1952), and *Materialien zu Brechts "Mutter Courage und ihre Kinder"* (Frankfurt am Main: Suhrkamp, 1964).

[6] The positive studies far outnumber the negative ones, most of which have appeared in the last fifteen years. John Fuegi has spanned both extremes: from Brecht as hero of *The Essential Brecht* (Los Angeles: Hennessey & Ingalls, 1972) to Brecht as villain of *Brecht and Company: Sex, Politics and the Making of the Modern Drama* (New York: Grove, 1994) and *Life and Lies of Bertolt Brecht* (London: Flamingo, 1995).

[7] Strindberg's *Charles XII,* as Göran Stockenström shows, does not present the Swedish monarch as the active agent of historical events; instead, Charles remains asleep in bed throughout the play while great, fatal events occur offstage. The play thus ironizes the heroic, nationalistic history play that was so popular in nineteenth-century Europe: official history is exposed as ideological discourse written and staged as a pageant for the benefit of those in power. See Göran Stockenström, *"Charles XII* as Historical Drama," in *Strindberg's Dramaturgy,* ed. Stockenström (Minneapolis: U of Minnesota P, 1988), 41–55.

[8] In "An Expression of Faith in Wedekind," a eulogy published in the *Augsburger Neueste Nachrichten,* March 1918, Brecht writes: "He was together with Tolstoy and Strindberg one of the great educators of the new Europe." Trans. Erich Albrecht, in *The Tulane Drama Review* 6 (September 1961): 26–27.

[9] See for example: John Rouse, *Brecht and the West German Theatre* (Ann Arbor: UMI Research P, 1989); James K. Lyon, *Bertolt Brecht in America* (Princeton UP, 1980); Margaret Eddershaw, *Performing Brecht: Forty Years of British Performances* (London and New York: Routledge, 1996); Janelle Reinelt, *After Brecht: British Epic Theatre* (Ann Arbor: U of Michigan P, 1995); Michael Patterson, "Brecht's Legacy," in *The Cambridge Companion to Brecht,* eds. Peter Thomson and Glendyr Sacks (Cambridge: Cambridge UP, 1994), 273–287.

[10] Many scholars have documented and theoretically explored feminist theater's extensive incorporation of epic principles into its own practice. See Iris Smith, "Brecht and the Mothers of Epic Theatre," *Theatre Journal* 43 (December 1991): 491–505; Jill Dolan, "Materialist Feminism: Apparatus-Based Theory and Practice," in her *The Feminist Spectator as Critic* (Ann Arbor: UMI Research P, 1988), 100–117; Elin Diamond, "Brechtian Theory/Feminist Theory: Toward a Gestic Feminist Criticism," in *A Sourcebook of Feminist Theatre and Performance,* ed. Carol Martin (London and New York: Routledge, 1996), 120–135; Janelle Reinelt, "Rethinking Brecht: Deconstruction, Feminism, and the Politics of Form," in *Essays on Brecht/Versuche*

über Brecht: The Brecht Yearbook 15, eds. Marc Silberman, John Fuegi, Renate Voris, and Carl Weber (College Park, Md.: International Brecht Society, 1990), 99–110; and Reinelt's chapter on Caryl Churchill in *After Brecht*.

[11] Some examples: Lorena B. Ellis, *Brecht's Reception in Brazil* (New York: Peter Lang, 1995); Antony Tatlow, "Analysis and Countertransference," in *The Other Brecht I/Der andere Brecht: Brecht Yearbook* 17, eds. Hans-Thies Lehmann and Renate Voris, (Madison, WI.: International Brecht Society, 1992), 125–133; Tatlow, *The Mask of Evil* (Bern: Peter Lang, 1977); *Brecht in Asia and Africa/Brecht in Asien und Afrika: Brecht Yearbook* 14, eds. John Fuegi, Renata Voris, Carl Weber, Marc Silberman (College Park, Md.: International Brecht Society, 1989).

[12] *The Brecht Yearbook*, International Brecht Society Symposia, *New Theatre Quarterly, Theatre Journal*, and *The Drama Review* have for years been disseminating information about this important intercultural work.

[13] Immanuel Kant, "The Critique of Pure Reason" (1781), excerpted in *The Enduring Questions: Main Problems of Philosophy*, 5th edition, eds. Melvin Rader and Jerry Hill (New York: Holt, Rinehart and Winston, 1991), 106–111.

[14] Gottfried Wilhelm Friedrich Hegel, *The Philosophy of History* (1837), trans. F. Sibree (New York: Dow, 1965); and *Reason in History*, trans. Robert S. Hartman (Indianapolis: Bobbs-Merrill, 1953).

[15] Introduction, *Reason in History*, xii. Subsequent page numbers of citations from this source are indicated in parentheses in the text.

[16] Gaston Bachelard, *The Poetics of Space* (1958), trans. Maria Jolas (Boston: Beacon, 1994), 9, 8. Further citations are indicated by page numbers in parentheses in the text.

[17] Jean Hippolite, spoken commentary on Freud's *Verneinung* (negation), quoted by Bachelard, in *The Poetics of Space*, 212.

[18] Yi-Fu Tuan, *Space and Place: The Perspective of Experience* (Minneapolis: U of Minnesota P, 1977); and *Topophilia* (Minneapolis: U of Minnesota P, 1974).

[19] Maurice Merleau-Ponty, *Phénoménologie de la perception* (Paris: Gallimard, 1976).

[20] Michel de Certeau, *The Practice of Everyday Life*, trans. Steven Rendall (Berkeley, Los Angeles, and London: U of California P, 1984).

[21] Mikhail Bakhtin, "Forms of Time and of the Chronotope in the Novel: Notes Toward a Historical Poetics," in his *The Dialogic Imagination*, trans. Michael Holquist (Austin: U of Texas P, 1981), 84–258.

[22] Bakhtin, "Forms of Time and of the Chronotope in the Novel: Notes Toward a Historical Poetics," 84, 85.

[23] De Certeau, "Tactics and Strategies," 26–39, and "Walking in the City," 91–110, in *The Practice of Everyday Life*.

[24] Michel Foucault, "Discipline and Punish: The Birth of the Prison," in *The Foucault Reader*, ed. Paul Rabinow, trans. Alan Sheridan (New York: Pantheon, 1984), 169–256.

[25] De Certeau, "Walking in the City," *The Practice of Everyday Life*, 93–98. Like Brecht, de Certeau admires Charlie Chaplin as a virtuoso pedestrian, the little man with nothing but his cane, but a cane he uses with great inventiveness in every crisis to "do other things with the same thing." (98)

[26] Brecht, entry March 17, 1942, *BBJ*, 208–209.

[27] Brecht, entry March 18, 1942, *BBJ*, 209.

[28] Brecht, "The Modern Theatre is the Epic Theatre" (1930), in *Brecht on Theatre: The Development of an Aesthetic*, ed. and trans. John Willett (London: Methuen, 1986), 37–38. Brecht is commenting specifically on his epic opera *Mahagonny*.

[29] Ibid.

[30] Barthes, *Roland Barthes by Roland Barthes*, trans. Richard Howard (New York: Hill and Wang, 1977), 177.

[31] Barthes, *On Racine*, trans. Richard Howard (New York: Hill and Wang, 1964).

[32] The figure of Brecht helps Barthes measure his own work. In the essay *"Reproche de Brecht à R. B.,"* Brecht's criticism of R. B.," in *Roland Barthes by Roland Barthes*, Barthes writes: "R. B. . . . always wants to *limit* politics. Doesn't he know what Brecht seems to have written especially for him? 'Now one must be either the object or the subject of politics; there is no other choice. . . . It is quite possible that my whole life must be dedicated [or even sacrificed] to politics.' [Barthes's] milieu . . . is language: . . . To sacrifice his life-as-language to political discourse? He is . . . willing to be a political *subject* but not a political *speaker*. . . . Yet . . . he can at least make the *political* meaning of what he writes" (52–53).

[33] John Willett notes in *Brecht on Theatre*: "It can hardly be a coincidence that *Verfremdungseffekt* should have entered Brecht's vocabulary after his Moscow visit," where he saw a performance of Mei Lan-Fang's company in 1935, attended by Russian artists and intellectuals. The term first appears in print in "Alienation Effects in Chinese Theatre," written after that performance (99).

[34] Vincent M. Colapietro, *Glossary of Semiotics* (New York: Paragon, 1993), 84, 151–152.

[35] See Michael L. Quinn's excellent study, *The Semiotic Stage: The Prague School Theorists* (New York: Peter Lang, 1995).

[36] The old charge of formalism as a pejorative appears again in the poststructuralists' critique of structuralism, though realism is now often discounted by both structuralists and poststructuralists— even the self-critical realism of epic theater. In turn, the poststructuralists themselves are now accused of reducing

all to a solipsistic play of texts as mere forms from which history is emptied out.

[37] Barthes, "To Learn and to Teach" (1975), in his *The Rustle of Language,* trans. Richard Howard (Berkeley and Los Angeles: U of California P, 1989),178.

[38] *BBJ,* 11.

[39] Marvin Carlson, *Places of Performance: The Semiotics of Theatre Architecture* (Ithaca, N.Y. and London: Cornell UP, 1989).

[40] Jan Mukařovsky, *Structure, Sign, and Function,* trans. and ed. John Burbank and Peter Steiner (New Haven and London: Yale UP, 1978).

[41] Petr Bogatyrev, "Signs in the Theater," *Sign, Sound, and Meaning: Quinquagenary of the Prague Linguistic Circle* (Ann Arbor: U of Michigan P, 1976).

[42] Tadeusz Kowzan, "The Sign in the Theatre," *Diogenes* 61 (1968), 52–80.

[43] Anne Ubersfeld, "The Space of Phèdre," *Poetics Today* 2:3 (Spring 1981), 201–10; *L'Espace théâtral,* with Georges Banu (Paris: CNDP, 1978); *Lire le Théâtre* (Paris: Éditions sociales, 1982).

[44] Michael Issacharoff, "Space and Reference in Drama," *Poetics Today* 2 (Spring 1981), 211–224.

[45] Patrice Pavis, "Toward a Semiology of the *Mise en Scène?"* in his *Languages of the Stage: Essays in the Semiology of Theatre* (New York: Performing Arts Journal Publications, 1982), 138–139.

[46] Ibid., 139.

[47] These connotations are often attached to Brecht as a person and have combined with the hostility against all things Marxist, especially during the Cold War. This situation heightened the suspicion of epic theater in the 1950s. Margaret Eddershaw documents this suspicion and misunderstanding in *Performing Brecht: Forty Years of British Performances* (London and New York: Routledge, 1996).

[48] Georges Banu, *Bertolt Brecht* (Paris: Subier Montaigne, 1981).

[49] Carl Weber, "Brecht as Director" (1967), *The Director in a Changing Theatre,* ed. J. Robert Wills (Palo Alto, Ca.: Mayfield, 1976), 72.

[50] Idem, 74.

[51] Louis Althusser, "Piccolo Teatro: Bertolazzi and Brecht. Notes on a Materialist Theatre," in his *For Marx,* trans. Ben Brewster (New York: Pantheon, 1969), quoted in Mohammad Kowsar's "Althusser on Theatre," *Theatre Journal* 35 (December 1983): 461–474. Althusser discusses the relationship between Marxist theory and the work of Brecht and that of the Italian director Giorgio Strehler of the Piccolo Teatro of Milan.

[52] Ibid.

[53] Yi-Fu Tuan, *Space and Place,* 16.

[54] Roland Barthes, "The Grain of the Voice" (1972), *Image - Music - Text*, trans. Stephen Heath (New York: Hill and Wang, 1977), 179–189.

[55] Sergei Eisenstein, "A Dialectical Approach to Film Form," (1929) *Film Form*, ed. and trans. Jay Leyda (New York: Harcourt Brace Jovanovich, 1949), 101–122.

[56] Barthes is the first to give this famous example of the social *Gestus* in "Diderot, Brecht, Eisenstein," *Image - Music - Text*, 73: "When Mother Courage bites on the coin offered by the recruiting sergeant and, as a result of this brief interval of distrust, loses her son, she demonstrates at once her past as tradeswoman and the future that awaits her — all her children dead in consequence of her money-making blindness."

[57] Mikhail Bakhtin, *Rabelais and His World*, trans. H. Iswolsky (Cambridge, Ma.: M.I.T. P, 1968).

[58] Michel Foucault, "Discipline and Punish: The Birth of the Prison," *The Foucault Reader*.

[59] Teresa de Lauretis, *Technologies of Gender: Essays on Theory, Film, and Fiction* (Bloomington: Indiana UP, 1987).

[60] Teresa de Lauretis, *Alice Doesn't: Feminism, Semiotics, Cinema* (Bloomington: Indiana UP, 1984).

[61] Judith Butler, *Gender Trouble: Feminism and the Subversion of Identity.* (London and New York: Routledge, 1990), 147.

[62] Judith Butler, "Bodies That Matter," in her *Bodies That Matter: On the Discursive Limits of "Sex."* (London and New York: Routledge, 1993), 27–56.

[63] Brecht, entry April 3, 1941, *BBJ*, 138.

Part I:
Defining Epic Theater:
Bertolt Brecht and Erwin Piscator

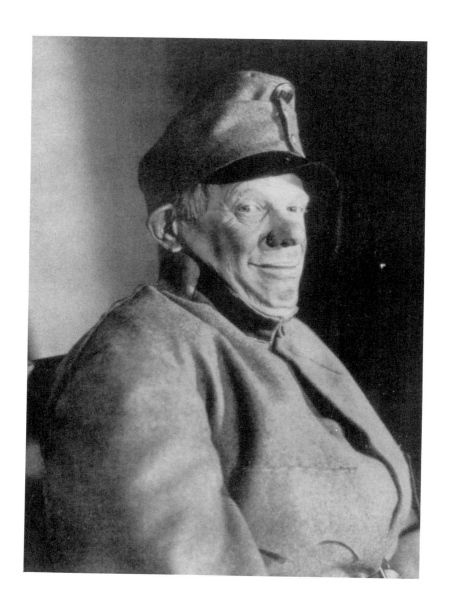

Max Pallenberg as Schwejk, *The Adventures
of the Good Soldier Schwejk*, Piscator-Bühne, 1928.
By permission of the Erwin Piscator Center, Berlin.

1: Theater for the Age of Mechanical Warfare: Piscator Directs *The Good Soldier Schwejk*

> My calculation of time begins on August 4, 1914. From that point the barometer registered:
>
> 13 million dead
> 11 million crippled
> 50 million soldiers in combat
> 6 billion shells fired
> 50 billion cubic meters of poison gas used
>
> Where is "personal development" in all this? No one develops in a personal way. Something else develops the person.[1]

THESE ARE THE OPENING WORDS of director Erwin Piscator's 1929 book *The Political Theater*. Significantly, Piscator's time did not begin with his own birth but was calculated impersonally, registered in mass statistics by a "barometer." In other words, human experience was being "written" in vastly expansive ideological discourses and through modern technology. In no production was that writing more powerfully and concretely staged than in *The Adventures of the Good Soldier Schwejk* of 1928 at the Piscator-Bühne in Berlin. This essay will show how, in *Schwejk*, the war itself took center stage, its time and space no longer smoothly contained within the dramatic form of classical comedy but openly and materially constructed before the spectators by a theater of the machine age — not only acted but also visibly and audibly written in the mass-media discourses of the twentieth century.

Piscator and Bertolt Brecht wanted to stage not only the "person" but also that "something else": the political, social, economic and ideological actants that determine the "personal." For their generation of radicalized artists the idealistic belief in the autonomy of the individual and of art had been exploded by several events: the massive death and destruction of the First World War; the involvement of German religious, judicial, and cultural institutions in promoting and prolonging the war; the Bolshevik Revolution; the German rightists' crushing of the Spartakus Revolt; and now, in the Weimar Republic (1917-1933), the rise again in popularity and power of the same right-wing, authoritarian, militaristic nationalism that had brought such destruction. During more than a decade after the end of the war in 1918 only the Communists took this rising tide seriously enough to struggle against it; by the time the hopefully compromising moderates finally faced what was happening in the early 1930s, it was too late to stop the National Socialists from taking power. But in 1928 there still seemed to be a chance to turn this tide, and leftist artists joined Communists in an attempt to awaken the public. This awakening was the aim of the Piscator Collective in producing *The Good Soldier Schwejk*.

Piscator and Brecht tried to show that the ideological discourses driving and legitimizing these "fateful" events were still within the power of human beings to change, even if beyond the power of the individual. To this end, the epic theater did not want to naively reflect the prevailing images of historical change, causality, and agency but to expose these images as ideological discourse — to catch them in the act of mechanical self-reproduction, so to speak. The "dialectical" theater would demonstrate human existence as a work in progress by openly pointing to itself as an operating model of that work. Stage events were related to the sociopolitical and economic situation of the characters and spectators, but not in the manner of naturalism, which presented these situations as impenetrable *milieus* that completely filled the stage and thus obscured their relationship to the larger world. Instead, the epic theater functioned as a kind of narrating podium, using both the old and by now "organic" media of actors, dialogue, and music on a proscenium stage, along with cut-out wooden marionettes and the new technological media of the conveyor-belt stage, documentary slides and film footage, animated cartoons, the radio, phonograph, telegraph, electric signs, and loudspeakers.

Piscator's practice of epic theater was not identical to that of Brecht: as Piscator noted, Brecht presented political processes "in miniature" and "sought the parable," while he himself worked "on the big scale" and "sought the essence."[2] The two different approaches only worked to the good in their many collaborations, however, and they shared the conviction from early on that epic theater should practice dialectical materialism in Marx's sense. Achieving a dialectical materialist critique was not merely a matter of appropriate subject matter and ideological aims, however; after all, socialist realism already fulfilled these criteria. Instead, for Piscator and Brecht's epic theater, every element of the theater apparatus had to be dialectical. The theater was to historicize its own means of production — material, cultural, social, and ideological. Piscator and Brecht also recognized that there was considerable humor of a liberating or even revolutionary kind in Marx's own writing. *The Communist Manifesto* ironically parodies German idealist philosophy,[3] while *The Eighteenth Brumaire of Louis Bonaparte* chronicles the theatrical process by which the bourgeois state legitimized itself by weaving the slogans of the French Revolution into its own discourse, all the time securing its power by reinstating the institutions of the *ancien régime,* albeit under new titles. In the preface to the second edition of *The Eighteenth Brumaire* Marx stated that his intention was to "demonstrate how the *class struggle* in France created circumstances and relationships that made it possible for *a grotesque mediocrity to play a hero's part* [italics mine]."[4]

Long before the production of *The Good Soldier Schwejk,* Piscator had begun exploring the comic potential of the dialectical theater. Berlin Dadaism of 1917–1920, in which Piscator and several *Schwejk* collaborators had taken part, contributed to the important comic element of epic theater. The driving impetus for the highly political Berlin Dada was outrage at the hypocritical business of "fine art" and at its adherents, who professed humanist ideals yet valued art above human lives. This outrage, expressed as incisive ironic humor, was passed on to epic theater. The *Schwejk* collaborators George Grosz and John Heartfield, also former Berlin Dadaists, are credited with inventing the photomontage, which visually condensed the unsettling experience of living in the twentieth-century metropolis: the perspective of the individual was shattered and multiplied through technology, and the montages offered a simultaneous collective view of such surfaces as the battlefield and the city streets.[5] The Dada perspective recognized that a reproduction of great art might share a wall with graffiti and bullet holes. As Walter Benjamin noted, Dada's juxtaposition of high art with material reality "hit the spectator like a bullet." It acquired this "ballistic quality" through *abrupt shifts in spatial orientation:* "The distracting element [of Dada] . . . is . . . primarily tactile, being based on changes of place and focus which periodically assail the spectator."[6] In contrast to the expressionists, who presented the technological machine as an uncontrollable monster, and the futurists, who glorified it, Dada treated the machine and technology with comic irony, as would *Schwejk.*

One Dada performance of 1918 clearly demonstrates the movement's self-reflective critical spirit. It was advertised as a contest between a sewing machine and a typewriter and was held in an overcrowded auditorium, with George Grosz as master of ceremonies. The actor/playwright Richard Huelsenbeck manned the typewriter while the artist Raoul Haussmann sat at the sewing machine. After a half hour of furious typing Huelsenbeck had to rest; the sewing machine was thus declared the winner, since Haussmann had only to keep pedaling as the machine stitched around and around an endless mourning crepe whose two ends were sewn together. Huelsenbeck, always the ungraceful loser, threw the typewriter onto the floor and destroyed it — which turned out to be unfortunate, since it belonged to his publisher.[7] The two machines displaced the human protagonist and antagonist of the traditional theater and carried out a parody of the dramatic conflict between them. In addition, the triumphant sewing machine and defeated typewriter comically and literally *materialized* the fall of language from a transcendental medium of truth to a meaningless stream of noisy type.

Piscator relates that such juxtaposition had become fundamental to his view of the world even before Dada. As a young draftee into the army during the First World War he volunteered to become an actor in the German Front Theater, which featured folk comedy and operettas. The bizarre irony of acting in plays such as *Charley's Aunt* amid the bombed ruins of Flanders, with shells exploding in the distance, had an impact that is discernible in all his later work. The real contradictions of life at the Front were the source of his vision of a theater that would not ignore the realities all around it but would bring them onto the stage.[8]

For his earlier theater productions Piscator had used film and stage machinery to create a documentary montage and to lend the proletariat mechanical, architectural, or geographical strength, as in *Flags* of 1924, which was strongly influenced by Eisenstein's film *The Battleship Potemkin*. The sailors in the film were a collective protagonist set down upon the ship as a powerful, high-speed "people mover," so to speak; thus the old spatio-temporality defined by human speech and bodily movement was expanded and accelerated by a huge machine with superhuman rhythms. A new rhythm and space would also be defined by *Schwejk*'s rolling conveyor-belt stage, but not to amplify organic human rhythms or the human body. Instead, both the organic and the machine spatio-temporality were juxtaposed on the same stage. Piscator thus broke through the self-containedness of dramatic space and time and, with it, the "enchanted circle" of illusion that the theater of Richard Wagner and that of the director Max Reinhardt had tried to create. By 1929, a year after the *Schwejk* production, Piscator could evaluate the source and significance of his innovations over the past decade:

> The two most important results of our theater, stage design and dramaturgy, came about through its *lack of architecture* and *lack of new drama*.
>
> Four of my productions, *Hoppla, Rasputin, Schwejk,* and *Konjunktur,* each had a different type of stage design. This was not the result of a restless technical fantasy constantly looking for new sensations, but was based, strange as it may sound, on Karl Marx's historical materialism. . . . [W]e needed to relate each individual scene to political

events of world importance, and thus to raise it to a level of historical significance. . . . In the stage construction a dynamic principle was developed: [In *Schwejk*] the *rolling stage* or conveyor belt and the dramatic-dynamic construction of the play . . . represented a comic moment in revolutionary theater architectonics . . . it became an integral part of the play's action and thus represents a true *dialectic,* that is, an oscillating interplay between dramatic and technical events.

Similarly, the use of film should be understood . . . as a means to demonstrate the drama's great historical significance, as well as to place the play itself into a historical process. The same ideas apply to our new *dramaturgy*. . . . [A] private fate or individual . . . is no longer the center of the action. *The function of the human being has been changed.* The social aspect of existence is now in the foreground. . . . [If] this . . . produce[s] a caricature human being, . . . it is [because of] the disharmony under which human beings live today, which makes every aspect of life political.[9]

Adapting *Schwejk:* Epic Novel to Epic Theater

The political, comic potential of dialectical montage, with its juxtaposition of actors, mass media, marionettes, and machine, was realized in *The Good Soldier Schwejk*. Of all Piscator's productions, *Schwejk* most strikingly demonstrates why epic theater effected such a revolution in representation. In *The Political Theatre* he explains that he wanted to translate into theatrical terms the anti-heroic, sweeping, bitterly comic portrayal of the First World War in Jaroslav Hašek's epic novel "in order to expose the whole complex of the war under the spotlight of satire, and to illustrate the revolutionary power of humor."[10]

Max Brod, champion of Kafka and other Eastern European writers, discovered the novel of the obscure Bohemian writer, who had died before its completion. Brod and Hans Reimann wrote the first stage adaptation, which disappointed the Piscator collective because it turned the episodic, multilocale narrative into a three-act drama, destroying the sense of restless flux and imposing the formal symmetry of a classical comedy. This treatment effectively *contained* the epic novel, pushing the war into the background, outside the dramatic action. The treatment of space and time in the two versions was at the heart of their difference. The axis of Brod and Reimann's plot was now a romantic triangle involving Schwejk's aristocratic young Lieutenant, the Lieutenant's true love, and the villain to whom she was engaged. Like the age-old comic servant, Schwejk, through no less a venerable cliche than the misplaced confessional letter, accidentally foiled the villain, brought the lovers together, and ended the play by asking to be the godfather of their children.[11] Felix Gasbarra, also a collaborator, explained the group's objections to this first adaptation:

> The flow of a dramatic plot narrowed and shrank everything. . . . No longer were the environment and its representatives the decisive factors, but rather the insignificant individual characters brought in to fulfill the scenic requirements of the comedy. Hašek's thrusts at the monarchy, the bureaucracy, the military, and the church thereby lost all their power. Instead of the Schwejk who takes everything so seriously that it becomes ridiculous, who obeys every order to the point that it becomes sabotage, who affirms everything, but in a manner that negates it, there was now an idiotic orderly who unknowingly turns the fate of his lieutenant to the good![12]

Placing the episodes of the novel into a three-act format destroyed what Bakhtin would have called their *dialogic* quality, making them appear to be isolated from the spatio-temporality of the war, which was now relegated to a static *outside*. Schwejk was spatially and ideologically trapped *inside* each institution in turn, which meant that the church, the military, the court, and the police systems each seemed self-contained and unconnected to the other domains. But Piscator sought a way to present these institutions as the tunnel-visioned drivers of the action and Schwejk as the passenger who is carried along. He explained why he was attracted to the novel: "Other writers consciously 'make a stand' and attempt to formulate an attitude to the war, but the war in Hašek's novel cancels itself out."[13] In other words, the novel presented the war as a montage of many juxtaposed facets rather than reducing it to one individual perspective. It was thus necessary for the collective to go beyond the single-room space and cause-and-effect linear time of the dramatic theater, so that the war could be presented as pieces of a montage that the spectators were entrusted to connect as a system in process. The stage design was simple and economical, as, Hugh Rorrison, the translator of Piscator's book, describes it:

> Two pairs of white flats joined by borders stood 10 and 20 feet behind the proscenium arch, masking the flies and side stage. . . . [Two conveyor belts 9 feet wide ran parallel with each other across the length of the stage.] At the back was a huge white backdrop. The electric conveyor belts . . . were controlled independently. They served as a treadmill on which Schwejk marched, and brought in props like the . . . latrine or the bar. . . . Large pieces . . . came . . . [on the back conveyor belt]. The [white side flats] and backdrop were used for projections (the contents of letters or orders written onstage) and filmed scenery (the streets of Prague) or commentary (George Grosz's cartoons).[14]

When Schwejk was presented as the *picaro* walking from one institution to another across an ideologically neutral space, the spectators saw the church, the military, and the court as actors rather than as inertly stable backdrops or interiors. These institutions — represented by Grosz's cartoonesque wooden cut-outs of an officer's quarters, a courtroom, a pulpit, an army prison, all rolling on and off the stage on the conveyor belts — now became like obstacles in a steeplechase terrain, absurdly arbitrary but still dangerous. Between these rolling obstacles, in the empty expanses of the conveyor belt stage, a *system* could now become apparent, in contrast to the first adaptation, where the sequence of episodes was determined only by a generic formula.

The connection of episodes into a system of war is not in conflict with Brecht's insistence that in epic theater each scene must be able to stand by itself, unlike "Aristotelian" theater, where each scene "inexorably" flows into the next with all subordinated to a centralized plot driven by individual characters. Instead, the independence of the episodes is the very condition allowing the spectator to connect them in more than one way — to use semiotic terms, they are signifiers in process. The world of war as *signification* rather than dramatic *expression* is immediately established in the opening scene; Grosz's cartoon figures representing the army, the justice system, and the church were drawn before the spectators on what Grosz called the "moving notebook," i.e., the screen upon which pictures and texts were projected:

> The play opened with a Czech folk song accompanied by a hurdy-gurdy, then an erratic black line traveled across the screen, eventually forming the figure of a bloated Austrian general, quickly joined by a scowling, bemedaled Prussian general, then between the two a judge with a death's head and a whip, and finally an obese, unshaven clergyman balancing a crucifix on his nose.[15]

Staging the Dialectic

The new, dynamic principle upon which the plot moved was Schwejk's picaresque march from Prague to Belgrade toward Budweis and, finally, to the Front. Schwejk walked, always staying on the same spot, meeting one institution after another as set pieces. The smaller properties, too, often attained the status of living actors: in one scene, for instance, all dialogue stopped as a chair rolled in by itself and halted just behind the person who had expressed a need to sit down. Monty Jacobs, in his opening-night review in *Die Vossische Zeitung,* a liberal Berlin newspaper, recognized the revolution effected by *Schwejk* in its staging of time and space:

> Piscator has obviously conquered the standstill of the narrative by banishing all standing still from his scene. . . . [H]e has replaced the floor with two conveyer belts . . . separated from each other only by a narrow strip of solid land. When the stage manager pushes a button, the earth marches forth. Sets, people, and clouds wander by, quickly or slowly, whisking past or staying. . . . Everything is still in flux. . . . [N]othing was more effective last night than the mute wandering of Schwejk through the countryside, in search of his battalion. The conveyor belt, precipitating the body in one direction, proportionately slows its march in the other direction. The actor walks on and on, and a distance that can be traversed in ten steps becomes the path of a whole life. On the second conveyor belt the world rolls by with its phenomena, the snow falls from the sky, and *it seems as if the stage has conquered time and space.*[16]

This was not the first production to use the conveyor-belt stage; it had been introduced by the Königliche Oper in 1900, and was nearly always employed only to shift quickly from one illusionistic scene to another. The conveyor-belt stage was just one of many technological advances made in Germany during this era. Indeed, by the end of the nineteenth century the German stage apparatus had become the most mechanized in the world, largely in response to the demands of Wagnerian opera, and its financing was guaranteed by a strong economy, government subsidies, and the subscription system. The Piscator-Bühne's conveyor belts were much too loud to produce an illusory self-contained world, however. Instead, they revealed the stage as a means of *representing* the world, the "world" being a field of ideological conflict and Schwejk's life a perilous walk through it. This was a happy accident, however, and not initially intended. In fact, desperate efforts were made to quiet the belts at first, and it took the company some time to realize their full significance for *Schwejk,* as Piscator vividly recalls:

> When we heard the belts in action for the first time . . . they sounded like a traction engine under full steam. They rattled and snorted and pounded so that the whole house quaked. Even at the top of your voice you could hardly make yourself heard. The idea of dialogue on these raging monsters was quite unthinkable. I seem to remember we just sank into the orchestra seats and laughed hysterically. There were twelve days to opening night. The technicians assured us that they could cut down the noise, but there was no longer any mention of silent operation. . . . [Max] Pallenberg [, as Schwejk, was] an actor of unheard-of good will who would make any sacrifice to cooperate, but he was [also]

a very temperamental artist, and naturally apprehensive about the unusual apparatus, especially if it was not even going to work. . . .

It seemed to me that this apparatus had a quality of its own; it was
inherently comic. Every application of the machinery somehow made
you want to laugh. There seemed to be absolute harmony between
subject and machinery. And for the whole thing I had in mind a sort
of knockabout style, reminiscent of Chaplin or vaudeville.[17]

The treadmills became a materialization of our ancient concepts of
life as a road and time as a river — no quietly flowing natural river here,
but a visible and extremely loud mechanical contraption of wood, cloth,
ropes, and pulleys. It is one thing to speak figuratively of our lives being
taken over by the machine, of war sweeping over us, or of being com-
pelled to walk down a certain fateful road. But it is quite another to see
these familiar images materialize as actual machinery in operation. The
Piscator-Bühne had accidentally discovered the potential for subversive
humor inherent in the modern stage apparatus itself. In one stroke not
only was the arbitrariness of spatio-temporal construction made apparent
as ideological but the mystical *aura* of the machine also evaporated. Because the conveyor belts were able to signify lived experience but still
remain a rumbling, screeching contraption, the ideological discourses
carried by the machine could be demystified and deconstructed. No one
spatial or temporal dimension was allowed to physically fill the stage,
time and space were in flux, and thus no integrated, continuous world
was presented: neither the institutions nor the filmed landscapes and city
streets could fill the stage, *not even the open road,* although this was the
chronotope through which all signs intersected. The empty neutrality of
the stage as sign remained visible and audible.

Besides human actors, there were wooden cutout puppets designed
by Grosz that ranged from life-sized to ten or twelve feet tall. There
were also varying degrees of artificiality, from actors with masks and
stylized costumes to life-size cartoonesque marionettes and cartoon
figures on the screen; the aim was to create a hierarchy of familiar bureaucratic and military types. Sometimes the human figures projected
on the screens were large, threatening shadows looming over or following Schwejk, while at other moments they became a line of weary
soldiers marching silently in silhouette over the horizon projected on
the screen. Like the sets, the films and human figures were a mixture of
the naturalistic with the mechanistic and the cartoonesque. Again, instead of a seamless fictional world, an *ideological apparatus* was shown,
a representation of the social, military, and bureaucratic systems.

Schwejk as Speaker of Discourse

As an anti-heroic protagonist, Schwejk "affirmed everything" in the system of war; that is, he performed the discourses of nationalism, tyrannical politics, the military, and the church with a gusto unbefitting their pawn and victim. The discourses thus became conspicuous in their artifice but also in their deadly historical agency. Schwejk's language was full of military slogans, patriotic homilies, and propaganda, but in the context of this character and his experiences they became a satiric weapon against the war rhetoric: coming from the cheerful, peaceable Schwejk, such graffiti slogans as "Jeder Schuß ein Ruß" and "Jeder Stoß ein Franzos" (every shot a Russian, every thrust a Frenchman) attained a comic horror. Schwejk was a walking loudspeaker parroting the discourses of war and thus subjecting them to the *Verfremdungseffekt*. These discourses were also literally "objectified": they entered the scene as objects met on Schwejk's way — cartoon-drawn set pieces of a judge in his chair, a pastor in his pulpit, or a police commissioner at his desk, rolling out from the wings and across the stage on the conveyor belt to meet Schwejk — each representing an institution. The objects here were not set pieces or props as in the dramatic theater, where they serve an illustrative function. In *Schwejk* they presented themselves as signs out to *dominate* space and time, with no pretense of a transcendental aura.

In one scene Schwejk zealously adopted the same discourse of numbers that was used to obfuscate the operations of war and dehumanize the war casualties by rhetorically representing them as statistics. The scene took place beside an army transport train of the type that moved millions of men — an inexhaustible flow of human statistics — to the Front. After a long walk in search of his battalion, Schwejk was glad to finally be riding a train again — not realizing that he was being sent into the battle zone by the military, who hoped to get rid of him. His enthusiastic obedience and unflagging praise of the war had convinced them that he was not only a deserter but quite possibly a master spy for the Allies, cleverly disguising himself behind a stupid appearance. Schwejk's virtuoso command of the discourse of numbers allowed him to temporarily conquer his oppressors: he aroused the suspicions of the officers by voluntarily going through a routine of military exercises on his own so as "not to waste their precious time." The bullying Sergeant Nasakla was subsequently assigned to fill Schwejk's time by drilling him in rifle maneuvers to the point of exhaustion. As the Sergeant finished with the drill and was lighting a cigarette, however, Schwejk examined the number on the rifle and launched into a numerical dissertation that would bring his opponent to the floor:

Schwejk talks the Sergeant to the ground. The Adventures of the Good Soldier Schwejk, Piscator-Bühne, 1928. *By permission of the Erwin Piscator Center, Berlin.*

SCHWEJK: 4268! A locomotive in Petschek on track 16 had that number. It
             was to be towed away, to Lissa on the Elbe, to the repair shop,
             but that wasn't so easily done, Sergeant, because the engineer
             that was supposed to drag it away had a very bad memory for
             numbers. So the Station Master called him into his office and said
             to him: "On track 16 is number 4268. I know you got a very bad
             memory for numbers and if somebody writes it down for you . . .
             you only lose the paper. Now pay close attention to me. . . . The
             first number is a 4, the second a 2. So alright, you can already
             memorize 42, that's 2 times 2, starting at the beginning with the
             first number, is four divided by 2 is 2, and what have you got, 4
             and 2. Now, don't be frightened, how much is 2 times 4 — 8,
             ain't it?. . . Now [it] will never be lost out of your memory . . . or
             can you think of a simpler way of getting the same result?"

NASAKLA: Cap off!

SCHWEJK: So then he began to explain to him in a simpler way . . . .
             "Remember," the Station Master said, "that 2 times 42 is 84.
             The year has 12 months. . . . With division . . . it's just as easy.
             You figure the lowest common denominator out by taking the
             tariff duties." Ain't you feeling well, Sergeant? If you want, I'll
             begin all over again with the rifle discharge. . . . For heaven's sake
             . . . I got to get a stretcher.

(People arrive . . . with a stretcher . . . Nasakla is quite ill . . .) [He has
collapsed and is being carried away as Schwejk bends over him,
continuing to speak]

             But I don't want you to miss the end of this story, Sergeant. You
             think maybe the engineer remembered it, don't you? He got all
             mixed up and multiplied everything by three — because all he
             could remember was the Holy Trinity . . . and he never even
             found the locomotive and it's still standing there on track 16.[18]

Was Schwejk actually talking to the "real" Sergeant when he said,
"Now pay close attention"? If it could be proven that he were doing
so, then he might be accused of insubordination; but, instead, he had
removed himself from his story to the safe distance of the *fictional stage
present* and was only quoting another storyteller's words, impersonating
the narrator within the narration. Not accidentally, Schwejk was
speaking in the persona of the Station Master, who had an overview of
the whereabouts of the trains, their schedules, the numbers of the cars,
and, of course, the human miscalculations — in short, of the entire
network of operations imposed on the territory in wartime. Schwejk
played the role of the Station Master down to the last exhausting detail
and thrust the Sergeant into the role of hapless listener. A reversal of

power was signaled by a radical shift in their spatial relationship, with Schwejk looking down at his superior, who was now lying prone on a stretcher — in effect, trading places with the common soldier, for whom it was "normal" to be carried off dead or wounded from the battlefield. In the fictional stage present, Schwejk was just a military prisoner being railroaded to his trial, a statistic at the mercy of his *Vorgesetzte*, conventionally translated as "superiors," but literally "those who have been set in front of him" — in short, obstacles. The narrative he enacted put the unseen persona of the Station Master, and thus Schwejk himself, in control of the movements of his listeners. Although the two actors were physically on a treadmill representing a piece of land in front of a stopped railroad car, Schwejk had trapped the Sergeant in the position of the diegetic "Locomotive Driver" in the office of the panoptic Station Master.

A Gestic Object Reports

Like certain other objects, both visible and invisible, the rifle was *gestic:* it could be appropriated by more than one discourse and was therefore treacherous. Here it defined a social relationship and was a focal point both of the military's strategic propaganda and of the real killing that this propaganda was attempting to obscure. Discursively, it could and did backfire: in the first instance, the Sergeant forced Schwejk to perform the ritual movements of the military with the rifle, loading, shouldering, and firing it, in time with his commands. In the second, the mimetic rifle remained innocent and passive in Schwejk's hands during his whole narrative. But by using its serial number alone, Schwejk succeeded in *killing time*, especially the time of his adversary. Thus the rifle remained a weapon even twice removed from the battlefield, because it did, after all, set off the first and second rounds of discourse, the latter numerical narrative in effect defeating the previous military ritual. The number on the rifle was taken on a dizzy trip through Schwejk's subversive narrative. He never had to fire the gun, because the complex — indeed almost mystical — numerical connections in the story between guns, railroad cars, the calendar, and the tariff duties brought the Sergeant down. As a figure of authority, the Sergeant had at his command only the limited ritual of the military. He was no match for the rhetorical figure of *enumeratio* that Schwejk marshaled against him — that is, the endless proliferation of numbers by which any claim whatsoever can be "proven." *Enumeratio* is the principle of endless semiosis itself, the proliferation of chains of signifiers and signifieds that are never arrested anywhere as meaning, and so can be channeled towards any meaning at all. Schwejk functioned here as a kind of switchboard vandal who headed the discourse of numbers off into all sorts of directions and systems, thereby rendering unintelligible the central "intelligence" of the military, who thought to maintain control of the whole semiotic process of the war.

As the Sergeant lay on the ground, Schwejk, good sport that he was, asked if he should "begin the rifle charge" again; this would allow his adversary to have a head start in one last defense of himself and his authority. But the Sergeant was by now incapable of replying at all. As a climactic finale Schwejk, still impersonating the Station Master, performed the Last Rites for the Sergeant by letting his numbers dramatically stop at the Trinity. Thus Schwejk managed to temporarily derail and reroute the system by which railroad cars and common soldiers were hauled away to the Front.

Maneuvers on the Railway

In an earlier train ride Schwejk had literally stopped the train that was carrying him from Prague to Budweis to join his company. This was another scene that the collaborators agreed was all-important to the translating of the epic from the literary to the theatrical medium. Here the gestic object was the emergency brake, which in effect moved from the immediate mimetic space to the narrativized diegetic space and then abruptly back into the mimetic. Like the rifle, the emergency brake was a passive prop on stage until Schwejk whisked it away into his "off the track" story, after which it reemerged into the stage present and mysteriously seemed to pull itself, bringing the train to an abrupt and screeching halt.

(Schwejk walks to the end of the corridor, where a Conductor is stationed)

SCHWEJK: Can I have your permission to ask you something?

CONDUCTOR: (nods weakly and apathetically)

SCHWEJK: A very fine man comes to see me now and then, a fellow named Hoffmann and he always claimed that . . . the emergency brake, if you pull it, just won't work. To tell the truth, I never bothered about it, but now that this emergency alarm gadget is right in front of my eye, I'd like to know just where I am, in case I ever have to use it.

CONDUCTOR: He told you that right, that you have to pull this brake, but he lied that it don't work. The train always stops when this signal is connected with the locomotive. . . . (During their discussion both have taken hold of the emergency signal and pulled it. The train stops suddenly, with an earsplitting screech.)

CONDUCTOR: That was you.

SCHWEJK: That wasn't me.

CONDUCTOR: You pulled it.

SCHWEJK: That's impossible. I'm surprised myself that the train suddenly stopped. Why? It's traveling along and all of a sudden it stops. That annoys me more than it annoys you.

CONDUCTOR: The station master in Tabor will explain it to you, all right. That's going to cost you twenty crowns.

SCHWEJK: It really stops for twenty crowns . . . that's awful cheap. But we don't have to stand here anymore, we can go on now. It's not so agreeable if the train is late. If it was peace time now, it wouldn't make much difference. But in a war, everybody ought to know that army people, major generals, lieutenant's orderlies are on every train. Making a train late like this is a very crafty trick. Napoleon was five minutes late at Waterloo and by that time he and his fame were down the drain. . . .

[to his lieutenant] . . . Beg to report, Lieutenant sir, they blamed me for stopping the train. Beg to report, they're taking me to the Station Master.

(the scene changes)

— Act II, Scene 1–2, p. 3–4 [Italics mine.]

Again Schwejk had succeeded in (inadvertently?) *subverting the timetable and spatial track of the war,* by killing the time of the *Conductor,* who would have conducted him to the battlefield. Schwejk's subsequent meeting with the Station Master in Tabor was not seen, but it is learned that his military papers were accidentally taken away by his superior officer on the train to Budweis. With no papers and no money, he was not allowed to take another train and was arrested at the train station by the military police for having no papers:

CORPORAL: I beg to report, Lieutenant, we picked this man up at the station without any papers.

LIEUTENANT: Aha . . . and what were you doing at the station?

SCHWEJK: Beg to report, Lieutenant, I was waiting for the train to Budweis so that I could get to my regiment, the Ninety-First where I'm orderly for Lieutenant Lukasch, who they forced me to leave because I was taken to the Station Master after I was suspected of stopping the train in which we was going to Budweis by pulling the emergency brake after I just had the conductor explain it to me.

LIEUTENANT: You're driving me crazy, I can't make head or tail of a thing
              you're saying. Now tell me in a few words and in simple
              language and stop spouting nonsense! . . .

SCHWEJK: Beg to report, Lieutenant sir, I got to tell everything. I got to
              let it all out so that I have a whole view of it, to get the entire
              thing spread out clear in front of me. . . .

                           — Act II, Scene 3, p. 11 [Italics mine.]

By "letting it all out" through the story of his journey, Schwejk was creating a kind of *map*, a "whole view" that would perhaps be "spread out
clear in front" of the spectator at least, if not Schwejk himself. Throughout the play, Schwejk tried to place the events of his life into one narrative frame after another and thereby gain a measure of control over the
territory; he had represented and re-represented his journey through it:
we see the power of irony causing one momentary breakdown after another in the systems of representation in this *theater of war*.

As the picaro in search of his company, traveling on foot, in his
wheelchair, or on the trains, Schwejk showed a special affection for
train *stations*, in contrast to the flux going past them. A train station for
Schwejk seemed more a steadfast friend than an inanimate, passive locale. Ironically, as the only space that became familiar to him, the train
station was also the most dangerous space, since it was from here that
his enemies, the police and the military, carried out their strategy of
control and surveillance. In the persona of the elusive Station Master
(elusive to the spectator, that is, since the Station Master appears only
in Schwejk's dialogue), Schwejk seemed to gain an aerial view of the
whole topography of his journey.

The War into Focus: *Camera Lucida*

Each encounter with a train station became more dangerous than the
last. After a long walk through the peaceful countryside passing by him
on film, Schwejk found himself in the same village he had left the night
before; to his annoyance, he realized that he had only walked in a wide
circle. This time his arrival was foreshadowed ominously by silhouettes
of policemen seen behind the projection of a map with moving arrows
tracing his path. He was met at the village crossroads by the security
police, who had already received a message identifying him as a deserter
and spy. This time it was an *absent* train station that became the locus
of the action, the *scene of a crime* committed by those representing the
law. This time too, appropriately, it was not a *real object* but a hypo-
thetical one that carried the Gestus. The object was a camera, a pro-

ducer of representations. Even though it was a camera that did not exist, the policeman used it to fabricate an incriminating narrative of Schwejk as master spy:

> (Again a town approaches. It is slowly becoming lighter. Policemen are seen through the map. The arrow shows that Schwejk is making a wide detour around the town. The map fades, the landscape moves forward until the crossroad is reached. Policemen (drawn if necessary) appear and then disappear again. Film stops. Signpost with four arms rolls on.) . . . (Police station rolls on.). . . .

> POLICEMAN: (to desk sergeant) . . . The fellow is as slick as an eel. . . . Who would have suspected that. . . ? He looks stupid, doesn't he, like a halfwit. But they're just the kind — you've got to sneak up on. . . . He must be one of their higher officers. . . .

> (to Schwejk) Do you know how to take pictures?

> SCHWEJK: Yes.

> POLICEMAN: And why haven't you a camera with you?

> SCHWEJK: Because I ain't got one.

> POLICEMAN: But if you had one, you'd take pictures, wouldn't you? Do you find it difficult, for example, to photograph a railroad station?

> SCHWEJK: That's easier than some other things, because it don't move and you don't have to say: hold it, now smile.

> POLICEMAN: (writes) "During my cross-examination, he admitted, among other things, that he was not only able to take pictures but that he likes to photograph railroad stations most of all. Beyond a doubt, only the fact that he had no camera in his possession prevented him from making photographs of the station structure. The fact that he did not have a camera at hand is directly responsible for the fact that [it was] impossible to find any photographs on his person."

> — Act II, Scene 2, p. 11 [Italics mine.]

As the Policeman wrote this report in his notebook, his writing was also projected on the screen: in short, the writing was being *mechanically reproduced at the same moment that it was being produced*. In his report the Policeman was accusing Schwejk of photographing — mechanically reproducing — the railroad stations. While Schwejk had no camera on his person, the Policeman was not wrong to suspect the presence of one. In fact, the whole production of *The Good Soldier Schwejk* was the "camera" — both the image and the apparatus that produced it. *The stage was at once the interior chamber of the camera, the camera as machine, the moving film, the "original subject," and that subject's image.* This complex Gestus of the epic stage as a camera attests to Roland

Barthes's assertion that photography is a *camera lucida,* a chamber of light, and not a *camera obscura,* or chamber of darkness:

> It is *camera lucida* that we should say (such was the name of that apparatus, anterior to Photography, which permitted drawing an object through a prism, one eye on the model and the other on the paper). . . .[19]

The epic stage itself was such a *camera lucida,* producing the slides, films, and animated cartoons that laid out Schwejk's journey before the spectators. These technological media were in *dialectical oscillation* with Schwejk's spoken narratives; physical aspect; the manner, speed, and direction of his movement; and his spatial relationship to the objects and persons on stage. All of this constituted a *counter-discourse:* Schwejk walked against the forces rushing toward or towering over him.

Pedestrian Tactics, Territorial Strategies

In Michel de Certeau's terms, Schwejk employed one *tactic* after another in an attempt to walk safely through the great *strategy* of the war that was laid out as a deadly terrain before him. His situation vis à vis the war is clearly described in de Certeau's definitions of strategy and tactic:

> I call a *strategy* the calculation (or manipulation) of power relationships that becomes possible as soon as a subject with will and power (a business, an army, a city, [an] institution) can be isolated. It postulates a *place* that can be delimited as its *own* and serve as the base from which relations with an *exteriority* composed of targets or threats . . . can be managed. . . . It is also a mastery of places through sign. The division of space makes possible a *panoptic practice* proceeding from a place whence the eye can transform foreign forces into objects that can be observed and measured, and thus control . . . them. . . . (35–36)
> By contrast, . . . a *tactic* is a calculated action determined by the absence of a proper locus. . . . The space of a tactic is the space of the other. Thus it must play on and with a terrain imposed on it and organized by the law of a foreign power. It . . . is a maneuver "within the enemy's field of vision.". . . In short, a tactic is an art of the weak. . . . Lacking its own place, lacking a view of the whole, limited by the blindness (which may lead to perspicacity) resulting from combat at close quarters, limited by the possibilities of the moment, a tactic is determined by the *absence of power* just as strategy is organized by the postulation of power. . . . (37–39)[20]

Schwejk is the tactician and pedestrian par excellence, in de Certeau's terms. Yet he was already crippled for this march before he began it: no longer young, he had already served in the army and had rheumatism in his legs and feet. However, the Austro-Hungarian government was now calling everyone from teenage boys to crippled veterans. Accordingly, in the third scene of the play Schwejk had received a draft notice and immediately wanted to join his company. He called his landlady for crutches and a wheelchair and set off into the streets of Prague. The path of his journey was shown by traveling film footage of the city and countryside, which actually proceeded in the same direction as the treadmill, with Schwejk rolling against it yet staying in the same spot. Amid all this fruitless effort, he could be seen cheerfully pointing his crutch forward and upward like a saber, rolling off in his wheelchair to join his company. This iconic pose communicated the Gestus of the entire *Fabel* with all its contradictions, and the photo taken of it would become the most widely reproduced sign of this historic production.

SCHWEJK: Fight! . . . Except for my feet, I'm a good healthy piece of cannon fodder and in times like this . . . every cripple has got to be in his place. Mrs. Müller, I need a pair of crutches! Ain't the confectioner across the street got some? He has? Get them! He's got a little go-cart too, ain't he? Get it! And a flower for my buttonhole.

MRS. MÜLLER: (crying) I'll buy it.

SCHWEJK: And my Army cap!

MRS. MÜLLER: I'll get that too. (Begins to sob loudly)

(Scene: Street in Prague . . .)

SCHWEJK: (in a wheelchair . . . he is waving his crutches . . .) On to Belgrade! On to Belgrade!

— Act I, Scenes 3, 4, p. 5–6

It ultimately could not be decided whether Schwejk was a fool who unwittingly subverted the discourses of the war, or whether he was only playing the fool. The spectators were divided in their reactions: some reported that Max Pallenberg's naïveté showed "something of the good, innocent, long-suffering animal who does not know," while others, like Piscator and Brecht themselves, saw an edge of "vicious irony" beneath the innocent manner. Even though the performance included revolutionary songs and clearly sided with the powerless, reserving its sharpest caricatures for those with power, Piscator realized that Schwejk's power of negation went beyond any one political ideology, including Marxism:

This was Schwejk's significance: he was not just a clown whose antics ultimately affirm the state of things, but a grand skeptic whose rigid, untiring affirmation of reality reduces reality to nullity. Schwejk, we argued, is a deeply asocial element: not a revolutionary who wants a new order, but a type without any social links who would be destructive even in a Communist society.[21]

The crucial point is that Schwejk's character acted as an unlikely sounding board upon which the discourses bounced back to reverberate in his quotation of militaristic slogans, and that his mobile face all too faithfully reflected the enthusiasm of militaristic, patriotic propaganda. He was the epic character par excellence, able to "play back" the discourses mechanically, revealing their contradictions, their inane terror, through *Verfremdung*. But to do so he had to be suspended between multiple dimensions of space and time and between the human and the machine, as described by Barthes and Walter Benjamin.[22]

Barthes also explains the status of walking as a social sign: "To walk is perhaps — mythologically — the most trivial, hence the most human gesture. Every dream, every ideal image, every social preferment first suppresses the legs."[23] If the walking of Schwejk established his disruptive force as an anti-heroic character, it was the epic stage that allowed him to do so. On the stage of the traditional dramatic theater, the actor cannot walk long or far, only off into the wings to the left or right, in circles, or, at most, up and down stairs. Walking over long distances cannot be represented on such a stage. Even though Max Pallenberg actually moved only along a horizontal line parallel with the front of the stage, Schwejk was represented as walking for weeks and over miles of territory that was materialized through film and a few set pieces. Adding to the multidimensional complexity of the representation, the audience knew that the horizontal span of the conveyor belts was short-lived and relative, since they circled immediately under the stage at one side and back up on the other — like the mourning crepe in the Dadaist contest between the sewing machine and the typewriter.

Schwejk's long march to Budweis, titled *The Anabasis,* used the Dadaistic montage of multiple spatial and temporal dimensions juxtaposed in one work. Here time and space were overtly constructed by the stage and juxtaposed before the spectators. The stage was set into dialectical flux by the movement of Schwejk, the conveyor belts, and the scenes in the film. Schwejk said little here, and the apparatus of the stage became the sole narrator of his journey. In this last march, which he believed was still in the direction of Budweis but was actually in the direction of the front, the territory shown in the moving film was gradually transformed. The filmed landscape changed from railroad track to highway to woods and in the process became *a moving away from the temporalities and spaces of the war.* Schwejk's erratic journey to the Front was "followed" by a dotted line moving over a large map projected onto the screen. As the *Anabasis* scene began, a typewritten narrative appeared on the screen with a message that credited Xenophon, "a Greek historian and general," with having proven by "marching around the north without a map for a long time, that all roads lead to Rome." The historical Anabasis was the march of the Greeks through Asia Minor, which Xenophon wrote about but did not experience first-hand. This partly real and partly fictional march became a satirical version of the "great histories" that rely on the historian's reconstruction of the spatio-temporal map. Schwejk's walk "wrote" such a history of the Great War in Europe.

THE ANABASIS-THE MARCH TO BUDWEIS:

SCENE 5   FILM

Railroad tracks, then a Highway, then a Forest. Railroad tracks, signal lamps, signal posts, a watchman's shack, gates at a grade crossing and then the highway, from which the lights of Tabor can be seen. . . . The lights travel along for a stretch, keeping pace and shifting toward the middle, slip back into the distance and disappear entirely, as if behind a hill. In the background, the night sky, against which a hilly landscape with woods is dimly silhouetted. Fade into a map showing Budweis. The arrows point out Schwejk's direction. The following appears in white print on the screen:

(SCHWEJK MARCHES) "Xenophon, a general of ancient times hastened
        through entire Asia Minor, and ended up, without maps, God
        knows where. Continuous marching in a straight line is called
        Anabasis. Far off, somewhere . . . on the Gallic Sea, Caesar's
        legions, which had also arrived there without the aid of maps,
        decided to return to Rome by a different route and were
        successful. Since then . . . it has been said that all roads lead to
        Rome. It might just as easily be said that all roads lead to
        Budweis, a statement which Schwejk fully believed. And the
        devil knows how it happened that he, instead of going south to
        Budweis, marched straight toward the west.". . .

(SCHWEJK SINGS A MELANCHOLY AIR. . . . STOPS AND LIGHTS HIS PIPE.) The shots
        of the distant landscape have continued to travel past
        throughout the titles. The landscape in the distance begins to
        move faster and faster, while the scene in the immediate
        proximity retains Schwejk's marching tempo. . . . Fadeout. Cut
        into shot of snowy wood.

— Act II, Scene 3, p. 5–6

For the *Anabasis* scene several temporalities appeared simultaneously on stage: Schwejk walked at his usual marching tempo, while the conveyor-belt "road" under him accelerated the passing by of the world around him. Here the familiar concept of life as a passage — a passing through time and space — was materialized and *defamiliarized:* Schwejk and the scenes passed by each other, both the filmed scenes and the set pieces on the conveyor belts. The stage was in flux, nothing *stood* in relation to anything else; instead, everything was *underway*. The film footage passed by at differing rhythms, with all but the nearest landscape following a faster tempo than Schwejk's. The film at first followed the line of a railroad track but appeared to turn away from it as Schwejk became lost; that is, the train track no longer ran parallel with the conveyor-belt highway taken by Schwejk.

A larger image of the war-crossed territory of Europe gradually emerged over the course of the production: the clearing of "a whole view of it, the entire thing spread out clear in front" of the spectators, to borrow Schwejk's words. The expanding *war machine* had appropriated railroads first and highways second, transforming them into the "arteries" of its own abstract organism, which was imposed on the natural terrain. Soldiers and ammunition were conveyed in mass quantities via the railroads and highways — these now fatal arteries — to the Front, transforming the land in the process. The lines of the railroad and highways were used to redraw this terrain as a military map, a steeplechase of danger zones. By contrast, the spatio-temporality of the woods and fields was not represented by lines: it did not follow the tempo of the military or of the news media's march of events, and its space seemed remote from the strategized war zone.

The temporality of "official history" was literally written on the screen by a projector, and the space of the stage was thus visibly traversed by historical discourse moving in a certain tempo: the travels of Xenophon, Caesar, and Schwejk marched by in white printed letters on the screen, a mechanized realization of the proverbial writing on the wall. This "march of living history" was time as represented by the twentieth-century newsreel — which had appropriated and was now mechanically animating the time line of the history book. Schwejk's journey was also transcribed into the military's writing of space and time: his maneuvers were reduced to dotted lines, maps and arrows, abstract geometrical designs projected on the screen. The stage conveyed the sad irony of this map being superimposed on the slowly moving landscape. Schwejk's song — the voicing of human temporality — was sad. In the same slow rhythm as the song, the films of a starry night sky and of snow falling in a forest presented time as the cycle of seasons. These temporalities were sharply juxtaposed with both the newsreel's reduction of time to links in a chain of incongruous events forced into contiguity, and with the military's image of time as a moving line.

The Ending in Dispute

Because the author Jaroslav Hašek died before he could finish his novel, the Piscator-Bühne Collective had to invent an ending. Reimann and Brod's ending was clearly unacceptable, since it forced the events into a classically symmetrical, static circle with an archetypal comic ending: marriage and the birth of a child "rounding off" the events, a ritual of social stability wherein the traditional values were reinstated and their continuation assured for the future. Several different endings were considered, none of them satisfactory to everyone. Their struggle illuminates how difficult it was — and is — to confront and shift the ideological meanings entrenched in our theatrical conventions. Grosz's idea was "A slapstick scene: 'everything in ruins.' Or: The characters sit around as skeletons with death's head masks. They drink each other's health."[24]

Piscator, however, decided to end the play with a scene called "Schwejk in Heaven," wherein the protagonist faced God, represented by a projected cartoon figure that Grosz made to resemble another scowling, mustachioed military authority in a pointed helmet: this face initially filled the whole screen, and loomed gigantically over the stage and the small figure of Schwejk, but, confronted with Schwejk's discourse, it shrank smaller and smaller and finally dwindled to nothing. As a part of this final scene there was also a "parade of cripples before God," played partly by human actors and partly by cutout cartoon marionettes, wherein wounded, disemboweled, and disfigured soldiers and civilians rolled across the stage on the front conveyor belt. Piscator's description makes it understandable why the audience at the preview was so shocked by this scene that it was only played once:

> CASTING NOTES FOR THE LAST SCENE
>   Cripples before God.
> Sign up legless beggars.
> 20 life-size dolls as extras.
> 5–6 real cripples.
> One constantly treading on his own entrails.
> One shouldering a leg.
> One with his head under his arm.
> Arms and legs hanging out of rucksacks, smeared with mud and blood.
> Two little girls, hand in hand, with bloody faces.[25]

Piscator does not clearly say what was substituted for this ending, but a typescript preserved by Brecht indicates Schwejk crouching with another soldier behind two mounds on the battlefield. Schwejk says he wants to stick it out so that his bones can be turned into ashes for the sugar refinery to "sweeten his children's coffee." The other soldier leaves, preferring the hospital. A cartoon shows a Russian soldier swimming in a pond; a bush with the Russian's clothes hanging on it rolls onto the stage, after which the cartoon shows him running away. Schwejk tries on the Russian soldier's uniform and is arrested by a Hungarian soldier who does not understand that Schwejk is also Hungarian and on his side. A shell explodes and Schwejk falls. Then a film of a line of crosses is projected onto the back screen, which makes them seem to "march" from the horizon toward the spectators: they first appear at the top of this screen, then grow larger in perspective as they reach the bottom of it, after which the film is picked up by a gauze lowered downstage near the spectators, causing the crosses to suddenly loom up just in front of them.[26]

The violence of this ending was no longer naturalistic but was effected by an abrupt shift in the spatio-temporal orientation. The dominant movement of the play had been from side to side across the stage, like the traveling of the eye over lines of type. But without warning the "page" exploded in the middle of Schwejk's speech. The war had finally killed Schwejk's time and space. The treadmills representing time as a river came to a standstill, and the landscape that had always followed parallel to Schwejk's path, but at a far distance, suddenly seemed to wheel around toward the audience and advance from the back of the stage. It "stepped over" the tracks of Schwejk's picaresque journey at a perpendicular angle, poured over the edge of the stage, and invaded the space of the spectators. In this ultimate moment the spectators achieved a "station-master's view" of the topography and discourses of war. Piscator represented the writing of history not as a finished and unchangeable book whose pages he merely opened one after another, revealing still-life scenes. Instead, the whole stage was turned into a mobile epic actor suspended and oscillating between the human and the mechanical.

Epic Space and Time, Contained and Released

The question may arise here of how both the novel and Piscator's production were able to signify the epic "sweep" of continuous movement if the episodes were clearly separated from each other, as Brecht emphasized that they must be. A clue to the answer lies in Felix Gasbarra's remark that in a three-act dramatic structure "the air of the epic is lost." The existence of "air" as *atmosphere* or breathing space appears to be necessary, both in reading and in watching the staged event. There cannot be an unbroken string of fully present events; instead, *a rhythm of absences* is needed — visible absences following a certain tempo — in

order for the spatio-temporality to signify continuity, or, for that matter, to signify any movement at all. This pattern of presence and absence is also what Derrida calls *spacing,* which is endemic to the
Western concept of reading and writing as a continuum.[27] In our inevitably geometrical perception of this process, we *see* meaning as a
chain of writing where words alternate with *empty spaces,* or "air." We
are able to connect and expand the segments of the writ-
ing/reading/meaning because there is "air." Like *signification, spacing*
is a verb as well as a noun, the *temporal process* of writing/reading as
well as the *text* as a thing. *Spacing* in Derrida's sense is also the habit of
thinking in the terms of what Bachelard called *container space,* with its
attendant myth of inside and outside, as established in Euclid's geometry. In his own way, Derrida recognizes the persistent hold of container
space on the very process of reading and writing signs. It is this *signification as spacing* that *Schwejk* made material, visible, and audible for us
through the *Verfremdungseffekt.* This was a new, deconstructive *writing of history,* which the epic theater staged in order to show that real
politics and wars are theatrical productions as well, and that it is within
the spectators' power to dismantle the entire machine.

In *The Good Soldier Schwejk* the picaresque travels of its hero over
the First World War landscape brought together the European continent as a topography under the temporary control of an anarchic humor and a political imagination that transgressed the lines set up by
nationalistic and military zoning. Indeed, the humor of *Schwejk* was
powerful enough to momentarily halt the flow of ideological discourse
and to obscure the borders dividing the original Weimar audience:
spectators from the left, right, and center of the increasingly polarized
political spectrum were able to laugh at Schwejk's adventures. But as
we know from the newspaper reviews, they could not appropriate them
for or against any single political ideology.

Bernard Dort, France's foremost Brecht scholar,[28] and Walter Huder, founding director of the Erwin-Piscator-Center in Berlin,[29] when
asked to contemplate why Piscator and Brecht effected such a revolution of theatrical time and space, offered strikingly similar answers.
They explained that *epic time is both contained and released through spatial images.* In other words, epic theater *demonstrates* that *space and
time are imagined as container and contained,* and in the acknowledg-
ment it *releases them.* It is clear that innumerable contemporary politically engaged directors, including Peter Stein, Ariane Mnouchkine,
Patrice Chéreau, Giorgio Strehler, and JoAnne Akalaitis, owe a great
debt to the work of Piscator and his collective. Indeed, Brecht himself
often attested to the profound importance to his own work of all of

Piscator's stagings, especially *The Adventures of the Good Soldier Schwejk*. Brecht's production of *Mother Courage* twenty-one years later stands as eloquent testimony to this fact.

Notes

[1] Erwin Piscator, *Das politische Theater* (Berlin: Adelbert Schultz, 1929), 1. After fifty years this important book finally became available in English: *The Political Theatre*, trans. and with introductions by Hugh Rorrison (London: Avon, 1978). Rorrison's commentary supplies more information about the productions than Piscator originally included. Wherever I have supplied my own translation, as here, the note will list the German version first. Where Rorrison's translation is used, the English version will be listed first.

[2] Erwin Piscator, "Wie unterscheidet sich das *Epische* bei Brecht — bei mir?" Diary 15, 1955 or 1956. Cited by John Willett in his informative study *The Theatre of Erwin Piscator: Fifty Years of Politics in the Theatre* (London: Eyre Methuen, 1978), 187. C. D. Innes's *Piscator's Political Theatre* (London: Cambridge UP, 1972), the first major study of the director in English, is also extremely valuable. It aroused the interest of the Anglophone world in Piscator and sparked a reevaluation of his work.

[3] Karl Marx, *Manifesto of the Communist Party* (1848), in *The Marx-Engels Reader*, ed. and trans. Robert C. Tucker (New York: Norton, 1979), 469–500.

[4] Marx, *The Eighteenth Brumaire of Louis Bonaparte.* (1851), in *The Marx-Engels Reader*, 594–617. Citation from 594.

[5] By 1928 Grosz and Heartfield had become well known for their satirical poster montages linking Nazism with Big Capitalism, the latter instantly recognizable as the cartoon figure of a corpulent, red-faced, balding, cigar-smoking, rich bourgeois with a frock coat and diamond stickpin.

[6] Walter Benjamin, "The Work of Art in the Age of Mechanical Reproduction," in his *Illuminations*, trans. Harry Zohn, ed. Hannah Arendt (New York: Schocken, 1969), 238. The last line of this essay is also relevant to the *Schwejk* production: "[M]ass movements, including war, constitute a form of human behavior which particularly favors mechanical equipment" (251).

[7] Account given by Wieland Herzfelde in "Dada-Show," Summer 1918. Printed in Franz Jung, *Der Weg Nach Unten* (Neuwied: Berlin-West, 1977), 1242. Another Dada Show at the Charlottenburg Palace is recalled by Piscator in "Piscator über den Dadaismus," recorded October 6, 1959. In the Erwin-Piscator-Center, Akademie der Künste, Berlin.

[8] Piscator, *The Political Theatre*, 14–15.

[9] Piscator, "Rechenschaft (1)," an account of the work of the Piscator-Bühne in Berlin, lecture at the former Berlin "Herrenhaus," March 25, 1929. In *Erwin Piscator: Schriften 2. Aufsätze, Reden, Gespräche* (Berlin: Henschelverlag

Kunst und Gesellschaft, 1968), 51–52. An English version appears under the title "An Account of our Work 1929," in *Erwin Piscator: Political Theatre, 1920–1966* (London: London Arts Council, 1971).

[10] Piscator, *Das politische Theater*, 188. *(The Political Theatre, 254)*.

[11] Herbert Knust, ed., *Materialien zu Bertolt Brechts "Schweyk im zweiten Weltkrieg"* (Frankfurt am Main: Suhrkamp, 1974), 17–18. Knust includes a summary of the Brod-Reimann script, the full original 1928 version *Die Abenteuer des braven Soldaten Schwejk* by the Piscator collective, photos, an essay, a few surviving drawings by George Grosz, Brecht's 1943 script *Schweyk im zweiten Weltkrieg*, and editorial markings in Brecht's personal copy of Hašek's novel. In 1967 Brod published a "revision" of the 1928 Brod-Reimann adaptation, for which he incorporated almost all of the Piscator-Bühne's changes and left little of his own text.

[12] Felix Gasbarra, in *Die Welt am Abend* (Berlin newspaper), January 1928. Quoted by Piscator, *Das politische Theater*, 190–191.

[13] Erwin Piscator, *Das politische Theater*, 187. (*The Political Theatre*, 256.)

[14] Hugh Rorrison, Introduction to Piscator's chapter XIX, "Epic Satire: The Adventures of the Good Soldier Schwejk," in *The Political Theatre*, 250–251.

[15] Rorrison, Introduction to *Schwejk*, 251. Several of George Grosz's graffiti-like, satirical cartoons outraged the right wing. Grosz and Heartfield were bitterly critical of the role of Germany's "humanitarian" institutions in promoting the war. One drawing depicted a fragile Christ nailed to a cross in a devastated battlefield; on his head is a crown of thorns and on his face a gas mask. The caption reads: "Shut up and keep serving." This drawing was used as evidence to accuse Grosz and Heartfield of blasphemy, an archaic charge that allowed the police to confiscate the drawings and destroy all the plates. After several trials for blasphemy and insulting the military, the two were acquitted. They became a rallying cause for liberals and leftists.

[16] Monty Jacobs, "Pallenberg auf Rollen. 'Schwejk' auf der Piscator-Bühne," review in *Die Vossische Zeitung*, January 24, 1928; in the Erwin-Piscator-Center, Berlin. This review is included, with excerpts from other press reviews of the production, in Günther Rühle's collection of reviews for every major German production during the Weimar Republic, *Theater für die Republik 1917–1933 im Spiegel der Kritik*. (Frankfurt am Main: Fischer, 1967), 840–848.

[17] Piscator, *The Political Theatre*, 260–261. (*Das politische Theater*, 182.)

[18] Act II, Scene 5 (e), "*Schweik — The Good Soldier*. Dramatized from the novel by Jaroslav Hašek. As revised and staged by Erwin Piscator" (18–20. Manuscript in the Erwin-Piscator-Center. All quotations are from this version, with minor changes to conform with the original German. Subsequent quotations will be identified by act, scene, and page number.

[19] Roland Barthes, *Camera Lucida: Reflections on Photography*, trans. Richard Howard (New York: Hill and Wang, 1981), 106. Barthes's remarks on the

historical structure of the photograph also apply to epic theater: "The Photograph then becomes a bizarre [new] *medium* . . . : false on the level of perception, true on the level of time: a temporal hallucination, . . . a modest, *shared* hallucination (on the one hand 'it is not there,' on the other 'but it has indeed been') (115). . . . Such are the two ways of the Photograph. The choice is mine: to subject its spectacle to the civilized code of perfect illusions, or to confront in it the wakening of intractable reality" (119).

[20] Michel de Certeau, *The Practice of Everyday Life,* trans. Steven Rendall (Berkeley, Los Angeles, and London: U of California P, 1984). See "Strategies and Tactics," 34–39, and "Walking in the City," 91–110.

[21] Piscator, *The Political Theatre,* 268. *(Das politische Theater,* 202.)

[22] Walter Benjamin and Roland Barthes offer profound insights into the aesthetic and ideological significance of the epic theater. See for example: Walter Benjamin, "What is Epic Theater?" in *Illuminations,* trans. Harry Zohn, ed. Hannah Arendt (New York: Schocken, 1969), 147–154, and "The Author as Producer," in *Reflections,* trans. Edmund Jephcott, ed. Peter Demetz (New York: Harcourt Brace Jovanovich, 1978), 220–283; and Roland Barthes, "Diderot, Brecht, Eisenstein," in *Image – Music – Text,* trans. Stephen Heath (New York: Hill and Wang, 1977), 69–78.

[23] Roland Barthes, "The Harcourt Actor," in *The Eiffel Tower and Other Mythologies,* trans. Richard Howard (New York: Hill and Wang, 1979), 20.

[24] Piscator, *The Political Theatre,* 261–262.

[25] Piscator, *The Political Theatre,* 262.

[26] Hugh Rorrison takes this version of the new ending from Brecht's typescript in the Bertolt-Brecht-Archiv, Berlin, in *The Political Theatre,* 252–253.

[27] Jacques Derrida, *Of Grammatology,* trans. Gayatri Chakravorty Spivak (Baltimore and London: Johns Hopkins UP, 1974).

[28] Bernard Dort, conversation in Paris, February 1985. Dort's influential essays on Brecht appeared with those by Barthes in issues of the journal *Théâtre populaire* during the 1950s. Other discussions of Brecht and epic theater are found in Dort's *Lecture de Brecht* (1960), *Théâtre public* (1967), *Théâtre réel* (1971), and *Théâtre en jeu* (1979), all published by Éditions du Seuil, Paris.

[29] Walter Huder, conversation in Berlin, June 1985. Dr. Huder was professor of theater at the Freie Universität-Berlin and founding director of the Erwin-Piscator-Center at the Akademie der Künste, Berlin. This archive has organized world exhibitions and produced catalogues and other publications on Piscator.

Mother Courage and Her Children, *Berliner Ensemble, 1949.*
By permission of the Bertolt Brecht Archive, Berlin. Photo by Wolfgang Meyenfels.

Mother Courage and the Cook, with Helene Weigel as Courage.
Mother Courage and Her Children, *Berliner Ensemble, 1949.*
By permission of the Bertolt Brecht Archive, Berlin.
Photo by Wolfgang Meyenfels.

2: Into the Whirlwind: Brecht Directs *Mother Courage*

> Sometimes I see myself driving through hell with this wagon and sell-
> ing brimstone. And sometimes I'm driving through heaven handing
> out provisions to wandering souls! If only we could find a place where
> there's no shooting, me and my children — what's left of 'em — we
> might rest up a while.
>
> — Mother Courage, Scene 9[1]

MOTHER COURAGE PULLS HER WAGON over a treadmill. Kattrin climbs atop a house to beat her drum and warn a village of attack. The pregnant Sophie is thrown to the ground by her lover Baal. Queen Anne leaves her throne in pursuit of her husband Edward IV and "runs through the forest like a she-wolf." Pirate Jenny sails away from the burning town on a black ship. Grusha flees into the mountains with a baby boy she has rescued. These are framed moments of women moving through the Brechtian theatrical space that defines them and that they conversely delineate. A basic premise for this study is that epic theatrical space is not a neutral container but an important participant in the temporal action. This chapter will look at the female characters of *Mother Courage* as part of the dialectic that makes the play move through the time and space it sets up.

Women on the Ideological Landscape: The Didactic Tradition.

We recall that Barthes read Racine's tragedies as a whole and deduced a primal space and narrative that would render all the characters and plots coherent in their motivation, even though the motivating myth itself is not "rational" and cannot be reduced any further.[2] When Brecht's works are read in this way, one is left not with a fixed space and contained design of time, as in Racine, but with a long series of "social landscapes," tableaux seen along the route of a traveler. From the stories of the individual female characters a metanarrative can be constructed that closely parallels, in particular, eighteenth-century models of the picaresque heroine, such as Daniel Defoe's Moll Flanders. Like Schwejk, the original Courage also first appeared as a picaresque character in a novel;

Brecht adapted her from the seventeenth-century novel by Hans Jacob Christoffel von Grimmelshausen, *Courage, the Adventuress.*[3]

Brecht's debt to the Piscator Collective's *The Good Soldier Schwejk* is also clear: in both plays and their performances the epic sweep results from the spectator following the walk of the protagonist through a hostile landscape of war. Brecht's protagonists are, with few exceptions, exiles, characters who live precariously and travel ceaselessly — often literally walk — through the social tableaux of their societies, and his women characters are exiles in an even more profound sense. Whatever Brecht's conscious attitudes toward women may have been, these characters serve the purpose of epic theater even better than he perhaps realized, because they are in a position to ironically reveal, to a more radical extent than is possible for male characters, the social systems in which they are relatively powerless. This is because throughout most of history women have had to move outside the centers of power even within their own class, whether peasant, bourgeois, or aristocrat; they are also, as Julia Kristeva notes, the proletariat of the proletariat.

It was a necessary first step for feminist studies to demonstrate that male writers have traditionally used women as stereotypes and, in the case of Brecht, also as "didactic objects" rather than as fully realized subjects.[4] The next step is to investigate women characters as important signs within the social tableaux depicted by artists and writers. The didactic stereotype, if read as a symptom, reveals political and ideological tensions within the social system. Brecht often uses women characters to demonstrate exemplary socialist selflessness, most notably in *The Mother, St. Joan of the Stockyards, The Caucasian Chalk Circle,* and *The Good Person of Setzuan,* and even went so far as to call socialism itself a "hard but loving mother" on several occasions. But in most of these plays, as in *Mother Courage and Her Children,* the "examples" are complex indeed.

Brecht's use of female characters in a didactic function follows a German literary and dramatic tradition that can be traced back at least to the seventeenth century but that reached the height of its popularity during the Enlightenment and *Sturm und Drang.* Women were used as a locus for the debates of political rationalism in Lessing's *Emilia Galotti,* Gellert's *The Delicate Sisters,* Schiller's *Cabal and Love* and *Maria Stuart,* and Lenz's *The Soldiers.* The plight of women in these plays is significant if looked at from a feminist perspective, because the role assigned to them by society and aesthetics is always strategically designed to harmonize the ideologically disharmonious and conceal the ruptures between those ideologies and the real conditions they attempt to justify. At the same time that women characters in these plays are exiled from power, they are, as didactic objects, accorded the double task of veiling society's seams and reflecting its values. In the didacticism of Brecht, as in that of the Enlightenment, the woman as a *figure*, whether she is mother, lover, or deity, is the favorite medium through which ideologies are displayed, disguised, and appropriated. She is often glimpsed as separate *parts* of a physical body-as-object. In Schiller's *Cabal and Love,* for instance, the eyes of the female figure are supposed to function as a metaphorical mirror in which the hero can verify his ideal selfhood as this is defined by bourgeois values. But since these eyes also belong to a character with her own narrative, they are an unstable sign. They can be used to constitute an "underground subject," from whose viewpoint the dominant ideologies of the text can be criticized.

Feminist Interventions

Simone de Beauvoir spoke for many when she insisted that the orthodox Marxist account of labor and politics is radically flawed because it stops at a point where it cannot see patriarchy itself as political; if patriarchy exists it is natural, outside the political realm.[5] This kind of orthodoxy does not recognize that the conventions of the family and marriage are a basic part of any political structure, nor does it accord the traditional work of women the status of labor. Sara Lennox,[6] in writing about Brecht's women characters, shares Simone de Beauvoir's disenchantment and faults Brecht with being blinded by the prejudices of Marxism itself, notwithstanding Engels' essays on the family structure under capitalism. Lennox is typical of the generation of feminists two decades ago who were rightly disillusioned with Brecht and many other male heroes of the left who were systematically blind to the injustices that women had historically suffered. In fact, many of these ex-heroes were helping to naturalize and perpetuate sexist and even misogynist attitudes. During the 1970s Brecht's real-life relationships with women came under attack, particularly his flagrant affairs with female collaborators and young actresses, affairs that he hardly bothered to conceal from his wife, the actress Helene Weigel. She took on the day-to-day management of the Berliner Ensemble while Brecht was free to do only the artistic work, as well as taking most of the credit for the success of the theater, as John Fuegi has documented.[7] Worse, Brecht took credit for some of his women collaborators' writings.

Fuegi, however, follows the earlier feminist generation in ignoring the immense contribution of Brecht's work as a model for feminist theater. In fact, the principles of epic theater have been extremely important to all theaters of social liberation, including postcolonialist, African-American, and gay and lesbian, as contemporary feminists such as Jill Dolan, Janelle Reinelt, and Elin Diamond have recognized.[8]

Yet the potential for a strong feminist critique exists in Brecht's own plays and productions, as well as in the principles of epic theory and stage practice that he and Piscator developed. In turn, both men recognized the great potential for epic characters and situations that existed in Marx's writings. Such is the case for *Mother Courage,* as well as *Schwejk.* There is, in *Das Kapital,* an *image* of the proletarian that distinctly applies to the picaresque figure, particularly the *pícara,* or female picaresque. Marx introduces the narrative and space of the marketplace:

> The proletarian is obliged to offer for sale as a commodity that very labor-power which exists only in his [/her] living self. [He/she] is mortal . . . and will eventually be withdrawn from the market by wear and tear and death.

Then he displays the protagonist and antagonist in an exemplary tableau:

> The capitalist . . . strides in front; the seller of labor-power follows . . . the one with an air of importance, smirking, intent on business; the other, timid and holding back, like one who is bringing his [/her] hide to market and has nothing to expect but — a hiding.[9]

In Marx's tableau we see movement, gesture, and attitude: the proletarian's skin is torn or worn away through the life-long walk to the market. This "market," or capitalist society as a whole, is presented by Brecht as a series of tableaux on the epic stage. Like Marx's proletarian, the epic characters in *Mother Courage* and *Schwejk* walk themselves to death.

The similarities among the life stories of various women characters also allow a metanarrative to be projected whose features are picaresque. Read syntagmatically, the metanarrative consists of four main segments, each of which is animated by a stereotyped character. Almost all of Brecht's female characters live out stories that have been familiar for centuries: the naive girl is seduced and abandoned, the prostitute avenges herself by gaining financial advantage, the entrepreneur becomes ruthless in her drive to make a profit, the martyr-mother sacrifices herself for the helpless. Sometimes a single character, such as Mother Courage, "travels" through several segments that are close variations on those listed above: as we know from her recitation in the opening scene, Courage has children by three different men who abandon or mistreat her and the children. In the "Song of the Great Capitulation," the unnamed mother — like Courage herself — must quickly learn to "march in step," in order to keep herself and her children alive:

And marching with the band you'll go
Keeping in step, now fast, now slow,
And piping out your little spiel.
Then one day the battalions wheel
(Two children round your neck and the price of bread and what all!)
When they were through with me, moreover,
They had me where they wanted me . . .
And [I went] down upon my [ass and upon my] knees.

— Mother Courage, Scene 4[10]

We never learn precisely what the "marching" entails, but we do know that the capitulation involves a lowering of expectations and a violent physical degradation. We know that during the long time span represented by the play, Anna Fierling, alias Mother Courage, has become ever more intent on profit. Finally, she inadvertently martyrs herself and her children by her inability to leave the battlefield/market, which is destroying itself. Jenny of *The Threepenny Opera,* on the other hand, moves from the role of a prostitute dominated by her pimp Macheath to that of an entrepreneur who allies herself with the capitalist Peachum. She was a mother briefly, but the baby's death cut this narrative short. Shen Te of *The Good Person of Setzuan* begins as a naïve virgin, proceeds to prostitution, and then splits into martyr-mother and capitalist entrepreneur. Interestingly, Brecht had his female protagonist disguise herself as a male so that the two stereotypes could appear within the same time frame. The two segments of the metanarrative, one featuring the naïve girl and the other the ruthless entrepeneur, usually appear as two stages of an economic developmental process, but in this play Brecht has collapsed them together without any "character development."

A character in one of Brecht's plays often could be an older or younger version of a character in another, as if one woman were changing her name many times. In *Baal,* we last see Sophie kneeling in the dark forest to pray for and curse Baal, her "child and lover." Perhaps Sophie found her way out of the forest and went to the city as Jenny, where she now plots her revenge against Baal, now grown into a middle-aged bourgeois called Macheath. Segments of the picaresque metanarrative are discernible as pasts and futures introduced into the dramatic present through songs, as in Macheath and Jenny's "Pimp's Ballad" and Courage's "Song of the Great Capitulation." Certain iconic tableaux also appear repeatedly, such as that of the pious mother on her knees praying for her child who is in danger. In *Mother Courage,* Kattrin visibly ironizes this icon by contradicting it move for move: while the peasant woman kneels on the ground to pray that the town will awaken before the soldiers kill them, Kattrin climbs up on the nearest roof and beats her drum to warn them. The juxtaposition of the two spatial movements is a pointedly ironic contradiction of the courses of political action versus inaction.

Women Travelers in Epic Territory: A Material History

The picaresque stories are not always verbally narrated but are often told through the language of movement through space. The main patterns of women characters' spatial movement indicated in Brecht's plays are a circling about at the outer edges of the stage (the prostitutes in *The Threepenny Opera);* a transversal of it (Mother Courage, Queen Anne in *Edward IV);* a descent (*Baal*'s Sophie, the mothers kneeling in prayer, and Joan Dark, who parodies Christ by descending three times into "the depths" of the stockyard workers' world); and last, an ascent (Grusha fleeing into the mountains to save the child, and Kattrin climbing onto the roof to warn the town). In these spatial movements women move through, past, or all around the center but do not claim it as a permanent base — in contrast to Galileo, Arturo Ui, and even Azdak (in his capacity as judge, not as wanderer). These patterns constitute a didactic stage rhetoric that speaks a semiotic language in its own right.

The use of concrete spatio-temporal narrative is one of the main distinguishing marks of Brecht's conscious practice as a playwright and director. The rhetorical tableaux of the epic stage recall the show wagons of the medieval theater, which was sometimes viewed by spectators walking about on a performance ground or over the space of a town, going from one wagon to the next, each tableau representing a station in the characters' — and also the spectators' — concrete journey through life. As a theatrical device, Mother Courage's wagon thus brings to mind the long history of the stage; the wagon-stage even has a curtain with the title "Mother Courage" written on it. It not only contains scenes and moves through and constitutes the theatrical "socioscapes" but also reminds us that our own time-space is part of the historical pageant.

To bring the theatrical space into a temporal dynamic, Brecht relied on what he called *details,* by which he meant the revelatory moments of contact between people and real objects, moments that reveal the story of a life in one *Gestus.* In his director's notes on the 1949 Berliner Ensemble production of *Mother Courage* Brecht writes that the empty stage with the cyclorama allows the spectator to imagine, by turns, a sky and landscape that first promise adventure and then an "immeasurable wasteland" in the final scenes of the play. Brecht allows the large picture to be approximate, but not the details involving people, objects, and the contact between them:

> Whereas there is a lovely vagueness in the large picture, there is none in what is small. For a realistic production the most painstaking detail in costume and properties is essential, for here the fantasy of the spectator can supply nothing. The work and eating utensils must be specified in the most loving way. . . .
>
> The details, even the smallest one, must of course be completely played out on our floodlit stage. This is especially true of procedures such as the moment of payment in a business exchange. [Helene] Weigel invented her own small gesture for this: she shut the leather money bag that was hanging around her neck with an audible snap. . . . In accordance with the fundamental principle of epic theater, the details must be worked out thoroughly and inventively *one after the other.*[11]

Such plays of signification — *details* — involve not only the material stage properties but also objects that appear in patterns of imagery in the dialogue; the two are always interrelated. In Brecht's work, in particular, objects give meaning to a character's acts by making those acts material. In Barthes's often quoted example, the whole social situation, life-attitude, and fate of Mother Courage are revealed at the moment when she bites down to test the coin.[12] "Mother Courage bites on the coin offered by the recruiting sergeant and, as a result of this brief interval of distrust, loses her son, and demonstrates at once her past as tradeswoman and the future that awaits her — all her children dead in consequence of her money-making blindness." But objects may and often do allow new readings that contradict and even *defamiliarize* Brecht's intended didactic framework, so far as we can determine his intentions from his production notes, essays, and other sources. The fact that epic theater is based on the principle of the dialectic allows such "critical seeing" at every moment, opening the possibility of a feminist critique that does not invalidate the Marxist one but *deploys* and extends it to include subjects and classes that had not been visible before as such.

Tactics and Strategies

Spatio-temporal patterns involving characters' relationships to objects and, in particular, material *details* of everyday work are signs capable of producing political meanings. Some meanings have been realized overtly, while others are potential. Michel de Certeau in *The Practice of Everyday Life* employs two useful terms for the analysis of epic spatio-temporality:

tactics and *strategies*. Tactics are the purview of those who lack political and economic power, while strategies are that of the powerful:

> [*A tactic*] operates in isolated actions, blow by blow. It takes advantage of "opportunities" and depends on them, being without any base. . . . [L]acking . . . a view of the whole, [with] blindness . . . resulting from combat at close quarters, . . . a tactic is determined by the *absence of power* just as strategy is organized by the postulation of power. . . . [A] *strategy* [makes it possible for] a subject with will and power [to create] *systems and totalizing discourses* [in] physical places [where] forces are distributed.[13]

Clearly, women have historically been limited to tactics. In this sense, Brecht's female characters are even more antiheroic and picaresque than such typical male protagonists as Schwejk, Galy Gay, and Azdak. Both male and female characters are, however, necessarily involved in complex tactical and tactile relationships with the objects around them; the work of survival is a series of tactics whose purpose is to avoid being overpowered by the great strategies that are all around them but of which they have no commanding overview. In this play the war can be seen as a strategy dictated by those with political and economic power. Religion in this work is an ideological discourse that strategists manipulate — and within which tacticians try to maneuver. The characters seen on stage do not dictate the strategy of war but are engaged in tactics through which they hope to survive it. The war in *Mother Courage* is ubiquitous, and the territories are constantly shifting from one power to another and are never safe for the powerless, even during the episodes when "peace breaks out." Thus strategies are even more bewildering than in a time of political stability, because they are shifting constantly, so that tactics that brought safety under one strategy suddenly bring danger or even death, as is the case for Eilif and Swiss Cheese. In fact, many tactics only perpetuate the war. Sometimes characters learn a tactic that helps them survive one strategy but that proves fatal when they are confronted with another. Eilif learns during wartime that murder and plunder make him a hero; however, as soon as "peace breaks out," he is condemned to death for the same acts. Brecht contends that survival tactics, if practiced collectively, can undermine oppressive strategies. The *details* of material, tactical existence have revolutionary potential, which is why epic theater tries to single them out.

The surprising complexity of these details is revealed in the 1961 film of the Berliner Ensemble production.[14] Most striking are complex tactics that every character in the play uses in trying to find and keep a place within a social network that cannot be kept safe any more but is only precariously held together. Death and starvation are always around the next turn of the scenery. In reading the play and from documentation and descriptions by spectators who were there, we might take for granted that the Cook is a naturally carefree type to whom women are always attracted. The film, however, shows a different picture: with great effort he puts on his carefree, rakish manner like a costume to please Mother Courage, but the moment she leaves he slumps down in total exhaustion, reverting to the starving, desperate old man that he has become. Such tactics, which were visible on stage but are lost in the reading, also bring unexpected humor even to the most tragic moments: in Kattrin's last minutes on the roof, she suddenly sees her mother's wagon below and hesitates before drumming, realizing that it will save the children but also endanger the wagon that is her mother's livelihood — a lifetime of protecting this wagon seems to flash by in a second of indecision, then regret. Then in one movement she rolls her eyes, pulls down her mouth with a puff, and waves her hand — a *Gestus* of dismissal — and drums with great glee as hard as she can. Seconds later she is dead of gunfire.

Such moments make every character more complex and human than expected, and the moments are powerful, even overwhelming, in their cumulative effect. It becomes evident that the characters are not amoral; in fact, they try their best to protect each other, but every tactic they employ to save one person seems to result in the death of another. It also becomes very clear that Courage never stops trying to protect her children, even when she haggles over the wagon and seals her son's doom. We see that neither she nor anyone else has any time to reflect but only to react to the next danger and the next. All this belies the impression, gained from decades of critical writings, that the action stops for each *Verfremdungseffekt,* giving time for the spectator — and actor — to reflect. This is not the case; the action is as unrelenting as the war it represents. The moment of Courage biting the coin stands out not because the play paused there, but only because by the end the spectator has witnessed so many similar moments that there is a powerful cumulative effect, that of looking back and seeing one crushing truth: *that the war did not have to happen.*

Spatio-Temporality in Multiple Dimensions

Mother Courage offers a complex interplay of spatio-temporal signification patterns and female stereotypes. Besides the characters on stage, there are several women from other spatio-temporal dimensions: the old woman in "The Song of the Wife and the Soldier," who watches the young man go to war and prays as the cold water is "eating" his body away; the child Kattrin who is made speechless when a soldier "puts something into her mouth"; the young Anna Fierling; and the young Yvette. In order to analyze more closely how the women characters interact as signs in an overall pattern of signification we turn to Umberto Eco, who explains in *A Theory of Semiotics* that semiotics is grounded in materialism and that it thus accepts all signs as empirically capable of meaning. Every text, whether explicitly or implicitly ideological, must call on a "semantic universe" for its signs and, therefore, from the outset must lay itself open for a potential reading that could "turn the ideological system on its head." That is, the signs once appropriated to support one ideology may speak on behalf of a counter-ideology. All that is needed for such a reading is to question the original ideology's equivalences. Because semiotics can reveal the construction of ideological texts, Eco says, it can be a form of *social criticism* and thus a kind of *social practice*. [15]

To analyze the spatio-temporality of the play, the dramatic space can be divided into the *mimetic* and the *diegetic* spaces. [16] All of the signification processes touch each other at every point, and every theatrical sign is a sign in the act of becoming. The rhythmic shifting of objects and characters between the mimetic and the diegetic space comprises the complex signification process that makes *Mutter Courage* seem to move under its own power. The interplay of signs between these two spaces gives a sense of the play's dialectical structure, and the overall spatio-temporal dynamic is the signifier that can be read as an integrated system or signified, which in turn *refers* to the real space of the spectator via his or her interpretation. To Brecht and the audience at the Berliner Ensemble production in 1949, the immediate referent was Europe during the World Wars. Berlin itself was still in ruins from the bombs of the Second World War, and spectators reportedly had to step over the rubble as they made their way into the theater; thus the war-torn city itself was certainly part of that original dramatic space.

The Wagon as Frame and Object

The most obviously significant object in the play is the wagon. It is always visible in the mimetic space and all spatial and temporal signification systems converge on it. It is the nexus that organizes the diegetic and mimetic space and their manifestation as a temporality. The characters' spatial relationships to it reveal the *Gestus* of their presence in the play. Mother Courage is initially "on top of the world" through which she travels: she rides with her daughter upon the seat singing like a vagabond in a folkloric idyll, her two sons in the harness pulling. The wagon is both house and business, and it provides for the family materially; but in the context of the war it also aids in brutalizing and short-ening their lives. By the end of the play all the children have disap-peared, and Mother Courage pulls the wagon by herself. Through the framework of this wagon Courage and the world, including that of the spectator, encounter each other. This "framework" is not like a picture frame that contains a scene within itself but is, rather, like a scaffolding: a small wooden wagon-stage that rolls like an ox at a turnstile around Brecht's revolving stage.

The wagon is the front that Courage presents to the world: her "stage name" is lettered on it. It is also the flimsy structure that sepa-rates the family from the ever more desolate scenes through which they travel. The sons, as the two "oxen" who first pull the wagon, are also the first to be killed, "slaughtered like cattle" for performing the tactics their mother has taught them to ensure their survival. At first Kattrin rides high beside her mother on the front seat of the wagon as a chariot of adventure; but as the war wears on and her hope and confidence di-minish, the wagon is transformed into a kind of enclosure where she retreats to hide her shame and disfigurement. As the sons disappear one after another, Courage and Kattrin take their places in the yoke and pull the wagon themselves, suggesting that they are, like the sons, also headed toward death. Kattrin, however, turns herself away from this route by spatially and figuratively rising above it at the end of the play. For his part, the Chaplain must sleep *under* the wagon, an efficient stage sign of his material dependence on Mother Courage, his lack of sexual privilege, and his lowered social status. The wagon, moving around and around the turntable stage representing the territory of the Thirty Years' War, is a platform stage, a curtained enclosure, and a backdrop for the physical action. It is the vehicle that animates and or-ganizes the story and promises to carry its meaning to us, the didactic vehicle that Brecht uses to represent the economic system, and the per-vasive image of the picaresque journey.

The Other Objects — *Details*

But more humble objects are also significant. If we look first at their simple frequency, we note that the largest number of objects in the mimetic space, i.e., objects visible onstage, fall into the classification of clothing and wrapping. The next largest group includes food, drink, and utensils connected to eating and food preparation. The last three groups, in descending order, are weapons, wood, and musical instru-ments: the fife, drums, harmonica, and bells. The significance of the musical instruments is of a different order than that of the other objects: their visible aspect is less important than their ability to mark out diverse spaces, narrate the events, evoke the past and future both objectively and emotionally, and set up effects of repetition.

Items of clothing and wrapping on stage are always costumes, always overt vehicles of meaning signifying beyond their utilitarian function, theatrical signs in both the mimetic and the diegetic space. And in *Mother Courage* they appear and reappear in a unique manner, because single articles physically "travel" from one character to another, changing hands — or feet or heads or backs — across both the mimetic and the diegetic space. The red boots, for example, pass from Yvette to Kattrin to Mother Courage. The boots connect Yvette's spatio-temporal narrative to that of the other women; the boots are needed for her picaresque march. They are an ambivalent sign: by long tradition, red signals the prostitute, is historically associated by the church with sin, and connotes female sexuality, menstruation, and fertility. But, drawing on the imagery of revolution, the shoes recall the marching Red Army. Yvette wears the boots for her journey along what Brecht calls the *Hurenlaufbahn*,[17] translated as "the whore's career," but literally the running track of the whore, her "beat." In terms of the encompassing picaresque epic space, which frames all of the above connotations, the red boots are a visual image of a traveler's bloody feet and strikingly recall Marx's figure of the worn and torn proletarian. Most important, however, is the fact that these boots will outlast the feet who wear them.

We see a woman's fur coat worn by a soldier and know the route it has traveled from the diegetic space to the mimetic: it was a hide cut off an animal, made into a coat that was bought by a wealthy woman, and probably stolen by the soldier, who now possesses nothing else. In the mimetic space, the soldier wearing it tries to escape with a bottle from Mother Courage's wagon. Already angry at losing the profit from the linen shirts, she takes the price of the bottle "out of his hide":

> MOTHER COURAGE: *Seeing First Soldier trying to make off with the bottle he's been drinking from:* Stop, you pig, if you want another victory you must pay for it!
>
> FIRST SOLDIER: I have nothing.
>
> MOTHER COURAGE: *Tearing the fur coat off him:* Then leave this, it's stolen anyhow.
>
> — Scene 5

The movement involving the fur coat is one of many similarly violent "business transactions" that gradually constitute themselves as the signs of a giant system of exchange — an economy. The German word *Schlacht* means both "battle" and "slaughter," and from this basic analogy a wealth of images are descended, many of which, unfortunately, must be lost in any translation. In Brecht's design, slaughter and battle become phases in a cycle that also includes cooking and eating:

[T]hey'll make hamburger of me.

— Eilif, Scene 2[18]

The knife impales/ And the water devours those who wade in it.

— Courage, Scene 2, 26

I'll chop you into cutlets!

— Young Soldier, Scene 4, 55

Poor people . . . have to hang each other one by one, they slaughter each other in the lump, so if they want to look each other in the face once in a while — well, it takes courage, that's all.

— Courage, Scene 6

The war will feed its man / As long as there is gunpowder and lead / From lead alone it can't live / Nor from powder; it needs human beings too!

— Courage, Scene 8, 89

Cloth and Clothing

Protective blankets cover the wagon and tents. To hide her scar, Kattrin not only retreats to the interior of the wagon but also puts a blanket over her head. At the end, Mother Courage uses a blanket to cradle and finally to cover Kattrin's dead body. It is women who most often handle the various kinds of cloth, which is one of the few forms of property that characters possess for any length of time. But it either wears away or is destined for the dead and dying. The linen shirts were intended to be sold to officers, but Kattrin and the Chaplain tear them into strips to try to stop the wounded from bleeding to death. Cloth and wrapping are used in an attempt to stop the freezing and bleeding of the war, but the blood comes through in spite of their efforts. The women spend a great deal of time on stage sewing, washing, mending, and carrying clothes about — at one point, Courage and Kattrin actually string a clothesline from the wagon to a cannon, on which they sit to fold their wash (Scene 3). Their activity and the stage images it evokes are deeply ambivalent: are they tying up the cannon or costuming it to give its deadliness a domestic disguise? Or are they laying a fuse; and, if so, are they forming an alliance with the cannon or aiming this cannon at their own wagon? The spectator is left to weave the contradictory signs into a text. In any case, all of this bandaging, weaving, and clothing is finally in vain, because it cannot keep pace with the war.

The most striking feature of women's mimetic action is that it consists almost entirely of repetitive and incessant physical work involving household objects: washing, mending, bandaging, preparing food, sharpening kitchen knives, bartering, and haggling over prices. Whether the country is Sweden, Poland, or Germany, in a camp or on the highway, this work continues. But all of the objects are drawn into the system of signs that come to mean slaughter. In Scene 3 we see Kattrin and the Chaplain cleaning kitchen knives, then he sings the "Song of the Hours," which includes a reference to Jesus being speared in the side: "Daraus Blut und Wasser ran" (Out of it blood and water ran). Soon Courage joins them in cleaning the knives, and shortly thereafter Swiss Cheese is carried back to them as a corpse and finally taken away to be "thrown into the carrion-pit." The mimetic knives were thus on display in their domestic context during the very time that the son was being murdered in the unseen diegetic space. The knives appear innocent, but as *signs* they have been mobilized for slaughter.

Animals

Animal imagery is another important sign system that constitutes Brecht's powerful materialist analogy between war and butchery. Animals in *Mother Courage* are neither "characters" nor "objects." Rather, in the diegetic space indicated by dialogue they function as characters, while in the mimetic space of the stage they function as objects. More than twenty species of animals appear in the dialogue, most of them in the form of textual imagery. When the term *imagery* is used here, it is not in the traditional literary sense. Imagery in the dramatic text is aimed much more at defining the material spatio-temporality than is imagery in any other form of literature; it has a material dimension that is not a device to "color" the language. Rather, it helps constitute *other scenes* that are just beyond the visible.

Once the diegetic and mimetic spaces are established as a *dialectical relationship* rather than two separate *containers,* the sign system involving animals takes on a life of its own. Animals are used as a topos of the *Fabel* in order to say something about the human world; these animals, however, are not wholly drawn into any aesthetic system, including the neat this-for-that economy of the traditional fable. Instead, they maintain an unrecuperated materiality by *returning in the form of meat.* At the outset of the play the sons are oxen in the diegetic space; that is, they are derisively referred to as such by the recruiting officer, but real pieces of beef and other meat soon physically appear on stage, i.e., in the mimetic space. In Scene 2 the Cook and Mother Courage argue over the value of his piece of beef compared to her freshly cleaned capon. The scene has a grisly comic effect as the meat "comes alive" in the dialogue of its two "parents": Mother Courage incongruously boasts about the capon as if it were her son, while the Cook claims to have been a "personal" acquaintance of the ox:

MOTHER COURAGE: Look, this is no ordinary capon. It was such a talented animal that it would only eat when they played it some music. It fact, it had its own way of marching. It was so intelligent it could count. Forty hellers is too much for all this? I know your problem: if you don't find something to eat and quick, the Chief will tear your head off.

THE COOK: All right, just watch. *He takes a piece of beef and lays his knife on it.* Here's a piece of beef, I'm going to roast it. I give you one more chance.

MOTHER COURAGE: Roast it, go ahead, it's only one year old.

THE COOK: One *day* old! Yesterday it was an ox. I personally saw him.

MOTHER COURAGE: In that case he must have started stinking before he died.

— Scene 3

The reference to marching connects the capon and the ox to the soldiers and to the pervasive walking of the picaresque. The fact that the ox and capon are both castrated male animals is also a comment on the mutilating effect of war: they are both marching to the slaughter, as the soldiers — indeed the whole population — are marching into battle. We can compare this scene to the description of the two sons earlier in the play: they were ridiculed for impersonating oxen and being trapped in their mother's harness, but the alternative was for the army to lead them like "calves to the slaughter":

THE OFFICER: And you two oxen pull the cart. Jacob Ox and Esau Ox. Do you ever get out of the harness?

— Scene 2

The most numerous animals in the diegetic space are cattle, followed by chickens, dogs, lice, wolves, hyenas, and snakes. There is significance in the order and mode of their appearance: cattle appear far more frequently than any other animal, and references to them are scattered throughout the play, whereas dogs are found in the latter half only. Wolves are mentioned only four times, always at a fatal crossroads, and thus act as "milestones" on the road to hell. Wolves are also the last animals we "see" in *Mother Courage,* as they are left to roam the now wild and ravaged landscape. The slaughter imagery is over-loaded with cattle:

> [They] want to run away from their mother, the devils, and off to war like calves to salt.
>> — *Courage,* Scene 5[19]

But dogs are also often victims:

> Chop up that dog, I'll advise you.
>> — *Courage,* Scene 4[20]

In general, the farther from civilization the animal stays, the more likely it is to be a survivor:

> then they have to be as sly as the snakes, or they're through.
>> — *Courage,* Scene 1, 25

Mother Courage herself is becoming more and more "brutalized." She sees her existence as a dog's life but seems blind to her own part in the slaughter economy:

> I'm tired of wandering too, I feel like a butcher's dog taking meat to my customers and getting none myself. . . . They say the villagers in Pommerschen have been eating the younger children.
>> — Scene 9[21]

The Chaplain reminds her that she does eat the meat from the war, even though she does not do the actual killing:

> You're a hyena of the battlefield. . . . You don't want peace, but war, so you can make your profit.
>> — Chaplain, Scene 8

The Dialectical Movement of Humans, Animals, and Objects

The movement of animals in relation to that of human characters re-solves itself into a distinct system: the animals are living when they appear in the diegetic space, but they are dead when they reach the mimetic space. For humans, this movement is exactly reversed: they are living characters in the mimetic space, but they disappear, are killed, and reverse their course *out of our sight* — in a blind spot, so to speak — and then reappear as corpses in the diegetic space. As the play's time proceeds, the dead begin to invade both the mimetic and diegetic spaces: human corpses appear onstage, while more and more animals die offstage and in imagery. The movement of signs is thus a clear dialectic, which resembles the figure of a *chiasmus*. Everything is drawn into this movement, which signifies the cycle or economy of war. All the activities of life are swept into the chiasmus, which is devouring everything, including itself. To fuel this movement, the soldiers always find a moment to "multiply" — to produce more flesh so that the resulting babies help "balance out" the loss of body parts and lives. And, after all, mutilated people can still hop around:

> You could have a leg shot off, at first you let out a big scream, as if it were something, but then you calm down . . . and finally you're hopping around again . . . and why can't you be fruitful and multiply in the very midst of all the slaughter? . . . and so the war has your offspring and can carry on with them.
>
> — Chaplain, Scene 6[22]

Like Marx's proletarian in the marketplace, the characters in *Mother Courage* try to keep on their feet as long as possible, even while they are going down "on their knees," as the woman in the "Song of the Great Capitulation" relates. The war calls on all to begin the march: "And what's not yet dead / gets out of bed . . . " (Mother Courage, Scene 1, 9). In the first scene of the play the Sergeant praises the war for bringing everything into the neat economic order of a balance sheet:

> Only where there's a war are people and cattle cleanly counted and taken away! Because everyone knows: no order, no war!
>
> — Sergeant, Scene 1[23]

The process that Brecht ironically has the Sergeant praise is also what happens semiotically in the play: everything — people, animals, and objects — is part of the "great capitulation." Humans, tame and wild animals, food, work tools, weapons and clothing are "put into order" — literally, their heads are counted and chopped off as they are pulled into the tornadic "march" to the slaughter/market place. The war draws everything into its orderly chiasmic cycle of destruction. Brecht uses the image of a whirlwind in connection with the war :

> I sometimes ask myself how it would be if our relation should be somewhat more firmly . . . cemented. I mean now that the wind of war has whirled us so strangely together.
>
> — Chaplain, Scene 6

The Breathing Space

Only in the diegetic space of imagery does there seem to be any rest, but these spaces are nearly always associated with death: the snow, a pond, an icy sea, and, appearing repeatedly, the grave. The forest is the

only place to rest that does not necessarily entail death, and this is
where another sign system, fainter than the others but still legible, is
located: that involving trees and wood. This sign system is set up in
opposition to that of the chiasmus that signifies war. All three of
Mother Courage's children are explicitly associated with trees. The
young sons are beautiful:

> I see these boys are straight as birch trees, broad in the chest, strong
> of limb—what are specimens like that doing out of the army I'd like
> to know?
>
> — Sergeant, Scene 1

But the daughter is deformed:

> It's like . . . the trees: the straight and tall ones are cut down for roof
> timber while the crooked ones are left to enjoy life.
>
> — Courage, Scene 6

The weapons of the righteous are all made of wood, not metal. As
Courage tries to block the way to her expensive linen shirts, which are
in the wagon, Kattrin threatens her mother with a board so that she can
get them out and tear them into strips to bandage the wounded. In
Scene 11 the soldiers order a peasant youth to knock Kattrin off the
roof with a board to stop her drumming; but he decides to help her by
disobeying the order, and the soldiers beat him to death. Kattrin uses a
wooden ladder to climb up to the roof, pulling it up after her so that
no one can follow her. As she beats her drum to awaken and warn the
town of attack, the cowardly peasants try to drown the sound of her
wooden drumsticks with the "innocent" and "unwarlike" noise of an ax
chopping wood. But this time the metal knives and axes fail to kill their
intended victim — the "victim" here being the wood that, as a group
of signifiers, converges around Kattrin to give her actions the meaning
of resistance to the overpowering dialectic of the chiasmus of war.
Again, it is Courage who first sets this chain of signs into motion:

> *to Catherine:* And now all I have left is you, you're a cross in yourself,
> but you have a kind heart. . . . Don't be *too* kind, never again, there's
> a cross in your path!
>
> — Courage, Scene 1

The political meaning, toward which Kattrin as cross/tree moves,
seems to be that she finally uses herself — the stunted tree — not as a
Christian cross that mutely iconizes suffering as a universal condition
but as a wooden weapon on behalf of the powerless. She chooses not to
remain stunted, covered, and therefore safe, but to grow taller in order
to rise — spatially and figuratively — against and above the pull of the

slaughter system, an act that saves the village from being devoured by the *whirlwind* of the war. The knives and axes do not succeed in chopping her down to construct a cross. Instead, this potential "cross inside her" is never realized, because she manages at last to *speak:* when she turns the wooden drumsticks into instruments of revolution they speak for her. Brecht himself adds another layer of significance to the drumming: he suggests in his production notes that the drums should "speak" the word *Gewalt* over and over again, a word that in German connotes power, violence, rape, and control.

> On the roof . . . she looks over to where the sleeping town would be and begins without hesitation to beat the drum. She holds a drumstick in each hand and drums in two-beat measures, with the accent as in the word *"Gewalt."* [24]

Mothers and Daughters: A Feminist Perspective

The question remains: what does the relationship between this mother and daughter signify in light of the analysis of the spatio-temporality? As Mother Courage is transformed into a "butcher's dog" and then a "hyena of the battlefield," she also unintentionally helps to destroy her own children. [25] The tactics she teaches her sons in order to stay alive turn back upon them, and they are executed. But she hurts her daughter in a different way. In trying to keep her safe from rape and murder, she allows Kattrin to be maimed, lonely, and childless. We know that Kattrin lost her speech when a soldier "stuck something into her mouth." This violation, carried out when Kattrin was a child, is as damaging and "real" as a sexual rape. It is evident that Kattrin is sexually assaulted when Courage sends her to the town to pick up some goods for the wagon in Scene 6: a few minutes before she left we heard a drunken soldier sing, "Your breast, girl, quick, make haste! A rider has no time to waste!" She later returns to the wagon traumatized and with a disfiguring wound on her face, drops the goods she was carrying onto the ground, and, most telling of all, does not want the red boots any longer. Her mother, who had hidden them from her, brings them out now in an attempt to comfort her, but the gesture has come too late: Kattrin "leaves the shoes and creeps into the wagon," writes Brecht in the stage directions. [26]

If one looks at Kattrin's spatial movement in terms of the picaresque metanarrative of women characters that was discussed at the outset of this essay, it can be seen that Courage unwittingly and helplessly sends her daughter onto the track of the whore (to the town alone and unprotected through the dangerous territory of a soldiers' camp) and also that of the entrepreneur: Kattrin goes to fetch the goods for her mother to sell. By the time she returns from her journey through these two segments of the metanarrative, she is doubly disfigured. As Courage notes, the wound on her face has taken away every chance of attracting a man and bearing children of her own. Kattrin thus becomes one of Brecht's "true" mothers, i.e., not in body but in spirit. It seems at this moment of her disfigurement and radical effacement as a woman, that the only way she can now keep on her feet within the narrative, is to walk the path of the martyr — there is, we recall, "a cross in her path." Like one assigned to mortify the martyr's flesh and deface her even more, Mother Courage smears dirt in her daughter's face and humiliates her for her deformities:

> I don't like it when you howl like a dog, what'll the Chaplain think of you? See how shocked he looks.
>
> — Scene 3

In light of what will happen later, this attack by her mother — which is happening at the very moment the last son is being slaughtered — marks the beginning of a reversal of Kattrin's direction, a path finally leading to her managing to *speak* against the war, while her mother becomes a "hyena of the battlefield" and is the one who shocks the Chaplain into leaving them.

In his commentary in *Theaterarbeit* Brecht reserves his sharpest criticism of Mother Courage for the way she fails her daughter. This fact belies the simplistic claim that Brecht's mothers exist primarily to nurture sons for the patriarchal society. He is emphatic that the lullaby that Courage sings after her daughter's death should not be interpreted sentimentally, but as bitter irony.[27] The mother herself, he says, is also responsible for Kattrin's now permanent silence:

> Lullay, lullay,
> what's that in the hay?
> The neighbor's kids cry
> but mine are gay.
> The neighbor's kids
> are dressed in dirt:
> Your silks were cut
> from an angel's skirt.
> They are all starving:
> you have a cake;
> If it's too stale,
> you need but speak.
>
> — Courage, Scene 12

Brecht insists that the song must be read from an orthodox Marxist standpoint, but the fact that this is a mother singing to her daughter, and not her son, makes another reading possible. The signifiers may be the same, but in a feminist reading the mother and daughter become subjects and not merely didactic objects serving to represent capitalism from a Marxist standpoint. All of the sign systems that have gone into the "weaving" of the main story are here again in the song: the unseen animals ("What is rustling in the straw?"), the clothing (originally *"Lumpen,"* or "rags," for other children but "silk" from "an angel's skirt" for her), the sewing, the work done in vain (in the original German the angel's skirt is *"umgearbeitet,"* or "reworked"), the food ("cake" for her and "not a crumb" for the other children). The song tells exactly how Courage did *not* treat Kattrin during her lifetime. As with the other children, Kattrin's clothes were worn down to rags and her crumbs, her gaiety, and even her voice were taken away by the war. Mothers, in spite of all their efforts, cannot protect their daughters from being dragged into the endless march of the market.

In a feminist reading, the irony in Kattrin's life and death turns back against Brecht's determinedly "straight" Marxist interpretation. Only through Kattrin's suffering and effacement as a woman does he allow her to be a political heroine. To be helpful, she must be destroyed. In this sense, Brecht has not varied from the traditional didactic formula that specifies that a woman must be the sacrifice that redeems the society. The widespread practice of using the feminine body as an image to *embody* the cosmic battle against sin and death occurs in countless icons and textual metaphors. Beginning in the third century A.D. and reaching its height in the medieval era, the sights and smells of "femininity" were rendered as loathsome yet fatally attractive, often as the incarnation of the Fall. Pieter Bruegel the Elder's 1563 painting *Dulle Griet,* which was a direct inspiration for the stage figure of Mother Courage, is a case in point: Dulle Griet ("Mad Meg") is an open-mouthed, raw-skinned peasant woman, the leader of a band of housewives who plunder and fight their way past devils over a devastated landscape, through torture machinery and, finally, a hellmouth. The peasant women, especially Griet herself, were interpreted by church authorities at the time as a personification of Greed. Bruegel scholar Walter Gibson suggests, however, that the painting can also be read in its sociohistorical context as a register of widespread male anxiety and hostility at the ascension of an unusual number of women to the thrones of Europe — in the Netherlands, France, England, and Scotland. Griet has also donned male armor and carries a sword, marking her as a shrew who dominates her husband and even gives the devil a difficult time. The painting thus speaks to the need to blame women for all the ills besetting Europe.[28] Trapped in Bruegel's ideological terrain, Dulle Griet's physical existence is subsumed into a universalizing allegory that suited the needs not only of that particular historical situation but of many others to come.

Like Dulle Griet, Mother Courage also walks a circular road over hellish and dangerous territory, at the end of which is destruction and death. Thus Bruegel's Dulle Griet, Grimmelshausen's Courasche, and Brecht's Mother Courage all suffer the same fate: their faces and bodies are appropriated as a surface, a space on which the culture and the invisible male author write the signs of an ideological system. For Bruegel's time it was "Greed," while for Grimmelshausen it was "Lust," "Greed," and "Barrenness." In both of the older works the dominant ideological discourse was moral rather than social — although *the moral discourse rationalized the social one*. Brecht's work, however, transferred "Greed" from the discourse of morality to that of the economic and social. And though a mother figure, Mother Courage was now barren physiologically — she was a biologically "natural" mother, unlike Grimmelshausen's Courasche, but she behaved like an unnatural one. In all three cases, the women are made to *embody* an entire ideological system.

Interestingly, the Marxist feminist British playwright Caryl Churchill, who has often stated her debt to Brechtian theory and practice, has in effect further revolutionized such pícaras as Dulle Griet, Courasche, and Mother Courage. That is, Churchill rescues women from such mythical constructs that entrap them by letting them speak from *within* the constructs themselves. Her play *Top Girls* includes a character called Dull Gret, who describes what is recognizably Bruegel's hellish landscape from the first-hand perspective of a woman placed there through no doing of her own.[29] Dull Gret's description shows what a woman of Griet's or Courage's class in the Thirty Years' War would have encountered. It is evident that she has survived through tactics, but we learn that her son and baby daughter were killed by churchmen and a soldier, respectively, and that she has roused her fellow peasant women to wreak revenge on these oppressors. For his part, Brecht tries, without total success, to deprive Mother Courage of revolutionary status and to bestow it instead on the daughter Kattrin, whom he also endows with all the qualities of a "true" mother that he took away from Courage.

How, then, can Brecht's female characters become subjects who speak in a feminist voice? The answer lies in the fact that Brecht, like Grimmelshausen and Bruegel before him, was a realist, and regardless of his conscious intentions, he carefully observed and faithfully preserved so many *details* of the *tangible, material* world and of *women moving within it.* Thus the traces of women's history are indelibly inscribed in the Brechtian details. Brecht's greatest value to feminists lies in the fact that he was, after all, a skeptical materialist who refused to close off the process of signification by offering a final solution. That is, he did not impose a definitive interpretation *in the work itself,* notwithstanding his statements *about* it. The metanarratives of his women characters are pieces of a montage to be constructed and, as such, the narratives are as open-ended as those of *Schwejk:* a series of pictures of women moving among objects that allow us to *touch* — to frame — their material, historical reality, as well as our own.

In 1934 Walter Benjamin visited his friend Brecht, who was then in exile in Denmark. Benjamin notes that Brecht had painted a slogan on a large beam in his study: "The truth is concrete."[30] This is the famous statement of his faith in material experience. In expressing his admiration for the work of his wife, Helene Weigel, in the role of Mother Courage in the 1949 Berliner Ensemble production, Brecht draws an illuminating parallel between women as *tactical* "connoisseurs of reality" and himself as a poet:

> As the millet planter chooses the heaviest seeds
> for his test field and the poet the well-aimed words
> for his poem, so she chooses the things that accompany
> her form over the stage.
>   . . . Every piece
> of her wares is chosen . . .
> the capon and the bedding that the old lady
> finally threads into the ball of yarn.
>   . . . all
> chosen according to age, purpose and beauty
> with the hands of the bread-baking, net-weaving
> soup-cooking connoisseur
> of reality.
>   — "The Stage Properties of Weigel"[31]

In Retrospect

Such material objects define the path of women characters across the epic stage. The characters are in one sense stereotypes and many of the narrative paths of these spectral figures have been definitively mapped out long ago by successive ideologies. But other paths may also be traced over these from the trail left by the same objects, the same *Gestus.* Out of these traces the spectral characters of women can *speak* in the voice of their history. By focusing on the tactile and tactical *details* of their material existence, Brecht has preserved a memory of women touching the *things* that constitute the everyday. Through their incessant work, the female characters bring the reader and spectator closer to a true realization — a concrete experiencing — of the chiasmic, destructive, self-destructing war economy.

Semiotic analysis enables us to follow the movement and destination of such details within the performance and reception as one metasign, because *it does not value conscious ideas over material objects and relationships;* thus it is able to avoid idealism, as Eco promised. But to make this leap, we have had at every turn to go "outside" of Brecht's conscious intentions and reenter the semantic universe, a leap Eco charts but does not actually make in *A Theory of Semiotics.* And this is the point at which the feminist reader and spectator can step in to interrogate and overturn the basic values on which the whole set of equivalences rests.

In *Mother Courage* the spatio-temporality is part of a cyclical economy, a *Wirbelsturm* — a whirlwind — whose dynamic is a destructive process but also a hopeful dialectical one that allows the spectator, who is also without a voice or face, to intervene anyway, like Kattrin with her drums warning of violence, calling for control, and finding the power to stop the destruction of people, animals, clothing, food, and all the other objects. The place of the three women characters — Courage, Kattrin, and Yvette — in this chiasmic dialectic or "Möbius strip" is precisely at the median, in the blind spot, at the invisible turning and intersection point where death occurs and where the signs meet in passing from the diegetic into the mimetic space and vice versa. The chiasmus is the dynamic interrelating of signs that we may call the signifier, while its signified is the war economy. The chiasmus here is not a static abstraction; all the signs in the play as text and staging are gradually drawn into it and disappear. Thus the play's action is the war's destruction of its own time and space: as a system the war-chiasmus is cannibalistic, eating everything away, even itself. Brecht does not offer the comforting assurance that a different ideological *strategy* could stop that of the war economy once it is started. The only course open is to engage in *tactics.*

Notes

[1] Bertolt Brecht, *Mother Courage and her Children: A Chronicle of the Thirty Years' War,* trans. Eric Bentley, in *Masters of Modern Drama,* eds. Haskell Block and Robert Shedd (New York: Random House, 1962), 843–890. The

passage quoted is from page 866. Subsequent passages will be identified by character and scene number in the body of the essay. Bentley's translation will be used unless otherwise indicated. In instances where Bentley departs from Brecht's patterns of imagery, I have retranslated the text to preserve them, using as primary source Bertolt Brecht, *Mutter Courage und ihre Kinder: Eine Chronik aus dem Dreißigjährigen Krieg* (Berlin: Suhrkamp, 1949). When my own translation is used, I indicate the character, scene, and page number in the original version.

[2] Roland Barthes, *On Racine*, trans. Richard Howard (New York: Hill and Wang, 1964).

[3] Hans Jacob Christoffel von Grimmelshausen, *Courage, the Adventuress*, trans. Hans Speier (Princeton: Princeton UP, 1964). Original version: *Die Landstörzerin Courasche* (1670); (Munich: Wilhelm Goldmann, 1969).

[4] See Gay Gibson Cima's *Performing Women: Female Characters, Male Playwrights, and the Modern Stage* (Ithaca, N.Y.: Cornell UP, 1993), which discusses the representation of women, as well as the real-life role of actresses, in the work of several male playwrights, including Brecht.

[5] Simone de Beauvoir, *The Second Sex*, trans. H. M. Parshley (New York: Vintage, 1952).

[6] Sara Lennox, "Women in Brecht's Work," *New German Critique* 14 (1978): 83–97.

[7] To his credit, John Fuegi was among the first critics to begin exposing Brecht's cavalier treatment of women in real life. See *Brecht: Women and Politics/Frauen und Politik. Brecht Yearbook 12,* eds. John Fuegi, Gisela Bahr, and John Willett (Detroit: Wayne State UP, 1983), which includes essays on Brecht's women characters and his personal and work relations with women. In *Brecht and Company: Sex, Politics and the Making of the Modern Drama* (New York: Grove, 1994) Fuegi goes further, claiming that Brecht plagiarized from his female collaborators' work and authored almost nothing himself, a claim that ignores his unmistakable writing style. Unfortunately, Fuegi undermines feminist aims, since he creates a patriarchal narrative of rescuing naive, dependent women who have "fallen" for Brecht, been abandoned, and naturally wish only to die. For a critique of the latter book, see Olga Taxidou, "Crude Thinking: John Fuegi and Recent Brecht Criticism," *New Theatre Quarterly* 11 (November 1995): 381–384.

[8] Jill Dolan, "Materialist Feminism: Apparatus-Based Theory and Practice," in *The Feminist Spectator as Critic* (Ann Arbor: UMI Research P, 1988), 100–117; Elin Diamond, "Brechtian Theory/Feminist Theory: Toward a Gestic Feminist Criticism," in *A Sourcebook of Feminist Theatre and Performance,* ed. Carol Martin (London and New York: Routledge, 1996) 120–135; Janelle Reinelt, "Rethinking Brecht: Deconstruction, Feminism, and the Politics of Form," in *Essays on Brecht/Versuche über Brecht. Brecht Yearbook* 15, eds. Marc Silberman, John Fuegi, Renate Voris, Carl Weber. (College Park, Md.:

International Brecht Society, 1990), 99–110; Reinelt, *After Brecht: British Epic Theatre* (Ann Arbor: U of Michigan P, 1995).

[9] Karl Marx, "The Buying and Selling of Labor Power," *Capital* (Chicago: Charles H. Kerr, 1912), 16, 25.

[10] Mother Courage, quoted from Bentley, *Mother Courage,* 857, except for the material in brackets, which Bentley truncated in his translation but which I have restored, as translated from *Mutter Courage,* 58–59. Throughout the chapter, dialogue excerpts will be identified by each character's name in roman type, and by the scene in which the dialogue appears.

[11] Bertolt Brecht, *Materialien zu Brechts "Mutter Courage und ihre Kinder"* (Frankfurt am Main: Suhrkamp, 1964), 16, 25 [Brecht's italics]. Translation mine.

[12] Roland Barthes gives this example of the social *Gestus* in "Diderot, Brecht, Eisenstein," in his *Image – Music – Text,* trans. Stephen Heath (New York: Hill and Wang, 1977), 73.

[13] Michel de Certeau, *The Practice of Everyday Life,* trans. Steven Rendall (Berkeley, Los Angeles, and London: U of California P, 1984), 28–39.

[14] *Mutter Courage und ihre Kinder,* film of the Berliner Ensemble production, with Helene Weigel as Courage, Angelika Hurwicz as Kattrin, Ernst Busch as Cook, and Ekkehard Schall as Eilif; directed by Peter Palitzch and Manfred Wekwerth (East Berlin: DEFA, 1961). Both the original German version and a version with English subtitles are presently held by the Goethe Institute.

[15] Umberto Eco, *A Theory of Semiotics* (Bloomington and London: Indiana UP, 1976) , 289–313.

[16] Michael Issacharoff, "Space and Reference in Drama," *Poetics Today* 2 (1981): 211–224.

[17] Bertolt Brecht, *Materialien,* 34.

[18] *Mutter Courage,* 24; my translation here and in three of the following passages. The excerpt from Scene 6 is Bentley's translation.

[19] *Mutter Courage,* 15; *Mother Courage,* 846, except for Bentley's last phrase, "Off to war like a cat to cream," which completely departs from the play's overall metaphorical pattern.

[20] *Mutter Courage,* 57; my translation, as is the next passage.

[21] *Mutter Courage,* 82; *Mother Courage,* 863. Bentley omits the line "in Pommerschen . . . Kinder aufgegessen," which I have restored.

[22] *Mutter Courage,* 68; *Mother Courage,* 860, except for the last two lines, which I have translated, as well as the next passage.

[23] *Mutter Courage,* 8; *Mother Courage,* 844, with minor changes.

[24] Bertolt Brecht, *Materialien,* 82–83.

[25] See Iris Smith, "Brecht and the Mothers of Epic Theatre," *Theatre Journal* 43 (December 1991), 491–505.

[26] *Mutter Courage,* 67, 72, 73; *Mother Courage,* 859, 860, 861.

[27] Bertolt Brecht, Ruth Berlau, et al., *Theaterarbeit: 6 Aufführungen des Berliner Ensembles* (Dresden: VVV Dresdner Verlag, 1952), 298–299. For reconstructing the performance, we are fortunate to have this written and pictorial documentation of the 1949 Berliner Ensemble's *Mother Courage* and five other productions. Ruth Berlau initiated this project and kept Brecht working on it; he continued to do so after she died and nearly up to his own death in 1956.

[28] Walter S. Gibson, *Bruegel* (New York and Toronto: Oxford UP, 1977), 102–108. This need to make women responsible for Europe's ills was exacerbated in *Dulle Griet's* case by the relative financial independence and better education of women in the Netherlands than elsewhere in the world. Against these facts stood the patriarchal belief that without the restraint of men, women were naturally prone to wastefulness, greed, lust, and bad temper.

[29] Caryl Churchill, *Top Girls* (London: Methuen), 1982: I:i. The Afterword of this book contains the passage wherein Dull Gret describes this landscape.

[30] Walter Benjamin, "Conversations with Brecht," *Reflections,* trans. Edmund Jephcott (New York: Harcourt Brace Jovanovich, 1978), 206.

[31] Bertolt Brecht, "Die Requisiten der Weigel," *Theaterarbeit: 6 Aufführungen,* 267. My translation.

The Tutor and the Schoolmaster, from The Tutor (Der Hofmeister), *Berliner Ensemble, 1950. By permission of the Bertolt Brecht Archive, Berlin. Photo by Wolfgang Meyenfels.*

3: Gestic Writing and the True-Real Body: Brecht Adapts *The Tutor*

IN THE BERLINER ENSEMBLE'S 1950 ADAPTATION of *The Tutor (Der Hofmeister)*, by J. M. R. Lenz, first published in 1774,[1] the young actor playing the main character stepped out from the proscenium arch to deliver a prologue composed by Brecht and directed toward his fellow Germans, who were just beginning to set the course of the newly declared socialist state, the German Democratic Republic. This first crucial year was a time when hope ran high that these Germans could disassociate themselves from the Nazism of the immediate past and prove worthy of their comrades who, under extreme persecution, had fought the longest and most openly against it. Typically, rather than celebrating a victory or congratulating those present, Brecht used a play from the past to send them a pointed warning.

J. M. R. Lenz had written *The Tutor* at a similarly crucial juncture just before the French Revolution, after which Europe, including Germany, would never be the same. The *Sturm und Drang* playwrights of the 1770s — including Lenz, who was the most innovative among them, invented a new dramaturgy that registered the sea change that was already underway. Their drama in fact was the direct forebear of the epic theater. Although they were still of the Enlightenment in their aim to educate, they were less optimistic that all social ills could be alleviated with scientific reason, and their theater reflected this disillusionment. They saw themselves as overthrowing the neoclassic theater associated with political absolutism and rigid social hierarchy. Consciously emulating Shakespeare, they turned from the French models and the three unities: their treatment of time and space was less symmetrical and contained, their acts and scenes sharply confronted each other rather than flowing unobtrusively from one to the other, their dialogue was not refined but a juxtaposition of idioms of various classes and regions, and their protagonists were less autonomous actors in charge of the events than pawns of social and historical forces over which they had little control.

It is not surprising, therefore, that Brecht was attracted to this play — indeed, his own work was descended from it. He wanted, however, to bring into sharper focus the contradictions of the social system and its legitimating discourses, contradictions that the prescient Lenz had brilliantly registered. Brecht's point in adding the prologue was to alert his

German audience that the play was a parallel to their present situa-
, to assure them that they did have control of it, and, above all, to
warn them of the danger of continuing to play the familiar role of the
"serving spirit," which in its German original, *der dienender Geist,* conveys
a second meaning of "the serving intellect" or "the intellectual servant."
In other words, Brecht was speaking directly to German intellectuals like
himself and trying to intervene in their disastrous habit of obeying the
call to serve the ruling class. The Berliner Ensemble adaptation of *Der
Hofmeister* showed the process of a training and education whose end result was the violent self-castration of a body and a mind:

> Dear public, our play today
> was written one hundred and fifty years ago
> Out of the portal of the past I step forward,
> the ancestor of the German schoolmaster.
> I am still in the service of the aristocrat
> and for a miserly profit, teach his offspring
> the Bible and a bit of manners,
> to look down his nose, be a smartass, and give orders.
> Skilled in all the higher arts,
> I myself have a low standing.
> True, the times are changing now:
> The bourgeois is gaining power in the state
> And day and night I consider
> entering his service.
> In me he'd always have, as it's called,
> a serving spirit:
> The aristocrat has trained me well,
> straightened me up and exercised me
> So I only teach what's appropriate.
> I'll tell you a secret:
> Nothing would change in what I teach:
> The ABCs of German misery.[2]

Brecht left several volumes of notes and essays on the rehearsal and
production of *The Tutor,* as well as photos, the annotated scripts of
some of the actors, and an invaluable script that belonged to the stage
manager and contains sketches and notes about every rotation of the
turntable stage. To mark the passage of time and the movement from
one space to another, the turntable was divided into quarters, each representing a season of the year and a different setting. Also noted were
changes in lighting, props, music, and the *Gestus* they all served. This
material, which rests in the Bertolt-Brecht-Archiv, makes it possible to
reconstruct the main outline of the production and to look at the proc-

ess of the adaptation from an old play to a contemporary one, and from a written critical discourse to a critical discourse carried by the stage.

During the Tutor's prologue the tones of a music box were heard, and the actor's voice and body had, according to Brecht's notes, the mechanical quality of a "Glockenspiel figure," in order "to represent the Tutor as a historical species." He seemed part of the turntable stage that moved periodically, with the music-box sound, to show the passage of time. His head and body moved jerkily, his speech was precisely measured, and his jaw snapped open and shut, dividing his face into two sections. Yet all this remained only a "disquieting effect" that did not completely take over the actor. "He was still there in all his liveliness," writes Brecht, even though the "puppet quality" would become more noticeable.[3]

Through the play of bodies in time and space, Brecht's theater articulates a social text marked by such contradictions. In *Postmodern Brecht* Elisabeth Wright finds that both Brecht and Artaud "subvert any simple opposition by showing that the biological body is not identical with the body image as granted to the subject by society." The body is never presented as complete or self-identical. For Brecht, its identity comes from its placement within a coded system of social relations. In the Gestus the body's gestures always show its relation to other bodies. Wright also points out that Brecht, like Artaud again, "dwells on the violence done to the body by the inscription of Law."[4] In *The Tutor* the "inscription of social law" is violent indeed: the price of the protagonist's financial and social security is self-castration. He is hired as a private tutor to teach the son and daughter of a country squire, who is also a retired major. Allowed no escape from his isolation, Läuffer is drawn into a sexual liaison with Gustchen, the daughter, who has been forcibly separated from her beloved cousin, Fritz. She becomes pregnant, a scandal ensues, and Läuffer flees from the Major's fury. He is given refuge by a village schoolmaster, who hires him as a teacher, but his new financial security and petit-bourgeois respectability are threatened when he is sexually aroused again — this time by Lise, the schoolmaster's servant. To avoid a second disaster, he castrates himself.

As a schoolman he teaches "the German ABCs of misery," underwriting the socioeconomic system with his own blood. Writing is already overtly thematized in Lenz's original version, but Brecht singles it out and makes it signify a whole ideological tradition that reproduces social injustice. Brecht's Tutor is a specialist in handwriting, and after his castration his major work becomes the surveillance of his pupils' copybooks, in which they reproduce his model. J. M. R. Lenz did not make the Marxist leap of explicitly locating the cause of the Tutor's fate in the class system, nor in the economic exploitation it supported; Lenz's final solution is an eminently liberal, Enlightenment one: a nobleman delivers the message that hope lies in universal democratic education and ethical responsibility on the part of the nobility. Nevertheless, Lenz provided all the necessary elements for a Marxist interpretation. He also introduced "montage" scenes and a new protagonist: a historical subject-in-process whose locus is a body that is subjugated and yet also resists.

I will explore this contradiction between the subjugated body and the resisting body as it was constituted through gestic writing in the Berliner Ensemble's staging of the play. Dominating the performance was the spectacle of an oppressive social writing upon the body, which managed, nonetheless, to act out scenes of resistance. As a collective, the actors' gestic writing not only politicized the Tutor's body but also displayed their work as the ongoing construction of a historical subject. This construction of the subject also allowed a deconstruction, a complex seeing of the whole process. The subject-in-process could resist, escaping into joyful abandon and comedy.

To elucidate the dominant spectacle of oppression Michel Foucault's *Discipline and Punish* is valuable,[5] but Foucault does not offer any way for those subjugated by a monolithic system to speak or act against it. Julia Kristeva and Michel de Certeau have taken up that task, however, each in a distinct way. In her essay "The True-Real" Kristeva finds a parallel between the language of psychotic patients and the work of modern artists such as Artaud.[6] She proposes a subject-in-process who experiences psychic and social castration rather than acceding to the Law of the Father and so stays in the realm of the true-real, where immediate perception *is* the meaning. De Certeau, on the other hand, in *The Practice of Everyday Life* and *Heterologies,* shows how subjects without a privileged space can resist a powerful apparatus at the "micro-level": with no overview of the system, they can still circumvent, foil, delay, subvert it, or watch for a chance to deflect it by taking a small advantage.[7] Between them, Kristeva and de Certeau map out tactics of resistance against the huge Foucauldian systems. We can find both subjugation and resistance in Brecht's production of *Der Hofmeister.* If Brecht is of interest to postmodernism, it is because much of his work, including this play, seems to follow two contradictory agendas, even in a staging whose overt aim was closer to the Enlightenment.[8]

The body, writes Foucault in *Discipline and Punish,* has been considered "the seat of needs and appetites" and "the locus of biological events," such as diseases and attacks by germs. But it is also "involved in political fields: power relations invest it, mark it, train it, torture it,

force it to carry out tasks, . . . to perform ceremonies, to emit signs."[9]
The Tutor's story is that of a body trained and forced to write and reproduce the structures of class, culture, and economy that interlock to
cause "the German Misery." He is forced to perform ceremonies that
make a spectacle of his own debasement. To be hired as tutor, he must
have an interview with the Major's wife. He demonstrates his French
and his drawings, and, as the Major's wife plays the spinet, he dances
the minuet. He forces his large, soldierly body through an awkward
performance of the dance, watched by the Major's wife and her
brother-in-law, the Privy Councillor. Brecht describes the scene: "The
poor devil fights for his life when he displays the minuet steps for the
Major's wife. He looks sharply at his own feet, as does she. He dries the
sweat from his forehead, and does a few more steps."[10]

In the course of the play the Tutor is charged first with instituting
the power of the aristocracy and then that of the bourgeoisie. He is an
extreme example of what Foucault calls the "docile body" that is useful
to a military, social, and economic apparatus of power because it is productive and yet remains subjected. Foucault notes that during the Enlightenment the methods for training soldiers began to be appropriated
for training workers, whose bodies would reach ultimate docility under
the factory system. The Tutor is also caught in this historical transfer-
ence. Brecht often describes his movements in military terms: "The
catechism lesson," he says, "shows Gustchen's social superiority. She
mixes all the means of her rank with those of her body, to make him
dance. . . . His advancing march [toward her] was his defeat. He turns
like a spindle . . . steps fearfully back and forth."[11] The Gestus of his
body as a turning spindle recurs throughout the production, the
"writing" of a body fixed to the glockenspiel mechanism of history.
The Tutor does not belong to either class but serves both: first he
teaches his aristocratic students to "look down their noses" and "give
orders"; then, in his village students, he inculcates the bourgeois value
of copying preset models. But it is his self-castration that illustrates the
operation of this repressive apparatus at the peak of its efficiency: the
castration signifies that the subjugated himself has taken over his own
surveillance, discipline, and punishment — he has made himself a docile
body.

From the beginning the spectator sees the Tutor surveying his own
behavior and trying to discipline himself. In the production this was
shown gestically by, for example, his handling of his pedagogical stick.
He uses it to point on the blackboard and to rap for his pupils' attention. But he also disciplines himself with it by placing it through the
crooks of both elbows, in effect pinning his own arms behind his back.

He first displays this gesture in the scene of Gustchen's catechism as he tries to hold back his sexual "advance" toward her. Through his posture and the stick he produces several signs: with the stick he holds his own arms back from embracing her, imprisons his own body, and, as Brecht notes, "fixes himself on a cross."[12]

The name of the Tutor is Läuffer, a homonym of *Läufer* which means "runner." Until the castration, the Gestus of running, hunting, and being hunted dominates his movement. In a pantomime scene added by Brecht, Läuffer has finally obtained a brief leave from the estate and taken Leopold, the Major's young son, to a skating rink in the village. Here he tries to make contact with the village girls by jumping, writing figures on the ice, and skating with furious speed to get their attention. The girls' adolescent sexual feelings are awakened (or, at least, this is what their giggling means to Brecht, according to his notes). But when Läuffer tries to strike up a conversation with them, he fails: "He skates backward from them, his teeth bared, showing the wildness he will finally direct toward himself."[13] He does not see Leopold in his path; the two collide and fall into a sprawl on the ice. Thus, another escape route — via a liaison with one of these "safe," non-forbidden girls of his own class — is cut off, and the writing of his fate continues.

The gestic text that leads to Läuffer's castration is written by several actors. In an early scene Läuffer encounters the Major outside the gate of his estate. The Tutor bows but the Major ignores him, pretending to study a plant. Later outside the Privy Councillor's wall, the Privy Councillor lectures Läuffer on freedom as he hacks down his own laurel bushes with a large set of shears. The castration is also mimed in advance by Gustchen's fiancé, Fritz. In bemoaning his absence from Gustchen and his helplessness to change the situation, Fritz makes what Brecht calls a gesture of *Entmannung,* or castration, on himself.[14]

Brecht drew a parallel between Läuffer's physical self-castration and the German intellectuals' habit of complying with systems they should recognize as unjust. In Brecht's view, with their "mental self-castration" the intellectuals have helped perpetuate a tradition in which art and philosophy serve to rationalize what is happening around them. In Lenz's text and Brecht's adaptation, Gustchen reads romantic novels, poetry, and drama. In a scene that takes place in her bedroom, she lies in bed imagining herself as Juliet and the Tutor — her Herrmann — as Romeo. He sits morosely on the side of the bed, not looking like a Romeo or even a "Herrmann," which is literally a "master-man" — ironically, she calls him her "Herrmannschen" or "little master-man." She is unmindful that, because of his lack of social and economic privilege, his danger is real. Gustchen's bed was framed by an arch with curtains that closed and opened, a miniature theater framing the sexual relations as spectacle, like one of the small backlit theaters in Foucault's panopticon.[15]

Lenz's text already contains several satirical attacks on German idealism. Brecht left all of these in his adaptation and, in addition, had characters quote passages from Klopstock and Kant that describe the body being sublimated into the spirit or melted into the soul. Care was taken not to ridicule the young people in such scenes but to show the power of poetry to seduce, unite, and also imprison them. As Läuffer takes Fritz's intended place in Gustchen's bed, Fritz, far away at the university, draws comfort from the Romantics, using them to persuade himself that he is having a "true" love affair with his beloved from a distance. Spiritually, Fritz is with her, whereas Läuffer is only with her materially, which for the idealist does not count in the grand scheme of Truth. Here we have a poignant, commedia-style burlesque of the body-spirit dichotomy.

At his engagement party near the end of the play Fritz has a moment of doubt as he meets, in its cradle, the physical result of Läuffer and Gustchen's affair. But he soon accepts the baby as his own son, with these words:

> (Kisses the baby) And nevertheless an endless treasure to me, because it is the picture of its mother. At least, my sweet boy, I'll never have you educated by private tutors.[16]

General laughter among the Burg family closes the scene. The Tutor is ironically but effectively annihilated: through his castration and Fritz's appropriation of his child, *his body has taken the subordinate position of a woman in relation to the patriarchy* and *a worker in relation to the owner*. His body has been used productively to give birth, but his child (his product) becomes the "endless treasure" of the aristocrat, a living security for the perpetuation of that class.

Foucault explains that the "soul" is a historical reality, that is, a "reality reference" produced by the power of discourses acting upon it, around which various concepts such as spirit, psyche, subjectivity, and consciousness have been constructed. The situation of *Der Hofmeister* might be summed up in a striking sentence from *Discipline and Punish:* "The soul is the prison of the body."[17]

Matters are not this simple, however. As we have just seen, the philosophical dilemma of who is *truly* in Gustchen's bed has been foregrounded as theater. The body/spirit dichotomy is shown not only as tragic but also as comic. Once this dichotomy collapses, another oppressive binary can be deconstructed: the binary of masculine and feminine, which has been forced to stand for the body versus the head and the sensual versus the intellectual. The student Pätus, in fact, tries to use these binaries to solve a love problem, to little but comic effect. Precisely because theater can *show* subjects being constructed by such ideological systems, those subjects are not subsumed. No system, including Brecht's own, can entirely write or erase the human body, because it is a "wild signifier" with a potential for multiple meanings.

The body provides the refuge for what Julia Kristeva calls the "subject-in-process," a provisional identity that in theater is invested by actor, spectator, reader, and playwright. This subject-in-process is a *positionality* arrested nowhere as a presence. In this shared positionality, our ability to shift positions within a coded system, even to change roles with each other, lies our potential for what Kristeva calls love.[18] Kristeva's "love" has something in common with Brecht's notion of "co-storytelling," in which the spectators have the freedom to "compose in imagination other ways of behaving and other situations and . . . compare them to the ones put forward by the fable."[19] For *The Tutor,* produced at a moment when the German Democratic Republic's cultural and educational policy was being decided, Brecht tried to put this co-storytelling into practice by leaving a trail of negatives — paths not taken — throughout the play, and in an epilogue he has the Tutor explicitly ask the audience to reflect on the past and at least not repeat the same mistakes. Even though these didactic aims were no less Enlightenment-based than Lenz's, the production allowed for contemporary spectators to be implicated in the story.

During rehearsals for *The Tutor* the actors gradually developed a finely inflected physical language, a gestic writing through which the story could be articulated even in its absences and contradictions. The actors' physiques helped make such articulation possible. Läuffer contrasted sharply with the characters in the higher classes: he was tall and straight (when he was not bowing or dancing the minuet) in contrast to the short, fat, red-faced Major and the wasp-thin Privy Councillor. Likewise, the upper-class older women were more grotesquely caricatured than the young and lower-class women. Overall, Brecht wanted to suggest the style of figures in a Hogarth engraving.

The actors experimented with the archaic code of bowing, not resurrecting it to seal the play with a patina of "authenticity" but using it historically in Brecht's sense, to mark the distance and nearness of Lenz's era to the Germany of 1950. Inserting themselves physically into the grammar of the bow, the actors inflected differences of gender, age, temperament, and, especially, class status. Through the bow, they also marked out boundaries of social space and time. The language of the bow as social Gestus surfaced most prominently in the work of the

actor playing Läuffer.[20] During rehearsals, Läuffer's bow became increasingly laden with meaning until it seemed for the actors, and later
for the spectators, to take on a life of its own. Läuffer bowed lower and
lower to his employers, becoming ever more obsequious. The distortion of his body visibly prevented him from behaving "like a man" in
the presence of his superiors. The bow also was an ominous miming of
the self-castration to come. When the crucial moment approached,
Läuffer suddenly "ripped down his coat," both signaling and curtaining
off the violence. Nevertheless, in spite of its gruesome climax, the exaggerated enunciation of the bow became a virtuoso comic performance in its own right, a story that the spectators followed with delight.
In de Certeau's terms, it was a tactical resistance, signaling subservience
with such excessive élan that it outplayed and subverted the social code
it was assigned to support. Läuffer was still subjugated by this code and
"forced to emit its signs," but through tactics, he could escape his
"normal" post, momentarily "free-float" over the dominating discourse, and expose it as a historical construct. This holds true not only
for the Tutor trapped in place at his teaching post but also for the actor
placed in a differential position within a collective of actors who are expected to articulate a political meaning determined by Brecht. In his
commentary, however, Brecht makes it clear that he delighted in such
playful abandon from the actors, even when it worked against the unity
of his ideological aims.

The scene of self-castration is worth looking at closely. Does it show
only the Tutor's transformation into a docile body, his capitulation
before the Law in order to secure a place in the social system? In Lenz's
text the castration takes place between scenes, but Brecht writes it out
on paper and through mostly pantomimed stage sequence, literally dividing it into three parts: "The Self-Castration: a, b, c" :

> This whole [sequence is] most delicate, and *it must stand out from
> the whole* to emphasize its poetic quality, so that the spectator is able
> to carry the self-mutilation out of the sexual sphere and place it in a
> more general intellectual one. We changed the lighting for this act;
> the projectors which indicated the locale are left off, and we got a very
> dark and strange background, even though the bright lights were still
> on. We also framed the three scenes with music. . . . Other than this,
> *we were especially conscious of emphasizing the realistic moment in the
> play. The event in itself, wholly standing for itself,* has no more meaning
> than the forced situation of a poor devil deciding between a sexual life
> or a professional life, characteristic enough for this social order.
>
> [In scene a] Lise comes in with a coffeepot. At the desk, Läuffer
> holds his pen in his hand to do a correction, and with it goes like a

sleepwalker to the door, opens it, takes the pot from Lise, turns back to the table, puts the pot down, begins to correct. . . .

[Strong wind at the beginning of scene b, then a quick dying down.] The scene shows Läuffer as in a nightmare. Again sexuality rises against him, so the scenic arrangement has to repeat that of the . . . catechism [of Gustchen, where he gave way to his desire for her]. His hunting down of himself. . . . The cursing at the window. The rolling gait from there to the wall, as if an invisible storm were blowing a leaf into destruction. . . .

Läuffer stood for his monologue before the blackness of an open window. He meditated, then . . . with the sentence . . . "if thine eye offend thee, pluck it out," the decision was born. . . .[21] [Finally he says,] "That I can say to the storm: if it comes by tomorrow, I won't be there anymore. So be it, exactly so. Let us give an example that makes her shudder." (Rips his coat down)[22] [italics mine].

Brecht insists that the self-castration *stand out from the whole,* stand *wholly for itself,* so that *the spectator can carry it out* of one sphere into another. He wants to detach it from discourse, relinquish it. Läuffer's sexual body becomes a leaf in the storm, but it does not really disappear. Instead, it is imagistically dispersed as fragments strewn about the stage. It remains as the "true-real," a term Kristeva coins as the *"vréel,"* joining the *"vrai"* (true) and the *"réel"* (real). Drawing on Lacan, she posits that for those who remain in the true-real, perception itself is the meaning. Signification proceeds directly from the "real" (the immediate physical perception) to the "true" (the symbolic), bypassing the imaginary. The only way to meet the Law (the realm of the father, of truth, of the symbolic) without taking up a post within it is to suffer castration. To proceed "normally" from the real through the imaginary to the symbolic would be to *appropriate* the phallus and let oneself be fixed into proper position within the patriarchal order.[23] Brecht, too, perhaps unconsciously, refuses to take the normal course of signification: the self-castration scene must *stand for itself.* It does not signify that the Tutor's castration is *like* the German intellectuals' reproduction of history. Instead, it shows that the Tutor's castration *is* the *on-going production* of history by the German intellectuals. If history is Brecht's Other, as Wright says, then one way to preserve its otherness is to erect a *provisional* identity for oneself, which is possible through self-castration. In this way the spectator also can remain a subject-in-process in Kristeva's sense and not have to close off meaning; the theatrical apparatus lies open, ready to present contradictory positions and directions in other audience contexts.

The positional play of identities is seen everywhere in *The Tutor:* Läuffer takes Fritz's place in Gustchen's bed, Gustchen substitutes Romeo for Fritz, and Fritz transports himself to her spiritually. The fact that the physical body can never actually be "spirited" away causes misery but also empowers and allows resistance. Läuffer's sexual body returns to part c of the scene as imagistic fragments in a montage left to the spectator to reassemble. At the end of the Tutor's monologue at the dark open window, the curtain closes as there is a blackout, then opens again to show the same schoolroom empty and silent but strewn with signs. The window is now closed, the copybooks are strewn over the blood-splattered floor, and Läuffer's chair, which was standing beside his desk, is lying on its back across the room — a sign and nearly animate body in its own right, a silent witness pointing to and embodying the violent act that has just occurred. The next scene is still the schoolroom, but the blood splatters have been washed away, and in their place is an excessive and comic proliferation of props of bourgeois comfort: pipe, slippers, coffee cups, saucers, and, as always, the copybooks, papers, and pens of the teaching — and writing — profession.

To end the essay I return to Läuffer's initial interview scene to describe an element not discussed before, one that seems incongruous in the Foucauldian spectacle of a body being disciplined. Läuffer is dancing the minuet, staring at his feet, and sweating, with the Major's wife at the spinet looking on. "Meanwhile," continues Brecht in his commentary, "Leopold, for the sake of whose education Läuffer is applying, is catching flies on the wall. He has seen a lot of such auditions."[24] Brecht notes that for the young actor playing Leopold this short pantomime was his one moment of glory: "The actor played the catching of the fly so well, so comically, that the attention to Läuffer's examination, going on at the same time, had to suffer as a result. We didn't have the heart to impose moderation on the young actor, so we at least had to dim the light a little." Brecht finally decided on an uncharacteristic gradation of lighting intensity, from a sharp white to half-light. "In general it is our strict policy to avoid atmospheric lighting effects," he writes in his notes, "but this time we made an exception."[25] The little scene of catching the fly, drawn directly from the *lazzi* of commedia dell'arte, was a tactic of resistance. Leopold threw off the *misery of his education* for the moment, and, following the fly, managed to write a path of escape for himself and the spectators, even if it was only written in the air and out of the bright light. Thus the epic theater staged a multiple spectacle, a production of contraries, where monolithic discourse was upstaged again by gestic writing.

Notes

[1] Jacob Michael Reinhold Lenz, *Der Hofmeister: oder Vortheile der Privater-ziehung. Eine Komödie* [The tutor: or advantages of private education. A comedy], Leipzig, 1774; (Frankfurt am Main: Stroemfeld/Roter Stern, 1986).

Bertolt Brecht, adaptation of J. M. R. Lenz's *Der Hofmeister,* Berliner Ensemble, 1950. *Hofmeister* material, manuscript 539/575, p. 27, in the Bertolt-Brecht-Archiv, Berlin. All translations from this source are mine. An English version of Brecht's adaptation is also in print: Bertolt Brecht, *The Tutor: An Adaptation of the Play by J. M. R. Lenz,* trans. Pip Broughton (New York: Applause Theatre Book Publishers, 1988).

[2] Brecht, *Hofmeister* material, 547/01.

[3] Brecht, *Hofmeister* material, 547/06.

[4] Elisabeth Wright, *Postmodern Brecht* (London and New York: Routledge, 1989), 17.

[5] Michel Foucault, "Discipline and Punish: The Birth of the Prison," in *The Foucault Reader,* ed. Paul Rabinow (New York: Pantheon Books, 1984), 169–256.

[6] Julia Kristeva, "The True-Real," in *The Kristeva Reader,* ed. Toril Moi (N.Y.: Columbia UP, 1988), 214–237.

[7] Michel de Certeau, *The Practice of Everyday Life,* trans. Steven Rendall (Berkeley, Los Angeles, and London: U of California P, 1984), and *Heterologies: Discourse on the Other,* trans. Brian Massumi (Minneapolis: University of Minnesota, 1986).

[8] For all its strengths, Wright's book falls into the familiar totalizing of Brecht into three historical phases: the pre-Marxist Brecht amenable to postmodernism, the predictable middle Brecht, and the *Lehrstücke* Brecht, amenable again.

[9] Foucault, "The Body of the Condemned," from *Discipline and Punish,* in *The Foucault Reader,* 173.

[10] Brecht, *Hofmeister* material, 546/04.

[11] Brecht, *Hofmeister* material, 547/75.

[12] Brecht, *Hofmeister* material, 547/75.

[13] Brecht, *Hofmeister* material, 547/15.

[14] Brecht, *Hofmeister* material, 547/75.

[15] Foucault, "Panopticism," from *Discipline and Punish,* in *The Foucault Reader,* 203–213.

[16] Lenz, *Der Hofmeister,* 183. Translation mine.

[17] Foucault, "The Body of the Condemned," 177.

[18] Julia Kristeva, "The True-Real," See especially 216–220, 224–227, and 230–236, as well as Toril Moi's excellent introduction to Kristeva's main concepts, 1–22.

[19] Brecht, *Gesammelte Werke* 16: 924. Quoted by John Rouse, "Brecht and the Question of the Audience," *Essays on Brecht/ Versuche über Brecht: The Brecht Yearbook* 15, ed. Marc Silberman, John Fuegi, Renate Voris, Carl Weber (College Park, Md.: International Brecht Society, 1990), 114.

[20] This is well described by John Rouse, in his *Brecht and the West German Theatre* (Ann Arbor, UMI Research P, 1989).

[21] Brecht, *Hofmeister* material, 547/49–54.

[22] Brecht, *Hofmeister* material, 546/110.

[23] Kristeva, "The True-Real," 231–236. Only as a subject-in-process, who refuses or is refused a proper place in the phallic order, can experience what Kristeva calls *jouissance,* an abandonment of order and truth in favor of free play.

[24] Brecht, *Hofmeister* material, 547/01.

[25] Brecht, *Hofmeister* material, 546/70.

The Tutor, on his day off, shows off for young girls at the ice rink. From The Tutor, Berliner Ensemble, 1950. By permission of the Bertolt Brecht Archive, Berlin. Photo by Wolfgang Meyenfels.

Part II:

The Epic Legacy in Contemporary Theater

The young Peer Gynt (center: Heinrich Gieskes) shows off for the villagers. From Peter Stein's production of Peer Gynt, Schaubühne am Hallischen Ufer, Berlin, 1972. Photo courtesy of and © Helga Kneidl.

*Peer Gynt (Bruno Ganz) meets the Troll King's
daughter as a Troll matron turns away.
Photo © and courtesy of Helga Kneidl.*

4: *Peer Gynt* as Epic Theater: Peter Stein in Berlin and Rustom Bharucha in India

The negative aspects of [Ibsen's] work contribute materially to its achievement. . . . To ask for the essence of Ibsen [or] quintessence of Ibsenism, is to formulate a wholly misleading question; there is nothing to be got by boiling down, there is no extract of wisdom. . . . If one must have an analogy, one might be a little nearer the truth by asking for the root of Ibsen; for just as the root of . . . 9 is not 3 but that more ambiguous entity mathematicians call ±3, so the root of Ibsen's view of life, however positively he may at times seem to express himself, conveys the impression of being similarly "plus or minus."

— James W. McFarlane[1]

In Ibsen's Hegelian aesthetic, that heirloom from the national past, its treasury of lyric ballads richly stocked with objectified emotion and collective spiritual inwardness, must be productively united with the epic consciousness of great events and vast historical forces to yield a drama worthy of the time. . . . [T]he world that Peer Gynt is poised to enter, the world of the future, . . . of international trade and mass exploitation, is epic, is history on the move; the world he tries to leave behind, the world of the past, of simple verities and home truths, small minds and smaller opportunities, is lyrical, a grieving celebration of lost possibilities. The unaccomplished synthesis of the two is one version of the dramatic conflict.

— Rolf Fjelde[2]

PEER GYNT HAS BEEN CALLED the first modern drama, the final flowering of Romanticism, and a forerunner of both the absurdist and the epic theater. Since its publication in 1867 and stage premiere in 1876, the history of *Peer Gynt*'s staging and reception has been marked by controversies that raise basic questions about representation itself. Its popularity, thematic complexity, episodic structure, and mixture of naturalistic, fantastic, and satiric elements helped precipitate the practice now called the *mise en scène:* an integrated spectacle involving a centralization of all performance elements under the control of one director's unifying vision, usually realized with the aid of a particular designer. In the mid-nineteenth century neither audiences nor critics nor directors nor stage design and technology were ready to deal with *Peer Gynt*'s unexpected juxtaposition of satire with poetry, the realistic with the fantastic, and topical politics with mythical folklore — which was precisely the kind of dialectical juxtaposition of genre, tone, language, and historical perspective that would characterize the epic theater. In fact, it was the advent of Brechtian practice and theory that allowed *Peer Gynt*'s contradictions in structure, themes, and ideologies to be understood and appreciated. This chapter will focus principally on productions by two modern directors whose work reflects twentieth-century understandings of *Peer Gynt* as epic in its ability to critically illuminate its social and political circumstances and its own role as theater in perpetuating them: Peter Stein, whose 1971 staging at the Berlin Schaubühne was epic in the Brechtian sense; and Rustom Bharucha, one of today's foremost postcolonial scholars of theater, who translated, adapted, and directed *Peer Gynt* for a 1990s staging in Mysore, India. Bharucha was drawn by the folk and epic elements of Ibsen's play and by its "translatability" into the Indian theater forms and sociopolitical context. Both directors recognized Ibsen's play as epic in the traditional as well as the Brechtian sense. To gain a historical perspective on *Peer Gynt* as epic in both these senses, the precedent-setting premiere production of 1876, as well as Hans-Jacob Nilsen's precedent-breaking staging of 1948 and the American premiere of 1905 will also be briefly discussed. These five productions clearly demonstrate what James McFarlane calls the dialectical "plus and minus" of the play, which is also at the heart of the dynamic structure of the epic theater.

Before turning to specific performances, however, the epic spatiotemporality of the dramatic text of *Peer Gynt* will be analyzed, employing a semiotic approach informed by Mikhail Bakhtin's work on the chronotope as it operates dynamically in the work of Rabelais. The term *dramatic text* is defined here as a text created by countless signifiers of concrete and abstract spatio-temporality that give it the dimension of a potential theater performance.

For years preceding *Peer Gynt* Ibsen had worked as a playwright and dramaturg creating and helping stage nationalistic folkloric spectacles for the Christiania (Oslo) Theater. In connection with this work he had received a government grant to collect Norwegian folktales, and *Peer Gynt* incorporated a good deal of this research. In fact, however, the play would throw a critical light on the very genre, i.e., the folkloric spectacle, to which it ostensibly belonged and on the conservative, nationalistic, mythicizing ideology supported by this genre. Ibsen's statement in 1881 that the work was a "dramatic poem," that was "in no way designed to be performed" has only helped perpetuate the controversy,[3] notwithstanding the fact that it had already enjoyed a successful stage premiere five years previously. When it appeared as a published text in 1867 *Peer Gynt* provoked a debate over the definition and limitations of dramatic versus poetic discourse.[4] It was faulted with being neither poetry nor drama, neither true nor beautiful. From the safe distance of his newly adopted Italy, Ibsen wrote a prophetic response:

> My work is poetry; and if it isn't, it shall become so. The concept of poetry in our country, in Norway, will come to conform to the work. *There is nothing stable in the world of concepts* [italics mine].[5]

To many, beauty was incompatible with the play's irreverence toward idealism, particularly nationalistic idealism. Sometimes — but not too convincingly — Ibsen himself tried to play down the "isolated satiric elements" and disclaimed responsibility for any irony that might be read into the play: "The satirical bits are fairly isolated. But if . . . the present-day Norwegians recognize themselves . . . that is those good people's own business."[6] *Peer Gynt's* stage productions and receptions through more than a century have never managed to totally suppress the irony and social critique, even if they have tended to resolve the play's contradictions in one distinct way or another. Each stage interpretation has attached these contradictions of the text's content and structure to its own set of culturally specific value systems that are being defended, attacked, or critiqued.

The Spatio-Temporal Dynamic of *Peer Gynt*

Mikhail Bakhtin's *Rabelais and His World* provides us with an example of the chronotope that helps illuminate the dialectical epic quality of *Peer Gynt*.[7] Bakhtin shows that Rabelais's novels are fundamentally structured upon the principle of ambivalence. That is, there is a contradictory meaning-structure whose valuations can never be resolved, and their very irresolvability is the source of the work's dynamism. This is the phenomenon that McFarlane notes when he describes the "root" of Ibsen as both positive and negative. The semiotic structure of *Peer Gynt's* spatio-temporality is at the heart of its dynamic contradictions. This eminently epic structure helps explain the volatility that has marked the history of the play's production and reception, especially in regard to its representation of ideology.[8]

From the overall narrative of Peer's physical movement through represented space and time we can extrapolate a particular topography. This "map" emerges only gradually. At the outset, the topography is a landscape of Norway: high mountains, fjords, and the sea. As the story continues, Peer's territory extends across the Atlantic and Pacific Oceans, the Mediterranean Sea, and the continents of Europe, the

Americas, and Africa. His movement over this space forms a large ir-
regular circle; this movement is the most all-encompassing signifier of
the spatio-temporal design: first, Peer proceeds outwards from his
mother Aase's hut in the upper valley to a neighboring farm, then up to
the tree line of the mountains, down again to lower land, then westward over the sea to America and southeastward to Africa, from which
he slowly makes his way northward back to Norway. In Norway again
after fifty years, he proceeds back upward past the same farm and past
his mother's hut. He tramps over the same paths that he took in the
first three acts, and finally, at the end of the play, climbs back up to the
same mountain hut to join Solveig (literally, "Sun-way"), the woman
who loves him and has been waiting for him for fifty years and whom
he at last calls his "mother and wife" as she cradles him in her arms.

This large circle is drawn not just through space but over time as
well. The "time line" representing fifty years of Peer Gynt's life is made
to curve and to close itself *nearly* into a circle by the order of events
and images: from the beginning of the play the *gestic* impetus of almost
every episode is Peer's avoidance of obstacles and entrapment. For instance, just as he is about to enter the mountain hut and an ecstatic
(and perhaps static) life with Solveig, the alluring Green Woman blocks
his path. He sidesteps the latter by going all around the world.

Repetition is also important: the events that occur during Peer's first
large curve through geographical space are paralleled by similar events
appearing in reverse order during the last half of the curve. One example of many: the monkeys of Act 4 pursue Peer and throw feces at him,
recalling the attack by the troll children in Act 2. The near repetition in
reverse order of certain sequences in effect *bends* Peer's fifty years of
time: the image of time as a straight line marked by serial events is bent
into a moving arc. Further, the arcing circle of Peer's life is not drawn
on a flat surface, but is also traced out vertically. Scholars have noted
the importance of the image of incomplete circularity in Romanticism,
but the origins of the circle image are much older; one need only recall
the German idiom for death: *man kommt um das Leben* — we "come
around life," rather than, as in English, "to the end of life."

In addition to the movements of the protagonist, other signifying
systems within the play also help to establish the moving, never-closing
circle as a "master signifier." The dialogue contains recurrent images of
climbing, falling, and circling through the air and on the land. As the
play opens, Peer is telling his mother a story of how he rode a reindeer
across a high cliff and fell into the fjord below as his own mirrored image
rose to meet him. His poetic narrative contains several spatial images in

which the contrast between height and depth is set up. This landscape of extreme heights and depths is "without a sound," "sleeping."

If read in isolation from the dialectical movement of the play, this passage would seem to signify nothing specific in terms of ideology. It has the stylistic and thematic markings of a "quintessential" Romanticism — that is, a piece of Romantic discourse not joined to a particular ideology: a description of a man and a reindeer racing along a sheer high cliff that rises straight up out of the sea. It is not just Peer the rider who moves, however, but the other animate and inanimate elements in the scene as well: suns "flash" and "come close by" the rider, space "reels," eagles "float midway between" and then "fall away," the rider's senses "swim," "swirl," and "weave in rings." Peer's poetic narrative is interrupted by the speech of Aase and thus becomes part of a dialogue. She calls out the names of Jesus and God, and we now have two ideological discourses in juxtaposition: folkloric Romanticism and pietistic Christianity, in what Bakhtin would call a *dialogical* relationship:

PEER GYNT

>And then with dizzy leaps he springs
>Along the brink of Gjendin ridge!

AASE (involuntarily)

>Oh, my Jesus — !

PEER GYNT

>>Have you seen
>The way the cliffs of Gjendin hang?
>They run out nearly four miles long,
>Lean as a scythe edge at the top.
>Past glaciers, ledges, rockslides,
>Herbs clinging to the gray-green slope,
>You can look down either side
>Straight into water, where in a slow
>Black heavy sleep it lies one
>Thousand yards, almost, below.
>>He and I, on that blade of ground,
>Cut a channel through the wind.
>>I've never had me such a run!
>Sometimes in the headlong pace
>The air seemed full of flashing suns.
>In the reeling gulfs of space
>Eagles with brown backs would float
>Midway between us and the water—
>Then fall away behind, like motes.
>>I could see ice floes crack and shatter
>On the shore, without a sound to hear.

>   Only the imps of swimming senses
>   Came singing, swirling, weaving dances
>   In rings around my eyes and ears.
>
> AASE (giddy)
>   Oh, God help me!
>   — Peer Gynt, I:1, 5 [9]

We learn later that the adventure did not even happen to Peer but is a folk legend. Thus, a basic ambiguity is introduced: should the narratives of the imagination (especially the nationalistic Romantic imagination) be valued as truth or falsehood, moral or immoral, negatively or positively? The play's spatio-temporal signifiers point in two directions at once. One image in this scene strikingly visualizes the dynamic, dialectical ambivalence: the man and reindeer fall off the cliff as their reflected doubles rise to meet them:

> PEER GYNT
>   Behind us, rock walls sheering up,
>   Beneath us, gaping nothingness —
>   And we two dropping, . . .
>   Downward, endlessly we go.
>   But in the depths something shows
>   Dim white, like reindeer's belly fleece.
>   Mother, it was *our* reflection
>   Shooting upward in the lake from
>   Silent darkness to the glassy calm
>   On top with the same breakneck
>   Speed as we were hurtling down.
>
> AASE (gasping for breath)
>   Peer! Dear Lord, what happened? Quick!
>   — *PG,* I:1, 6

Thus, the spatio-temporal oppositions of height and depth, falling and rising, are unstable and relative per se, latently volatile even in their "silent" and "sleeping" state, before any specific ideology is attached to them.

Another important signifier of movement through time and space is the Great Boyg, a mysterious being who remains invisible, a voice in the dark who, in their only direct encounter, tells Peer to "go round about." Throughout the rest of the play this advice is echoed several times in Peer's own voice; he quotes it whenever he wishes to avoid making an irrevocable decision. Its name is related to the Germanic verb *beugen,* which means to bend. Scholars of Nordic mythology have theorized that the Boyg is a modern descendent of the legendary Midgard Serpent, which lies at the bottom of the sea, coiled all around the earth (the Midgard, where humans dwell). Thor alone has seen the monster face to face, when with his great strength he pulled it momentarily up out of the sea. The Boyg is also related to the World Serpent that appears in many mythological traditions.[10] The Norwegian folktale that was Ibsen's most immediate source tells of an encounter between the Boyg of Etnedal and a hunter called Per Gynt:

> 'Who is that?' said Per, for he felt it moving.
>
> 'Ah, it's the Boyg', came the answer. This left Per Gynt none the wiser. But he skirted round the thing a little way, thinking he must be able to get by somewhere. Again he suddenly ran into something; and when he reached out, it was big and cold and slippery. . . .
>
> 'Well, whether you be straight or crooked, you must let me get past', said Per, for he realized he was going round in a circle, and that the Boyg had curled itself round the saeter [hut] . . . and he went fumbling round the walls, . . . and wherever he turned to go, he felt the encircling Boyg. It isn't very good being here, thought Per, since this Boyg is all over the place. . . . Then Per Gynt let fly and fired three shots right into its head.
>
> 'Fire one more!' said the Boyg. But Per knew better than to do that; for if he had fired one more shot, it would have back-fired on him.[11]

Ibsen's Peer, as the modern epic antihero, struggles with it even more inconclusively: once, early on, he fights it in the dark, and years later, as he is gazing for the first time at the Sphinx, he believes he has finally met it face to face. But it remains elusive throughout the play. In contrast to the folk tale, it is never presented in material terms such as "big and cold and slippery." Yet in Peer's perception it puts itself in his path several times, thus helping to determine his route around the world. It too makes Peer's path bend. The Boyg, then, is more than an isolated image. It is a powerful signifier of the dynamic principle by which time and space are structured in the play as a whole. The Boyg is not closed within the structure of the text; rather, it extends through two levels at once: it is "within" the textual signification system but also part of what is "outside" it, which Eco calls the *semantic universe*.[12] Likewise, it is part of the collective mythology of its first Norwegian readers and spectators, but it also draws from a broader mythological context. Its elusive, spiraling shape *animates* the spatio-temporality.

As noted, the great curving circle of Peer's life journey is not only a movement over a flat surface. Instead, the circling also descends and ascends, gradually developing into an image of a *moving spiral*. The spiral seems to move because it is not exposed all at once but only through the occurrence of "events" in what we accept, through theatrical and reading conventions, as a continuum of space and time — it is repre-

sentation as *spacing,* to use Derrida's term.[13] The spiraling "line" created by Peer's movement stops with his arrival back on the mountain
where Solveig, in contrast to Peer, has been immobile for the whole
fifty years of represented time.

It is not surprising that we would find the spiral as an organizing
principle of the spatio-temporality of *Peer Gynt,* because this shape is so
important to the Romantics from Tieck, Novalis, and the Schlegels
through Goethe and Shelley up to Yeats. And long before Romanticism
became a self-conscious movement, the spiral was already important in
Renaissance thought. Hegel chose this image to spatially visualize his
concept of the dialectical movement of history. Some scholars of Romanticism believe that the power of the moving spiral on the Western
imagination originated in the discovery of the earth's magnetism. Literally revolutionary was the idea that negative and positive poles created
an energy field wherein matter was put into motion. If matter was no
longer stable, no longer a permanent "quintessence," then the cosmos
itself was in a state of transformation. The spiral's appearances in Romantic literature are innumerable. Close in spirit to Ibsen is its use by
William Butler Yeats, for whom the spiraling gyre is a dialectical image
of the end of an old era with a stable center and the beginning of a
more uncertain one:

> Things thought too long can be no longer thought, . . .
> And ancient lineaments are blotted out . . . and all things run
> On that unfashionable gyre again.
>   — from "The Gyres," 1936[14]

> Turning and turning in the widening gyre
> The falcon cannot hear the falconer;
> Things fall apart; the centre cannot hold. . . .
>   — from "The Second Coming," 1921[15]

Several sequences in *Peer Gynt* clearly echo the German Romantics
Hegel and Goethe. Peer's encounter in Act 2 with the trolls on the
mountain recalls the *Walpurgisnacht* scene from *Faust* — and also
draws from a Hans Christian Andersen tale. A preoccupation with geography, seismic activity, geological formations, and, in particular,
mountain landscapes, is seen in the work of many Romantics. By contrast, for the Enlightenment philosopher Kant, the mountain peak is an
image for the unchanging Eternal Sublime. In *Peer Gynt* Hegelian discourse, as well as that of Herder, Goethe, and Shakespeare, appear as
misquotations and in ludicrous contexts. These "negative elements,"
satirizing Romanticism, idealistic philosophy, nationalism, and the
"great man" concept of historical agency, come strongly forward in Act

4, which presents Peer's years of travel around the world. For the first seventy years of the play's stage history, this act and much of Act 5 were considered a flaw in Ibsen's otherwise perfect design and were either omitted or severely truncated.

An example of the ironic *negation* of Romantic idealism is seen in Peer's relations with women. Pretending to be a holy prophet, he has the following encounter with the Arab temptress Anitra, a Sheik's daughter whom he meets in Egypt during his travels as a colonial empire builder:

> ANITRA (points at his turban)
>   That pretty opal!
>
> PEER GYNT (enraptured, giving her the jewel)
>   Anitra! Child! Eve's own daughter!
>   Like a magnet drawing me — for I'm a man;
>   And just as he said, that well-known writer:
>   *"Das Ewig-Weibliche zieht uns an!"*
>   — *PG*, IV:6, 120

Peer has misquoted the final line of *Faust*, which is *"Das Ewig-Weibliche zieht uns hinan."* Goethe's "The Eternal Feminine draws us upward" has become "The Eternal Feminine lures us on."[16] There is a confusion of "animal magnetism" with the magnetic pole that is supposed to attract the spirit to a higher plane; unlike Solveig on her mountaintop, Anitra as woman-magnet is not located at the proper Romantic height but on the same *horizontal* plane as Peer — namely, lying in a tent in the desert. The polarity between Solveig and Anitra represents them both as an *other* to Peer, with the function of *landmarks* in the geographical and existential topography. While Solveig is associated with Mary, goodness, virginity, self-sacrifice, the blond Nordic European, the high mountains, spirituality, and vertical movement, Anitra and the Green Woman are connected to Eve, sin, sexuality, greed, the dark exotic Oriental, the lowland, and horizontal movement. All the women in Peer's story, including his mother, Aase, mark out what Teresa de Lauretis calls a "mythic space" as the *stage upon which he acts:*

> [In traditional works] the mythical subject is constructed as human being and as male; he is the active principle of culture. . . . Female is what is . . . the womb, the earth, the space of his movement. . . . She . . . is an element of *plot space, a topos, a resistance, matrix and matter* [italics mine].[17]

Yet Peer's heroic manly status and the mythical and philosophical discourses supporting it are anything but stable; rather, at the very mo-

ments they assert themselves most confidently they are subverted by
contradictory irony.

After surviving a shipwreck on the Mediterranean and escaping from
Anitra and her angry father, Peer abruptly decides to become a philosopher-historian since he happens to be in ancient Egypt. At the site
of the Sphinx, he meets Dr. Begriffenfeldt, literally "field of concepts,"
a German philosopher-scientist who now directs an experimental institute for the insane, with the aim of raising their spiritual consciousness;
all of his patients are natives. By this time, philosophy and history have
become Begriffenfeldt's paranoiac obsessions:

BEGRIFFENFELDT
        Can you keep a secret? I have a confession —
PEER GYNT (increasingly uneasy)
        What's that?
BEGRIFFENFELDT
        You think you can stand the shock?
PEER GYNT
        Well, I'll try —
BEGRIFFENFELDT (draws him into a corner, whispers)
        Absolute Reason
        Died last night at eleven o'clock.
                            — *PG,* IV:8, 140

Despite this ominous scene, in which Begriffenfeldt's experiments
result in a patient's inadvertent suicide, Peer still tries to emulate the
idealist philosophical style and themes of Hegel and Herder. In attempting to do so, he employs a parodic language that is epic because it
draws attention to itself in the act of staging ideological discourse:

> What if I went as a wandering scholar
> To trace the past ages, the greed of mankind?
> Yes, that's it! There's my place!
> I always read legends as a child;
> And now, with the sciences I've distilled —
> I'll follow the course of the human race!
> I'll float like a feather on history's stream,
> Relive it all, as if in a dream —
> See the heroes battle for truth and right,
> But as an onlooker, safe in thought —
> See thinkers perish and martyrs bleed,
> See empires rise and sweep to doom,
> See the world epochs sprout from seed —
> In short, I'll skim off history's cream.
> . . . And become a strict chronological seeker.
>   — *PG,* IV:9, 132

Peer's speech as would-be philosopher-historian follows the cadence and lyrics of Hegelian discourse: "to trace the past ages," "the sciences I've distilled," "to follow the course of the human race," "history's stream." Peer also speaks of "world epochs sprouting from seed," echoing Herder's organic concept of great national cultures sprouting from seed, growing, flowering, dying, and leaving seeds for future civilizations. However, whereas Herder's image involves a flower, Peer philosophizes about his life and that of his country with a *wild onion,* whose layers he peels away one by one, searching in vain for a central kernel. As another image of Peer's time, the outermost layer of this sphere represents the most recent event, and each succeeding one goes further into the past — yet he arrives there last. The onion, often used as a symbol for human life, can be read here as a *mise en abyme,* an infinite regression/progression, a signifier pointing in opposite directions.

Seen as an abstract geometrical pattern, then, the unfolding of Peer's time and space resembles the dialectical *Aufhebung* of the World Spirit of History that Hegel describes as an *upward-moving spiral,* the progression of thesis, antithesis, and synthesis. Peer's restless spiraling is set in contrast to the timeless immobility of the high mountain hut where the pure, already perfected Solveig lives — it is significant that Peer is interested in history, while Solveig is not. But if Peer's actions and other events are judged in reference to prevailing social norms in our epoch as well as in Ibsen's, then the ideological or moral values that Hegel attached to this spiral are reversed.[18] Peer's spiral can no longer be unhesitatingly read as ascending in the sense of the positive progress of a World Spirit. As noted already in the discussion of the reindeer ride, *spatial signifiers of height and depth, ascent and descent can literally be turned upside down, thereby reversing the values attached to them.*

In Act 1 Peer ascends the mountain carrying the abducted bride Ingrid under his arm as if she were a pig, an action often read as his moral descent, a fall into animal nature. This action can be interpreted as antisocial or even anticomic: he violently disrupts a wedding, which could mark him as a sociopath who has aborted the ceremony by which the society assures its continuity. Yet the abduction can also be seen as beneficial for this society because it disrupts a sterile union: the groom was impotent anyway, too dependent upon his parents, too immature to perform his marital duty — which Peer does for him. It is also high in the mountains that Peer debauches with the Herd Girls and the Woman in Green. Further evidence of contradictory values attached to the signifiers of height and depth is the fact that Solveig's hut is not actually on the mountain peak but rather at the tree line of the mountains. Moreover, the trolls, figuratively relegated to the "subhuman" level, live at the foot of the mountain, which in topographic spatial terms is higher than the valley where the townspeople live.

In addition to the contradictory values of the spatial signifiers, the movement of time is also not at all a clear sign of positive spiritual or historical progress. Both Peer and Norway are moving historically, but the direction is questionable. Many critics have seen Act 5 as a move backward in time, the closing of a circle as Peer returns to his past. But if Norway, as portrayed in this act, were judged according to Darwinian precepts, we might also view it as a downwardly mobile society. In Act 5 Peer notices that the Norwegian children he meets have become more troll-like: children traditionally represent the future of a society, but here the citizens seem to be *regressing* on the evolutionary scale. This society does not grow upward into flower nor bear fruit: contrary to Herder's design, only wild onions emerge from its ground. Time reveals itself as devolution rather than evolution, and Hegel's history appears to be traveling in reverse, in a kind of burlesque of the dialectical *Aufhebung* — translated as "sublimation" but literally a *lifting up*. Another textual image likens Peer's life to a photographic plate whereon *no* trace has been registered, as opposed to either a positive or a negative imprint. Thus, Peer's final return to the mountain is profoundly contradictory, in Bakhtin's sense of a contradiction that is inherent in the dynamic structure of a work and allows it to be dialogical.

Therefore, we cannot really say, from a textual semiotic analysis of *Peer Gynt's* spatio-temporality, whether the ideological discourses that are represented by this spatio-temporal structure are to be valued positively or negatively by our own or any other social standard. Is the signified progression or regression? Romantic ideology has been textualized to signify and refer to what? Looking back from a post-Brechtian standpoint, one answer is that this ideology ironizes or even deconstructs itself, as Brian Johnston suggests in *Towards the Third Empire:*

> It is difficult not to conclude that the play quite consciously resurrects its great archetypal and literary models to reveal their devaluation by the modern spirit. Peer's journey above and beneath earth and sea is not a heroic quest but a lifelong evasion. He encounters enemies and monsters, yet flees conflict with them. . . . Unlike Everyman . . . Peer does not learn from the allegorical figures he encounters, and it is uncertain if he finally understands Solveig's answer to the riddle of his identity.[19]

Less idealistically but more optimistically, we might answer that the social, moral, and physical regression seen on stage sets off the dialectical process of a *Verfremdungseffekt,* through which the *spectators,* if not Peer himself, might progress toward enlightenment. In *Peer Gynt's* early history, however, this devaluation of philosophical and literary archetypes through irony happened only for the first *readers* of the published text, not on the stage.

The Epic Chronotope

As a chronotope, or time-space, the spiral that dominates *Peer Gynt* can be seen as a struggle between verticality and horizontality, but the movement of that spiral is fundamentally contradictory because it can be read as proceeding downward as well as upward. Bakhtin, in *Rabelais and His World,* explains that in the medieval era the dominant view of the cosmos and its ideological structures was organized along a two-poled vertical axis representing a hierarchy. This hierarchy devalued time and geographical space: it was possible, of course, to move "outward" in an exploratory way from one's birthplace through space, or "forward and backward" through historical (developmental, processual) time, but such a move was meaningless according to the ideology of the Church. Only up-and-down movement held meaning: that is, movement along the vertical axis that placed hell at the bottom and heaven at the top, a hierarchy wherein there were *no developing events but only simultaneous existences.*

> The medieval cosmos was built according to Aristotle. It was based on the precept of the four elements (earth, water, air, and fire), each of which had its special rank in the structure of the universe . . . all the elements were subject to a definite order from top to bottom. The nature and movement of each element were determined according to its position in relation to the center of the cosmos. . . . The basic principle of all physical phenomena [was] the transformation of one element into the element nearest it. . . . This [was] the law of creation and destruction to which all living things [were] subject. But above the earthly world there [rose] the world of celestial bodies, not ruled by this law [but] composed of a special kind of matter, *quinta essentia* [the fifth element], which [was] not subject to transformation. . . . The higher the element on the cosmic scale (that is, the nearer to the "immovable motor") the more nearly perfect was this element's quality.[20]

Bakhtin explains that with the Renaissance the concept of a vertically oriented cosmos began to be replaced with one that organized the cosmos horizontally. The horizontal was associated with the developmental and with historicity — in other words, with the new possibility

of meaningful human movement through terrestrial time and space.
The old value system, which had placed unchangeability at its apex, was
giving way to a system wherein transformability was no longer seen as
the unhappy fate of all sub-celestial existence but rather as its most desirable, "highest" value:

> This transfer of the world from the vertical to the horizontal was real-
> ized in the human body, which became the relative center of the cos-
> mos. And this cosmos was no longer moving from the bottom to the
> top but along the horizontal line of time, from the past to the future.[21]

Bakhtin points out, however, that this great shift from the hierarchical axis of verticality toward the historical axis of horizontality was not
effected without conflict and that many works register the tension between these two axes. Dante, for instance, still had the ideological intention of structuring his cosmos along the medieval vertical axis, but this
world was "already in a state of crisis and stands at the breaking point."
That is, Dante placed some values on the horizontal plane, and as a result there is a discernible clash between these two sets of polarities.[22]

If we now reflect on the spatio-temporal dynamic of *Peer Gynt* in
light of Bakhtin's insights, the dialectical spiral can be seen as a strikingly apt geometric image of a tension that pulls the line of human
destiny toward two opposing axes, the vertical and the horizontal:
therefore, the inevitable path of this line is a spiral. All of the conflicting
ideological discourses of Ibsen's play can now be seen as organized
along either the vertical or the horizontal axis: Solveig's unwavering
one-way climb to her place above the valley civilization is a meaningful
journey in terms of *any hierarchical ideology that values permanence and
immobility and devalues historical time and change.* Conversely, Peer's
horizontal exploration of the world beyond his birthplace is meaningful
in terms of the Renaissance values outlined by Bakhtin: *history, time,
freedom of choice, development, events.* But Peer does not merely travel
along the horizontal plane; instead, his path is pulled into a spiral
whose "top" — his final reunion with Solveig in the mountain hut — is
so contradictory that it is not able to secure a stable positive or negative
meaning. On the contrary, this precarious apex can reverse itself, thus
becoming the "bottom," or negative pole, in another system of values.

In our own times these axes are still in operation. Ideologies like that
of the medieval Church, which value being and devalue becoming, time,
change, and geographical space, are still often represented by means of
the vertical axis, while those ideologies that value becoming or historical
change tend to organize themselves around a horizontal axis. It should
be noted here that the concept of movement did exist in the medieval

hierarchical schema, but this movement had no duration; it occurred instantaneously. A human being could rise instantly to the position of an angel. And while it was always possible to explore real space on the horizontal plane, this activity was perceived as static. It becomes clear, then, that our perception of meaningful versus meaningless movement is arbitrary and depends on how ideological values are codified by a particular social context. Since the values of any semiotic code are volatile, the same spatio-temporal construct can be read differently according to the pragmatic ideological needs of a historically specific audience. A brief look at three highlights of *Peer Gynt's* early stage history will show how and why specific ideologies were textualized, i.e., aesthetically codified, along the polarities of these two axes. The earlier stagings will help to illuminate the historical significance of the two overtly epic contemporary productions that are the main focus of this chapter.

The Norwegian Premiere of *Peer Gynt*

Although Ibsen was initially skeptical that *Peer Gynt* could be staged, its premiere at the Christiania Theater on February 24, 1876, was surprisingly successful; it ran for more than ten months, until a fire forced it to close. From his new residence in Italy, Ibsen had contracted Edvard Grieg to write music for the play that would not only guide the mood, provide sound effects, and "describe" the landscape of Norway but, on a practical level, would cover the long and noisy set changes. Since it was taken for granted that all scene changes had to be literally represented, performing the whole text of the play was deemed impractical.[23] Indeed, nearly all of the fourth act — which anticipates the epic theater — and much of the fifth was cut.

But nothing in the theater is done for practical reasons alone. The chosen cutting allowed only one ideological discourse to dominate, and the "unwieldy" episodes of Acts 4 and 5 did not fit comfortably into its agenda. Here we return to the concepts of verticality and horizontality. In Act 4 we learn through exposition that Peer has spent the last thirty years traveling outward — horizontally — over the geographical, economic, and social terrain of the nineteenth century: he sails to America, becomes a trader in African slaves and oriental idols, a colonialist in Africa, and in the Mideast an empire builder, a religious charlatan, a historian-philosopher, and a mock emperor in turn. Because these topical episodes ironically subverted the Romantic, nationalistic ideology that seemed to pervade the rest of the play, they would be systematically omitted from the stage for more than seventy years.

Surprisingly, for the first production it was the author himself, not the director Ludvig Josephson, who wanted to cut these scenes and replace them with "a musical tone-picture." Ibsen wrote to Grieg with the following suggestions:

> More or less the whole of Act Four is to be omitted. . . . In its place I imagined a substantial musical tone-picture to represent Peer Gynt's wanderings about the world, in which American, English and French melodies might be heard as themes varying and fading . . . one will see like a distant dream-picture the tableau . . . where Solveig . . . sits singing in the sunlight outside her house. . . . [Act Five] . . . must be . . . abbreviated. . . . The scenes on the upturned boat and in the churchyard will be left out. . . . Solveig's song concludes the play, . . . the curtain falls and the singing of psalms is once more heard closer and louder.[24]

But Josephson tried to save as much of the text as possible, and a compromise was reached, with the scenes in question shortened but not transformed into a "musical dream picture." Yet more than any visual element, even more than the cuts in the text, it was Grieg's music that precluded an ironic reading by the audiences. Ibsen biographer Michael Meyer absolves the author of betraying his own intentions: "Few musical scores can have so softened an author's intentions as Grieg's *Peer Gynt* suite, which turns the play into a jolly Hans Andersen fairy tale; but Ibsen was too unmusical to perceive this, and was delighted with the result, though he might have been less so had he seen it."[25]

In another curious turnabout of what we might expect, while the music was overwhelmingly interpreted as folkloric, idealistic, even "sublime," Grieg himself had intended some of it to be taken as an ironic comment on smug, ethnocentric "Norwegiomania":

> Things are going very slowly with 'Peer Gynt,' . . . It is a frightfully intractable theme, apart from certain parts, for example where Solveig sings and where I have done it all. I've also done something of the Hall of the Dovre-Master which I literally can't bear to listen to — so full of cow platters, Norwegiomania and self-complacency! But I also expect that people will be able to sense the irony.[26]

This was difficult, considering the textual cuts and other totalizing elements such as the set design, acting style, and costumes: from production photographs it is evident that great effort was made to fill the stage space with a Romantic-sublime, recognizably Norwegian landscape, using real foliage, detailed interiors, and authentically grass-roofed huts, all backed by painted mountain-and-fjord vistas. In one photo a carefree Peer in bushy beard and mountain-man attire leans jauntily against a tree. The trolls look like merry elves rather than the grotesque, malevolent, primitive forest dwellers of mythology. In another photo a straight-backed Anitra, the Arabian temptress, stares solemnly into the camera in a long, multilayered, high-necked Victorian dress covered with medals.

Ibsen wrote the play in the verse form of the Norwegian folk ballad, whose rhythm ideologically defined the basic temporality of the play for its first readers and spectators. Rolf Fjelde explains the historical circumstance that made such an ideological effect possible: the folk ballad had been the "only continuous strand of Norwegian identity" to bridge more than 400 years of subjugation to Denmark, from 1380 to 1814.[27] The first staging radically suppressed Ibsen's attack on idealism and Norwegian nationalism that had so offended the readers of the published text nine years before. The rhythm of this folk ballad juxtaposed with the ironic dialogue is eminently epic. Grieg's music obscured the dialogue's irony, however, so that the balladic verse was overdetermined by the music, which would become an indispensable ideological signifier for its audiences. Together, the ballad verse form and Grieg's music would become increasingly associated with the Norwegian landscape and a collectively perceived "Norwegian spirit."

Peer's return to Solveig was interpreted as the upward spiral of his spirit, an ending that turned the narrative into an allegory on the order of *Everyman* or *Pilgrim's Progress*. Two ideological narratives were merged and represented by one spatio-temporal movement: the Christian narrative of the soul's journey upward to heaven was joined to the nationalistic narrative of the return of the Norwegian spirit to its heroic mythical past. As imagistic systems, both ideologies still operate on the medieval axis wherein historical time is devalued and mobility is only vertical: the goal of the ideal Christian is to climb steeply to the highest point in order to reach timeless perfection, while the goal of the nationalistic, mythic Norwegian is to go back to a past of Viking heroes and gods. Both narratives turn away from the historical present. As societies, both the Christian heaven and the nationalistic mythical past are rigidly hierarchical. All the meaningful acts have always already taken place; there is no longer any possibility of development — it is neither needed nor desired.

The original social context of the play assured the triumph of verticality, which was pragmatically necessary in order to aesthetically codify a national Norwegian identity. *Peer Gynt* would appear regularly in the repertory of the Norwegian State Theater, but in more severely cut form than the premiere production. Whatever the omissions, all the scenes with Solveig remained unabridged. Thus, the play was inevitably interpreted as a positive progression, albeit to an idealized past — an interpretation that ignored even the irony inherent in the Romantic aesthetic, according to which Peer's story could be seen as a negation of the negative. Instead, the Norwegian audiences saw the story as a glorification of themselves or, at worst, as a good-humored satire. In the rest of the world *Peer Gynt* would long be staged as a frolicsome yet pious Nordic operetta, a far remove from the dramatic poem attacked for its irreverence toward "Norwegiomania."[28]

The American Premiere

A striking example of how the spatio-temporality of *Peer Gynt* was staged to codify a particular ideology is the American premiere — indeed, the first English-language production — of *Peer Gynt,* which opened on October 29, 1906, at the Grand Opera House in Chicago.[29] The event began before the curtain opened. Richard Mansfield, as director, producer, and lead actor, had left New York with his company of 347 cast and crew, a full orchestra, and the set, in eleven railroad cars traveling westward to Chicago; according to the press it was the largest theatrical traveling company ever. The spatio-temporality of the performance event was set up through the social and geographical context of the trip westward. The company metaphorically traveled over the same ground as had the mythic wagon trains that were the pervasive image of Manifest Destiny in American nationalist ideology. Now, however, the tempo of the wagon train was accelerated and the space dramatized, expanded, and made more panoramic by the technological wonder of the steam locomotive — and, of course, the train could go straight *through* the mountains. In short, the ideology of Manifest Destiny could be joined to that of empire-building technological progress, through the newly shared spatio-temporal signifier of the train moving westward across the continent.

Mansfield's cuts in the text were much more drastic than those carried out by the Christiania Theater. He left the first three acts fairly intact but dropped every scene essential to the play's philosophical development: the finger-chopping scene; Peer's Darwinian encounter with the monkeys; the Memnon, Sphinx, and insane asylum scenes; the struggle in the shipwreck; the funeral elegy; the monologues of the threadball, straw, and yarn; and even the famous onion-peeling scene. The only sequences remaining in the epic Act 4 were the capitalist empire builders' dinner party and Anitra's dance. What was left emphasized Solveig as a personification of redemptive Christian love, while Ibsen's concise, direct balladic language was translated into the stilted prose of melodrama. In Act 4, Peer's world travels take place, during which we find the sequences that parallel those in the first three acts. With these parallel scenes omitted, the spiral pattern of time and space disappeared. Peer's encounter with the Boyg in Act 2 remained, but all his later references to it were omitted except for the one in the final scene. In effect, the Boyg is confined to the Norwegian mountain landscape for the entire time; it does not travel with Peer at all, and its power as a signifier of spatio-temporality is aborted. Little wonder, then, that Mansfield called the Boyg *shapeless*. In a typical gesture he assigned it an allegorical duty, namely as "the Spirit of compromise":

> There are no doubt many possible sub-intentions in the Boyg, and we may, if we please, understand it as the Spirit of compromise amongst other things. It is a vague, shapeless, ubiquitous, inevitable, invulnerable and invisible thing.[30]

Through these cuts Mansfield transformed the contradictory spiral of Peer's story into a straight line marked by a series of discrete events. The philosophical discourse of Hegel was now missing too, and along with it all references to the dialectical movement of history. The concept of history that emerged was a "straightened out" discourse, a line speeding toward a final climactic manifestation. Peer does not seem to regress at all but only to foray out into the world long enough to amass a fortune and encounter Anitra, after which he turns in his tracks and sails north again. Once in Norway, he proceeds upward without many detours to reach the high mountains and finally "runs straight through" to Solveig:

> PEER (approaches the hut).
> > Forward and back, and it's just as far.
> > Out and in, and it's just as strait. (Stops.)
> > No! — like a wild, an unending lament,
> > is the thought: to come back, to go in, to go home.
> (Takes a few steps on, but stops again.)
> > Round about, said the Boyg!
> (Hears singing in the hut.)
> > Ah no; this time at least
> > right through, though the path may be never so strait!
> (He runs towards the hut. . . .)[31]

Mansfield allowed the word *strait* to be spoken during performance, rather than using the unmistakable translation "narrow," thus further *straightening* the dialectical spatio-temporal structure of the play. Another telling detail is the decision to "correct" Ibsen's German; we find the following footnote in the acting script: "Ibsen writes '*[Das Ewig-*

Weibliche] ziehet uns an.' We have ventured to restore the exact wording of Goethe's lines [to *'Das Ewig-Weibliche zieht uns hinan'].*"[32] With such counter-movements eliminated, the work was no longer dialectical at all.

However, Mansfield's production was successful by all the standards of that historical context: ideological, technological, artistic, and economic. Thousands poured in night after night for weeks, many to see all the new technology: a "giant pig covered with real boar's hide and operated by two men inside its steel frame," the "steam curtain and other daring devices,"[33] and "the most realistic storm scene ever produced on the American stage."[34] As a semiotic process, the event of this production can be summarized as follows: the traditional American ideologies of Christian positivism and Manifest Destiny were codified by the stage signifiers of spatio-temporality, and a new ideological strand was also interwoven: the belief that new technology can hasten (white middle-class) civilization's proprietary journey across the continent toward self-manifestation.

Breaking with Grieg

The first major break with the idealized, folkloric stage tradition came from within a transformed Norwegian social context. In 1948 Hans-Jacob Nilsen directed a starkly anti-Romantic and antinationalistic production at the Norwegian Theater in Oslo that restored nearly the whole text and, most iconoclastic of all, jettisoned Grieg, which was a controversial, even painful omission. The picture-card mountain landscape was gone, replaced by dark, jagged, expressionistic cutout shapes. The trolls were dressed like guests at a modern costume party, and Grieg's music was replaced with an atonal score that put the stage events into an ironic light and precluded their interpretation as folkloric and nostalgic.[35] Though the original purpose of Grieg's music had been to cover the cumbersome scene changes, this function had long since been rendered obsolete by advances in stage technology. The music had come to stand for the spirit and body of Norway, evoking its landscape as an inviolable space, gathering the stage events under its temporality, and creating a Scandinavian *Gesamtkunstwerk*.

By the late 1940s this discourse of the "spirit of Norway" was sharing the same signifier — Grieg's music — with that of a more extreme political ideology. The music of Grieg, like that of Richard Wagner, had also come to signify Nazism. To use Foucault's terms, the new discourse of Nazism had "contaminated" the older discourse of Norwegian patriotism. In the wake of the Second World War, the Nazi occupation of the Norwegian coast, and the news of the Holocaust, a large number of Norwegians, including Nilsen, were ashamed of and embittered by their own past nationalism. Accordingly, Nilsen chose to radically amputate the whole contaminated signifier. Also weighing heavily into his decision was the fact that he himself had acted in a wartime production of *Peer Gynt* that was used as nationalistic propaganda. His experience strikingly recalls that of Piscator during the First World War: he too had participated in the use of his country's folk theater to bolster the nationalism deemed necessary in wartime. Nilsen's break with tradition released the sociopolitical critique that had lain dormant in *Peer Gynt* and registered the sea change in attitudes that epic theater had precipitated. But it was not until the generation of the radicalized 1960s that the play's deeply epic potential would be realized on the stage.

The Schaubühne's Brechtian Production

The theatre [is] a contradictory undertaking, in which the yearning for a rational explanation of the world (and this of course includes the desire to change the world) subsists side by side with the yearning to remember — to remember things as they once were, to recall possibilities, human possibilities deep in the past.

— Peter Stein[36]

Peter Stein's consciously epic production of *Peer Gynt* for the Berlin Schaubühne am Hallischen Ufer in 1971 is one of the most important of the twentieth century in its engagement with the play's epic structure and historical and ideological critique.[37] Like Nilsen in 1948, the Schaubühne company also chose a strong political interpretation and evoked a sharply divided audience response. The events of 1968 had radicalized the German theaters, as well as those of France and many other countries, especially in metropolitan areas. The Schaubühne had reorganized itself in 1969 in order to become a more politically engaged, Marxist-oriented theater and had became a showcase of the collectivist working method and democratic management. A major aim had been to raise the consciousness of the working class; to this end workers were given special discounts or free tickets, and some productions toured factories and union halls. However, it soon became obvious that this effort was not producing much perceptible result: the trade unions, with their own new policy of *Mitbestimmung,* or decision-making shared with management, were suspicious of the Schaubühne because they perceived it as too radical and leftist — too *linksradikal.* Stein finally concluded that the workers of the booming 1970s could not be reached anyway, being affluent and too much under the influence of the right-wing, anticommunist tabloid press. He called on the Schaubühne to stop pretending that it was representing the proletariat, because the working class was no longer conscious of itself as such:

> There is no possibility in the theatre of communicating something about the ideology of the working classes, because it does not exist as a reality which one could explore by means of a process of theatrical remembering. In the theatre one can only project optimistic ciphers about working-class ideology. . . . The theatre has the advantage over a book or a film that it retains a certain utopian potential that several people on a stage communicate directly and that one may witness this and imagine that one is participating in it. . . .[38]

Stein did not abandon a socially critical, even revolutionary political aim for the Schaubühne, but, just as Brecht had done with *The Threepenny Opera* in 1928, he decided that since its artists and audience were "eminently bourgeois," the theater would do well to reexamine bourgeois masterpieces, expose their underlying ideological assumptions, and thus engage in a kind of political self-analysis. Outside of Brecht's work there were few socialist plays that Stein and his company thought had any artistic merit. And "to present on the stage the technics of administration employed by the social-democratic state [West Germany] — everyone would fall asleep after five minutes! It can't be dramatized!"[39] Also like Brecht, Stein refused to produce propaganda, and to a large extent he allowed *Peer Gynt's* contradictions to stand. To stage this play, he thought, would allow artists and audiences to gain a more realistic picture of their own "bourgeois roots" and of the theater as a bourgeois institution. As might be expected, the right-wing press was delighted with this change of the Schaubühne's revised mission, while many on the left thought that Stein was betraying the original goals of his theater, was concerned only with securing government subsidies, and was turning the Schaubühne into a "delicatessen theater." This polarized atmosphere marked the performance and reception of Stein's *Peer Gynt.*

Considering these historical conditions, it is understandable that Stein was more divided in his political approach than Nilsen had been. On one hand, he wanted to show that the ambitions and values of nineteenth-century petit-bourgeois individualism were based on dangerous illusions that were still in force; but, on the other, he wished to load the production with all the powerful charm of these illusions. Clearly, this approach carried some risk of backfiring.

Stein was the first to use so many actors — six — for the role of Peer. Several reasons were given. It was an epic technique that could effectively be used to critique the notion of individualism. It was also more egalitarian and collectivist, giving more actors a role in the production. Finally, it would assure the continuity of the narrative as the story of a particular historical class, not just of an individual. In almost all previous productions Peer had been played by one actor who aged before the eyes of the spectators, but the Schaubühne group saw this as too "uncomfortable." Nevertheless, Stein did want Peer Gynt to age as a representative class *type*.

The critical representation of historicity was the cohering principle of this production. The temporal continuity — a rhythm of independent units in a series — was now that of an adventure book with lively pop-up illustrations.[40] The play was no longer divided into five acts but into eight "chapters" whose titles were announced in advance, in the style of a nineteenth-century playbill: "The Bride Abductor," "The Lord of the Mountains," "The Realm of the Trolls," "Free as a Bird and Fugitive in the Woods," "A Yankee in the Desert," "The Prophet in the Harem," "On the Track of the Past," and "Under the Sign of the Onion." In addition, the epic narrative unfolded over an unusually large playing area, thus literally and figuratively expanding both the time and the space over a wide horizon (at six and one-half hours, the actual playing time was also comparatively long — by contrast, Nilsen's Peer Gynt ran only five hours and still included almost all of the text).

Six months before the opening Stein and his troupe began placing the play into a large historical framework, whose shape begins to emerge from the list of subjects and works studied in the preparatory seminar: the play's reception history, the history of Norway in the nineteenth century, Marx's and Engels' discussions of the petite bourgeoisie, several Marxist-oriented histories of the nineteenth century, and histories of the empirical sciences and technology. In addition, the list included Ibsen's letters and biography and critical works on Ibsen's realism. More surprisingly, we see fairy tales, plays by Jarry, the adventure novels of Karl May, and pulp novels of the nineteenth century. Stein placed particular stress on the visual fantasy of the petite bourgeoisie, which was characterized by the fusion of industrial functionalism and decorative fantasy monumentalized in such works as the Eiffel Tower, the Crystal Palace, and the great metropolitan railroad stations. Peer Gynt had the kind of epic structure for which Stein had long been searching. The play allowed the theater to realize its dialectical power to bring back memories of a past world, to discover that world's continuities and discontinuities with the present, and at the same time to open a utopian dimension for the future:

[Peer Gynt] is like a grandfather in whom you partly recognize your-
self, but whom you view on balance as a stranger. It will not be
enough to know the nineteenth century on the basis of the facts that
you need for a Marxist analysis. Examination of the whole broad surface of the nineteenth century, of the . . . contradictions that it produced, will be more stimulating for our ideas: things we would call
kitsch today; the interlocking of . . . urban and rural culture; the ad-
mixture of fantasy in . . . European notions of the colonies. . . . [W]e
will have to touch on the vast flood of travel literature, which deals
with mountain landscapes and the problems of [mountain] people,
. . . utopian literature, . . . romantic orientalism. . . . An important aspect [of our research] will be the nineteenth century's remarkable
output of visual fantasy. . . . We should ignore everything that came
out of the drawing rooms of the haute bourgeoisie. We should ob-
serve the attempts to transform and domesticate technical objects . . .
how was a bridge or similar iron structure built (e.g. the Eiffel
Tower)? To what extent were technical requirements decisive and to
what extent were they overruled by . . . ornament? . . . Then of course
the illustrations in travel books and above all books for young people
. . . in which one can see how these things were presented to children
and to the lower orders of society.[41]

The Schaubühne's home theater was thought too confining for the
epic sweep of the play that was newly titled *Peer Gynt: A Play from the
Nineteenth Century* (Ein Schauspiel aus dem neunzehnten Jahrhun-
dert), so a rectangular arena was built ten meters wide and twenty-five
meters long, with the spectators in bleacher-like seating facing each
other along the two long sides; most of the action took place either
below or at their eye level. The profuse visual imagination of the nineteenth-century petite bourgeoisie was re-created in the scenography:
giant painted vistas of mountains, fjords, and sea extended the length
of the walls behind the audience. The floor of the acting area was covered with sand-colored canvas and transformed into an undulating
"mountainous" surface with a rise at one end and a dip at the other. At
both ends of the acting area were backdrop paintings of luminous bil-
lowing cloudbanks extending from horizon to zenith. Most of the acting took place in the middle area, and properties were either carried or
rolled onto the stage or pulled up out of the wooden floor. Solveig's
mountain hut was built by Peer on the rise at one end — in view of the
audience. This "mountain" was the highest point spatially but still was
only at eye level for most spectators. The foot of this mountain rise
opened out in one scene to reveal the troll palace. Likewise, a huge
cutout Sphinx was built into the floor and raised when needed, and the
hollow where it had lain became the insane asylum. The dip at the op-

posite end of the arena represented the farthest horizon from Solveig, who looked down on all the events while she knitted. The two shipwrecks took place here; in one of them a scale model steamship comically blew up with a crack and a cloud of smoke, snapped in two, gurgled, and sank below an undulating sea cloth.

In summary, the set had a colorful naive realism of detail and could be mechanically animated in a manner reminiscent of the pop-up scenery of children's books. The giant pig ridden by the daughter of the Troll King, the Arabian horse on which Peer flees from the Sheik, the desert lion, and other animals were taxidermists' creations pulled about the stage on wheels like exhibits in a natural-history museum or life-size children's toys. All of the costumes were historically accurate for the petite bourgeoisie of the late nineteenth century. In effect, the "clutter" of this class's imagination was "sorted out" into isolated objects and settings, scattered sporadically and often simultaneously over a wide, uncluttered topography viewed from above. All of this animated realistic detail brought back a *conscious* illusion of the past:

> [T]his staging . . . consciously represents . . . the nineteenth-century citizen's pleasure in panorama, in the view over mountain and valley. But papering over the environment with the visual world of that era finally evokes the impression of being in a museum where the art of illusion is carried out to such an extreme that even its people are brought back to life.[42]

The set, the actors, and the stage objects were spread over a wide and open space, in contrast to conventionally realistic scenography, which fits many elements together to fill a three-dimensional peepshow picture-in-the-box framed by a proscenium arch. The framed picture was now opened out horizontally — again like the animated pages of a picture book — so that the epic odyssey of Peer could cover more ground. Thus the vertical axis that had dominated past stagings of *Peer Gynt* was not obliterated but *reduced in size* by a new perspective: the mountains were still there but did not tower behind the actors and above the eye level of the spectators. Instead the spectators themselves were raised to the level of the highest mountain range, and presented with a panorama spread out below them. Peer's journey through space and time over this topography could now be followed in its entirety: the geometric shape of this journey could be traced out over an immediate material space that consciously "contained" it. Solveig's mountain hut remained visible in all but two scenes — this was all that remained of the eternal sublime. The imagistic power of this mountain was demystified not only because it was lowered in height but also because it was always visible: it was never al-

lowed to distance itself from the events taking place in the horizontal —
and thus *historical* — space of the play.

The referential power of a Christian ideology that in past productions had been textualized by a "timeless" hierarchical verticality was
accordingly diminished. In the medieval-based Christian view of the
cosmos Solveig's position represented the goal of unchanging perfection, the final reward for repentance or self-sacrifice. But the
Schaubühne's realignment of spatial signification deprived that goal of
its hierarchical superiority. Peer's final reunion with Solveig was also
given a new relation to the play's temporality: it was still the culminating point of the play's temporal design. Peer and Solveig took on the
pose of Michelangelo's *Pietà,* but this iconic image lost its elegiac
power and its position as the play's apex when it was suddenly frozen
and framed within a contemporary context of stage hands dismantling
the set. The reunion on the mountain could no longer be seen as an
absolute origin to which Peer was returning and thus could no longer
textualize the ideology of a nationalistic Romanticism whose goal was
to return to the mythic past. To make sure that the audience understood the *Pietà* image as an critical epic *Gestus,* the company even considered passing out white plastic dashboard-size reproductions of Peer
in Solveig's arms in this gestic pose.

Further diminishing the power of pietist Christian ideology was the
omission of the peasant whose life story is a counternarrative to Peer's.
The peasant's life is lived out in accordance with his moral duty. Born
at the same time and in similar circumstances as Peer, he chops off his
finger to escape military service and remain on his farm (located, naturally, in the high mountains), obeying a moral rather than a legal direc-
tive. He lives a humble, hard, and pious life and dies with the respect of
his family and neighbors. Stein called this character's self-mutilation too
"brutal" an alternative to Peer's illusions of grandeur. But brutality was
not the real issue, since the insane-asylum suicides were played out ex-
tensively and in bloody detail. The peasant's narrative, which is often
cut from productions, might in this case have been read as a Christian
questioning of the Marxist questioning of petit-bourgeois ideology —
one question too many for the Schaubühne.

In Ibsen's dramatic text Peer runs up into the mountains to sleep
with the three herd girls, apparently managing to satisfy them all, but
Stein's version makes Peer sexually — and financially — impotent, and
the girls run from him. Likewise, this Peer steals the bride and carries
her up the mountain because she is wealthy, not because he desires her.
In the original text Peer's sexual energy, represented in spatial images
as an "upward thrust," could also be seen as a positive force in the face

of the pious villagers' negation of it. The verticality signified not only a rigid Christian hierarchy but also the "animal" power of sexuality, and this was another fundamental contradiction of *Peer Gynt's* spatio-temporal structure. Therefore, the Schaubühne's devaluing of this ver-ticality also weakened the power of sexuality, literally flattening it out. Its "heights and depths" were reduced to an image and effect of the class and economic system.

Peer's final return to Solveig was given a new and unambiguous ideological interpretation by placing it within a new sociohistorical frame: uniformed workers invaded the stage to clear it for industrial con-struction, then paused in their work to watch and applaud the last mo-ments of Ibsen's play, wherein Peer rushed up the mountain to lay his head upon the lap of the now blind but joyous Solveig. None of the dialogue of the ending was changed, and Stein took care not to dismiss this scene with irony. When Peer asked where his true self had been, Sol-veig's answer to the riddle was still "In my hope, in my faith, in my love." In the original text Peer replies, *"O, gem mig, gem mig derinde!"* in idiomatic, direct language with a strongly sexual connotation, closer to *"O, hide me, hide me in there!"* than to its inevitably more refined translations.[43] At any rate, the construction workers appeared to be moved by the scene, but their presence ironized it. Peer first lay on Sol-veig's lap in a fetal position (calling her "My mother; my wife"), then they arranged themselves into the pose of the *Pietà*, after which Solveig's eyes seemed to glaze over like those of the statue. This was the moment, according to critic the Günther Rühle, when all that had gone before was reevaluated. Like the famous pose of Brecht's Mother Courage holding her dead daughter, it was a critically historicizing *Gestus*:

> [Stein's] cold use of this melancholy pose made us recognize . . . the unjust sacrifice of woman that her love concealed. . . . With this cold image Stein distanced himself [as if to say]: "I have shown you what was once beautiful but must no longer be regarded as such." In [Sol-veig's] eyes the drama suddenly seemed like a ghost, although because of its new-found freshness it had until then all seemed such fun.[44]

Then the uniformed workers wheeled the whole platform containing Peer and Solveig *down from the mountaintop* to be photographed as a curiosity of the past, frozen in the *Pietà* pose like the life-size taxider-mically preserved animals on their rolling platforms. The workers carted off all the stage properties — the "clutter" of this whole bourgeois tale was cleared away from view — as they went through the motions of disinfecting the playing area in preparation for a modern construction.

The performance, in spite of its clear ideological intentions, did not eliminate ambiguity for the spectators. Stein had wished to show that the petite bourgeoisie's great expenditure of energy and imagination upon the ideology of individualism had been self-destructive and had finally only helped the capitalist class to legitimize and consolidate its power. But the eloquence, color, humor, and energy of this staging stirred a sympathetic response to the fantasy it had intended to critique; the petit-bourgeois imagination was attractive: exotic foreign adventures, wild animals, entertaining mythical characters, colorful pornography, folkloric dance and music, and myths of the empire builders. Many spectators took that illusion at face value.

Nonetheless, when Brecht scholar Bernard Dort asked Stein whether he was returning to a theater of illusion like that of Max Reinhardt, Stein adamantly denied it:

> That's utter rubbish. . . . Don't forget that the horses that appear are completely fake — they're stuffed horses. Reinhardt would have had real horses. . . . Everything that is used, or let's rather say quoted, creates an illusion. . . . We deliberately and polemically emphasized that all that Peer Gynt does or thinks, all that a petit bourgeois with a little imagination can say, do, or think has already been said, done or thought . . . a hundred thousand times . . . and we have to approach these things like pictures, objects and mummies displayed in museums . . . . *Peer Gynt* describes an illusion.[45]

Stein apparently did not reckon with the possibility that the (bourgeois) audience might be able to have its past illusions placed into a contained topography, a toy landscape, or even a "museum," but still much prefer them to the bleak "present" animated by the industrial workers at the play's end. Perhaps these framing scenes set in a mechanized, efficient present were not quite vague *enough,* because they reminded some spectators of the Nazi concentration camps.

Stein's intention to critique bourgeois illusion with the *Verfremdungseffekt* succeeded with many spectators, while for others the staged fantasy was the final meaning, an illustration that overpowered its didactic aim. In any case, the political message was not universally received as intended, and for that reason some West German Marxists felt that Stein had betrayed their cause. But in the context of *Peer Gynt*'s stage history, the Schaubühne's production brilliantly illuminated the epic contradictions of the play and was able not only to uncover the dialectical historical vision of Ibsen but also to use this astonishing vision of the past century as a vantage point from which to critique the present.

This production would inspire a whole generation of future directors of *Peer Gynt,* including the postcolonialist critic Rustom Bharucha, who learned a great deal from the Schaubühne's strong sociopolitical engagement of the play with the theater's own historical situation. Bharucha rightly understood that *Peer Gynt* also has great relevance beyond its original European context. Because of its dialectical epic structure, its ability to allow folk tradition and political topicality to productively confront each other, and its far-sighted critique of the West's colonial empire-building, Bharucha was drawn to adapt and direct *Peer Gynt* for the sociohistorical context of his own contemporary India.

Peer Gynt in Postcolonial India

> Basically — and I trust that my perspective will not be interpreted as cultural chauvinism — I am convinced that the 'folk' and 'epic' dimensions of *Peer Gynt* are largely lost in western adaptations, for the critical (and historical) reason that there is no meaningful exposure of the 'folk' resources in these cultures. . . . The 'epic' is another context that can be encountered through diverse performative modes in [India] . . . which re-enact the epics through sharp juxtapositions of song, dance, music, and improvised dialogue.
>
> — Rustom Bharucha[46]

Through his 1993 book *Theatre of the World: Performance and the Politics of Culture*[47] and various articles, Rustom Bharucha has engaged in a postcolonial critique of the intercultural theater movement, including the "orientalist" borrowing from Asian theater forms by the Western directors Peter Brook, Eugenio Barba, and others. Based in India as a critic, director, and dramaturg, Bharucha has been controversial both in the West and in Asia for his view that intercultural theater is too often a hegemonic appropriation by the West of the cultural property of non-Western countries. Bharucha has sometimes been accused of reducing all theatrical borrowing between cultures to one-directional exploitative appropriation. In a May 1996 article in *New Theatre Quarterly*, however, he gives an account of his own experience directing *Peer Gynt* at the Rangayana Theatre in the city of Mysore, in Karnataka, India, which attests that such appropriation is carried out on both sides of the exchange and need not exploit one side but can benefit both.[48]

In reading about the stage history of *Peer Gynt* Bharucha was particularly impressed by the productions of Peter Stein and Ingmar Bergman but was convinced that Indian performance traditions could better address the play's epic qualities in both the new and the old sense of the term. Accordingly, he staged the epic and folkloric elements as interdependent. Bharucha elucidates his own process of borrowing as a translation and adaptation that involves both *intercultural* and *intracultural* theater; while intercultural theater involves exchange between countries and continents, intracultural theater engages the many artistic, social, religious, and political cultures within one country.

Bharucha takes issue with semiotician Patrice Pavis's definition of the intracultural as "the traditions of a single nation which have been almost forgotten or deformed and which need to be reconstructed."[49] Rather than this implied dichotomy between intracultural as a marginal, static, and dying theater tradition versus intercultural as a dominant, dynamic, and vital one, with all the influence going in one direction from the intercultural to the intracultural, Bharucha sees the relationship between the two as a delicate network of connections necessary to both. He defines this interrelationship through his own practical experience as director and dramaturg: several projects that began as intercultural became profoundly intracultural; that is, what began as the borrowing and exploration of a work from a foreign culture became a revelatory exploration of his own home culture of India.

He was drawn to *Peer Gynt* because he believed that this classic text had both the folk and epic qualities necessary to create an intracultural theater event with social and political relevance for the "rampantly multicultural" society of India:

> Ibsen's hybrid monster of an epic has pursued me for many years through my own meanderings across continents and cultures. For me it is . . . a saga of the secular self. Caught between forces of intolerance, fundamentalism, bigotry, and the giddy, irresponsible adventure of global capitalism, the play narrativizes a certain loss of the self, for which . . . there is no easy redemption. . . . (124)

Bharucha kept the basic structure of Ibsen's text, as well as what he called its "disjunctive logic." However, in defining the overall temporality of the play, he divided the story into three parts: first a preindustrial folk world, then an emergent capitalism culminating in the insane asylum at the site of the Sphinx, and finally a "metaphysics of self evoking the death of community" (124). The play was retitled *Gundegowdana Charitre*, literally *The History of Gundegowda*. It is important to note that calling the play a *history* already declares an epic approach in the Brechtian sense, as did Stein's added subtitle, *A Play from the Nineteenth Century*. That is, both directors took a critical position in regard to how and by whom history is represented. Both presented a history that extends beyond one individual and explored the mechanisms by which a nation, a class, and a culture are historicized through representation. While Stein's concept of history was dualist, with past and present directly confronting each other, Bharucha avoided this polar separation between temporal dimensions, as well as the Western dichotomy between "timeless" gods and heroes from religion and mythology on one hand, and "time-bound" human figures on the other. Instead, many characters existed in both dimensions. The Buttonmolder, for example, is presented by Ibsen as existing on both a mundane and a metaphysical plane: he appears to be an old-fashioned but ordinary artisan who melts down used buttons to make new ones, carrying his long-handled iron pan; however, because he speaks of melting down souls to make new ones, he also becomes a supernatural emissary of death, which in Norse myth was often imagined as a burning and melting together of bodies. By contrast, Stein's production depicted the Buttonmolder as a modern technocrat. Bharucha's Buttonmolder was more like Ibsen's: he was both the familiar blacksmith still found in Indian cities *and* a messenger of death in the service of *Yama*, an incarnation of compassion, or *daya* (124). This *Peer Gynt's* temporal dynamic thus represented an Indian history that encompassed both the secular and the sacred.

Long passages of time were often signified only through codes of costume or gesture, rather than by "miniature" time spans standing for larger ones, as is the usual practice in the Western tradition. In other words, time was *openly* coded in the Indian staging, rather than pretending that the miniature copy is identical to the original, only "shrunken." This aesthetic of miniaturization is pervasive in the bourgeois West, according to Roland Barthes, because it allows the artist and "consumer" patrons to feel like owners of property.[50] By contrast, in order to indicate that Solveig (Gulabi) had aged by many years since she began waiting for Peer (Gundegowda), the Indian actress simply reappeared on stage carrying a white wig on a stick.

Temporality was also signified by the language and idioms used in the production. Having no direct access to the Norwegian, Bharucha and his collaborator, the poet, director, dramaturg, and translator Raghunanda, used English as their "source language," which they translated into several dialects of Kannada, the language used widely in southwest India. While their main source text was Rolf Fjelde's eloquent, stageworthy, and well annotated English translation from 1980, they also drew from a much older verse translation that would be deemed unplayable in Western Anglophone countries. Yet a formal, rhetorical English from three centuries of colonial rule is still very much alive in today's India, and it continues to inflect many Indian languages. Thus, working from the old and new English translations helped Bharucha and Raghunanda to represent multiple historical dimensions as they translated the English into Kannada dialects. Although English and Hindi are the official languages of India, there is no standard English dialect that dominates; instead, many current and archaic forms exist side by side, preserving the traces of the diverse classes, occupations, races, cultures, and geographical origins of English-speaking people who have inhabited or passed through India over the centuries.

As Bharucha notes, the number three recurred throughout the mise en scène: besides the three parts of the narrative, there were also three actors who played Peer — but not as in Western stagings, where multiple casting has always meant one actor succeeding the next in linear chronology, whether there were two Peers or six. Instead, in the Indian version all three Peers were present throughout the play. They embodied three forms of energy: *sattva,* meaning purity, light, and truth; *rajas,* meaning passion or desire; and *tamas,* meaning darkness. Together they were, in Bharucha's words, "less a person than an ensemble of energies, a contradiction of multiple 'selves,' — unresolved, yet open to being negotiated" (124). This concept of the main character as a multiplicity of negotiable energies and selves was to the translator a way of being faithful to Ibsen's "structure of emotion." The recurrence of three throughout the performance gave a defining structure to this multiplicity. Solveig, for instance, to use Bharucha's words, faces the audience at the end of the play with her emotions "a combination of rage, grief, and loss" (129). The idea of the protagonist as a multiplicity of selves stands in contrast to the Western concept of the individual, literally the *undivided one.* By the same token, Solveig/Gulabi is no longer Woman as Other, no longer contained in the role of the pious, long-suffering, selfless, faithful virgin who is never allowed to show rage.

Not only are the characters' energies, emotions, and selves structured as triads; so is every other element, including the props. In the moment described above Solveig holds three objects: a miniature spinning wheel, the white wig, and an earthen lamp. All are equally powerful symbols, with the spinning wheel being a universal sign for the dignity of work but also a specific reference to Mahatma Gandhi's credo of *swadeshi,* or self-rule, under which he began a hand-weaving and -spinning program. At the end these three props are left on the floor where Solveig has placed them. Two of the Peers, *rajas* (passion) and *tamas* (darkness), are being rocked in the arms of Solveig and Aase, respectively, who sing a lullaby to them, while the third Peer, *sattva* (light and truth), looks at the three objects. In the last beat of the play he picks up the spinning wheel and is gazing at it in contemplation. The third Peer also parallels the spectator who searches for enlightenment — *for the third way in the epic dialectic.* The three Peers play out multiple qualities and choices for the multiplicity of spectators, rather than having all these qualities and choices *contained* within Peer as an individual or a class type.

In its triadic structure the temporality of the performance departed from the duality that has so deeply informed Western concepts of time and space, including concepts of the dialectical movement of history as theorized by Hegel, Marx, Brecht, and Ibsen himself. Even though the classic dialectic has three parts — thesis, antithesis, synthesis — only the first two have equal power. The third does not have the "autonomy" of the first two; rather, it is only their sum or offspring. Each new state arises after the last one, and in the process as a chain of events a singular albeit moving *line* is formed, which at any one moment is either ascending or descending. McFarlane's "plus and minus" is also an instance of this duality, as is Ibsen's spatial imagery of Peer's falling and rising life path, as well as the image of this life as either a positive photographic print or its negative counterpart, with the only alternative being to leave no trace at all. This duality extends also to the prevalent Saussurean theory of the sign itself as an either/or entity: one or zero, present or absent. It is, in fact, difficult for Westerners to conceive of a confrontation, a conflict, a *history,* or a progression of any kind as a triad, which we tend to "spatialize" by equating it with a triangle, representing strength and stability at best and stasis at worst. This equation also affects our concepts of countries and peoples, concepts that constitute the Western postcolonial imaginary: cultures such as India, because they do not share this dualistic, linear-geometric tradition of thought, are judged as static, entrenched in the past, without volition or a clear direction, and, thus, *by nature* unable to progress, to ever compete in the developmental "race" with the West.

Bharucha notes that his blocking was also based on the number three, and that the actors, rather than the set, were primarily responsible for defining the spatiality through their movement and placement. In contrast to most productions of *Peer Gynt,* the Indian version did not draw on verticality versus horizontality to structure the story, stage picture, or ideologies. In fact, there was no attempt to use spatial levels at all, whether to pictorially represent the landscape or to create abstract patterns and connect them to social, political, or cultural values in the Indian context. Instead, all the action took place on the flat, bare, wooden stage floor. In lieu of scenery, a few simple, lightweight objects were carried on and off by the actors to help designate various spaces: a small mound of straw for Peer and Aase's peasant dwelling, a painted two-dimensional palm tree from which the monkeys threw feces at Peer in Act 4, a light-colored block the size and shape of a doghouse to

stand for Solveig's mountain hut. A scrim was lowered behind the actors as a pictorial background for certain scenes, but it did not fill the
space; likewise, a partial curtain came down behind the "oriental" scene
where Peer stood as the false prophet Moosa Baba, wearing a sheik's
headdress and long robe that did not cover his white, expensive-
looking business suit and white shoes, and leering at a group of six
dancing girls with tambourines and whirling skirts who moved all
around him.

The triad is at the heart of the religious beliefs and philosophical
principles of Hinduism, whose most important and popular deities are
the Trinity of Brahma the creator, Shiva the destroyer, and Vishnu the
preserver. Together, the three equal Absolute Truth. The triads of
gods, heroes, social classes, things, states, qualities, and functions over-
lay and connect meaningfully with each other in what Bharucha, following Jakobsen, terms an *intersemiotic* relationship.[51] Typically each
member of a triad branches into three more entities. This triadic mode
of thinking contrasts sharply with Western dualism as seen in the polarities of destruction and creation, good and evil, living and dead, past
and present, West and East, bourgeoisie and proletariat. Theories of the
dialectic, posited by the Romantics and then by the Marxists, see such
polarities as inherently dynamic and generative of movement because
each pole in a set has a positive or negative "charge" of energy directed
toward one goal. Brecht's influential dialectical concept of the "not. .
.but" is a case in point; to stage an action dialectically is to show the
spectators both the way taken and the way not taken; *the third way is
left to the future and decided by the spectators*. It is inherent in Brecht's
formula but not articulated.

Triadic structures of spatio-temporality dominate not only Indian
religion, philosophy, art, and history but also topography and climatol-
ogy. The West marks the year as a cycle of four seasons consisting of
two polar sets: winter versus summer and spring versus fall. India, however, marks only three seasons: cool, hot and dry, and rainy. The geological map is likewise divided into three parts, with the sparsely
populated Himalayas in the north; the broad and fertile central Plain of
the Ganges, which has the highest population and prosperity; and the
dry, hilly Deccan plateau in the south. Thus, both the time and space of
the physical world itself are conceived as triadic.

The existence of these two distinct ways of structuring space and
time does not disprove but strengthens Bakhtin's thesis that chronotopes are culturally and historically specific, not universal or permanent. The society's cultural values are attached to these spatio-temporal
structures, but always with the possibility of shifting or overturning the

values while using the same spatio-temporal designs. Although Hinduism's ultimate aim is an *escape* from the cycle of life, death, and rebirth, it places great importance on the joys and responsibilities of life. This is not to argue that Bharucha uncritically venerated the Hindu tradition but rather to emphasize that India was not represented as *outside of history,* trapped by its religious and social tradition *within a closed circle of time,* and thus incapable of action, critique, or progress.

In fact, Bharucha's *Peer Gynt* held many religious, social, and political traditions of India up for critique, while respecting their complexity and all that was affirmative about them. For example, through the character Huhu in the insane-asylum scene in Act 4, Ibsen scathingly satirizes the Norwegian group who called for a return to "our forest tongue," "the primal language," and sought to return Norwegian to its "pure" state by eliminating all foreign elements. Bharucha had Huhu speak in a "heavily Sanskritized rhetoric" to satirically evoke the Indian fundamentalist groups who would return to "an absolute past that incarnates eternal Purity" (129). The production avoided narrowly targeting particular political or social groups, deciding, for example, not to identify the trolls *only* with Hindu fundamentalist extremists but to present them as "mixed signs," representing the silent, middle-class majority who voted the Hindu conservatives into power. The trolls were at once "fundamentalist," "bourgeois," and "ruralist," the latter being the Hindu Right's ideal of a "Village India" that rejects modernity. The actors developed concrete actions for the trolls that clearly evoked the reactionary Village India movement: chopping roots, pounding grain, lifting "authentically Indian" barbells, and chanting mystical tantras. Audiences were understandably more disturbed by the portrayal of the trolls than by the lampooning of Indian capitalists at a beach resort or Western tourists in Egypt.

The epic *Gestus* was located not in the narrative chronology but in primary motifs: homecoming, the death of a mother, madness, masking, cultural tourism, self-exposure, and self-mutilation (124). For each, resonances with Indian languages, everyday life, history, mythology, and religion were constructed. The Indian production's use of the folk and epic elements throughout *Peer Gynt* was unlike many Western stagings that relegate the folk to the first part of the play before Peer leaves home and the Brechtian epic elements to the second part, implying that these are two separate times and worlds.[52] This nonseparation of folk from epic is, in fact, much closer to Brecht — and Piscator as well — than the reduction of epic theater to a set of stage techniques. From his earliest plays and poetry until the end of his life Brecht drew from past and present popular culture, including folk tales, verse forms, and music. His dialogue is poetic yet startlingly direct, often colloquial, and inflected with German dialects signifying class and region. As for Piscator, his productions from the early agitprop *Russia's Day* of 1918 through the documentary *In Spite of All That* of 1925 to his last directorial work in the 1960s, always used a framework drawn from popular performance traditions rather than the classical three- or five-act play. He often used the framework of a cabaret revue to juxtapose documentation and political dialogues with comic skits, melodramatic scenes, and satirical music. Since Piscator and Brecht aimed to raise their audiences' sociopolitical consciousness, not to "elevate" their aesthetic taste, they used forms that were already popular — the music-hall revue, the theater of the fair, the carnival, and the street musicians, all of which constitute a vital folk culture. Thus the strict separation between folk and Brechtian epic theater that even Bharucha makes in his essay — although clearly not in his production — is a misconception that overemphasizes Brecht's abstracted formulae and ignores the multiplicity of performance traditions in his work. *Such a separation empties epic theory of its historical content.*

This, of course, is the last thing that Bharucha intended. What he rightly calls the "disjunctive logic of Ibsen's text" (124) also describes the juxtapositional structure of epic theater, even if he does not articulate this connection. Bharucha also does not problematize the relationship between epic theater and the traditional Indian epics but mentions them both without comment, once in the same paragraph. Yet Bharucha's production is clearly epic in that it follows the principle of dialectical contradiction. He explains that for *Peer Gynt* communication could not follow the norms of "a harmonious or omniscient discourse"; instead, differences and dissent were negotiated and became part of the performance:

> What concerns me increasingly as a director is the necessity of deconstructing the premises of my concept through an exchange of differences. The point is not to reflect one's assumptions of a particular frame, but to open them through contradiction. (125–126)

Bharucha's words are testimony not only to his directing credo but also to a basic principle shared by *Peer Gynt* and the epic theater. As this chapter has sought to show through highlights of its performance history, the energy of *Peer Gynt's* plus and minus comes to a great extent from its epic spatio-temporality. A dialectical structure of signification propels the work and is experienced by the spectator/reader as a dynamic event. Shifting historical values are collected around the *motion* of this event, and this is why, as Yeats said, the center cannot hold.

Notes

[1] James W. McFarlane, "Revaluations of Ibsen," in *Discussions of Henrik Ibsen,* ed. McFarlane (Boston: D.C. Heath, 1962), 24–25.

[2] Rolf Fjelde, in Henrik Ibsen, *Peer Gynt,* 2nd ed., trans. Fjelde (Minneapolis: U of Minnesota P, 1980), "Appendix I: Text/Translation/Script," 240. Fjelde includes useful appendices on the original text, translation, and resultant playscript of *Peer Gynt,* as well as a stage history.

[3] Henrik Ibsen, letter to Ludwig Passarge, August 17, 1881, in *The Oxford Ibsen,* vol. 3, ed. James W. McFarlane (New York: Oxford UP, 1972), 493. *The Oxford Ibsen* will hereafter be abbreviated as *Oxford Ibsen.*

[4] Clemens Petersen, November 13, 1867, *Faedrelandet, Oxford Ibsen,* 494–495.

[5] Ibsen, letter to Bjørnstjerne Bjørnson, December 9/10, 1867, *Oxford Ibsen,* 487–490.

[6] Ibsen, letter to Frederik Hegel, February 24, 1868, *Oxford Ibsen,* 49.

[7] Mikhail Bakhtin, *Rabelais and His World,* trans. H. Iswolsky (Cambridge, Mass.: M.I.T. P, 1968).

[8] Rolf Fjelde, in "Peer Gynt, Naturalism, and the Dissolving Self," *The Drama Review* 13 (Winter 1969), 28–43, sees Peer as representative of the gradual shift, starting in the late Renaissance and culminating in Kierkegaard's existentialism, from a *concept* of the self as *indivisible* to an *image* of the self as a *divided consciousness.* This "dissolving self" lives with the inability to *cohere* experiential time and space as a "solid" unity.

[9] This and all subsequent textual references from the play are taken from Fjelde's translation, hereafter abbreviated as *PG,* and identified by act, scene, and page number in the body of the essay.

[10] H. R. Ellis Davidson, *Gods and Myths of Northern Europe* (Harmondsworth, England: Penguin, 1964), 138–139.

[11] Per Fugleskjelle, *Norske Huldre-Eventyr og Folkesagn,* 190–196, quoted in *Oxford Ibsen,* 483–484.

[12] Umberto Eco, *A Theory of Semiotics* (Bloomington: Indiana UP, 1976).

[13] Jacques Derrida, *Of Grammatology,* trans. Gayatri Chakravorty Spivak (Baltimore and London: Johns Hopkins UP, 1974).

[14] William Butler Yeats, "The Gyres" 1938. Quoted in the frontspiece of Joseph Frank's *The Widening Gyre* (New Brunswick, N.J.: Rutgers UP, 1963), 35. Frank's work is the best discussion of the gyre in Yeats and other Romantic literature and a leading source on spatiality in general.

[15] Yeats, "The Second Coming," 1921, in *The Collected Poems of W. B. Yeats* (New York: Macmillan, 1956), 184–185.

[16] Rolf Fjelde, in "Appendix I" to his translation of *Peer Gynt,* 221.

[17] Teresa de Lauretis, *Technologies of Gender* (Bloomington: Indiana UP, 1987), 43–44. Italics mine.

[18] Georg Wilhelm Friedrich Hegel, *Philosophy of History* (1837), trans. F. Sibree (New York: Dow, 1965).

[19] Brian Johnston, *Towards the Third Empire* (Minneapolis: U of Minnesota P, 1980), 70.

[20] Bakhtin, *Rabelais and His World*, 362–363.

[21] Likewise, the human body was also divided into "higher" and "lower" functions. Ibid., 365.

[22] Ibid., 402.

[23] Rolf Fjelde, "Appendix I," *Peer Gynt*, 236.

[24] Henrik Ibsen, letter to Edvard Grieg, January 23, 1874, in *Oxford Ibsen*, 503.

[25] Michael Meyer, *Ibsen: A Biography* (Garden City, N.Y.: Doubleday, 1971), 410.

[26] Edvard Grieg, letter to Frantz Beyer, August 27, 1874, *Oxford Ibsen*, 503.

[27] Rolf Fjelde, "Appendix I," *Peer Gynt*, 263.

[28] The Norwegians' relations to *Peer Gynt* continue to evolve, but it holds its place as the most "national" work of art. Schoolchildren are taken in groups to see performances and warned beforehand to be respectful. As a modern Norwegian director put it, "For us Peer Gynt *is* Norway." (Interview on February 16, 1983, in Minneapolis with directors Kjetil Bang-Hanson, Tormod Skagestad, and Helge Hoff Monsen.)

[29] Fjelde briefly describes this production in the appendix to *Peer Gynt*. Also see "Peer Gynt," *The Dial*, Chicago (November 16, 1908): 309–311; and Montrose J. Moses, "Richard Mansfield and Peer Gynt," *The Times Magazine*, New York (February 1907): 313.

[30] Richard Mansfield, *The Richard Mansfield Acting Version of Peer Gynt by Henrik Ibsen* (Chicago: Reilly and Britton, 1906), 77. Based on William and Charles Archer's translation in *The Collected Works of Henrik Ibsen* (London: Heinemann, 1906).

[31] *Mansfield Acting Version*, 170.

[32] *Mansfield Acting Version*, 128.

[33] "Peer Gynt," *The Dial*, 311.

[34] Fjelde, "Appendix I," *Peer Gynt*, 272.

[35] Fjelde, "Appendix I," *Peer Gynt*, 272.

[36] Peter Stein, *Die Zeit*, January 2, 1976; quoted in Michael Patterson, *Peter Stein, Germany's Leading Theatre Director* (Cambridge and New York: Cambridge UP, 1982), 66.

[37] *Peer Gynt: Ein Schauspiel Aus Dem Neunzehnjahrhundert,* Schaubühne am Hallischen Ufer, West Berlin, opening April 27, 1971. Director: Peter Stein; scenographer: Karl Ernst Herrmann.

[38] Quoted by Michael Patterson in *Peter Stein, Germany's Leading Theatre Director,* 66–67.

[39] Stein, *Der Abend,* July 21, 1977. Quoted by Patterson, 67.

[40] Stein's setting an old story into a newer framework is strongly reminiscent of Brecht's epic adaptations of older works such as Lenz's *The Tutor,* Sophocles' *Antigone,* and Shakespeare's *Coriolanus,* and his own *The Caucasian Chalk Circle.*

[41] Stein, quoted by Hugh Rorrison, "Democratic Production Process in Practice on 'Peer Gynt,'" *Theatre Quarterly* 13 (February–April 1974), 24.

[42] Günther Rühle, "Was an uns ist noch Peer?," in *Theater Heute* 12 (1971), 29 (my translation). In the same issue see also "Aufführung des Jahres: Peer Gynt," 18–39 and 70–71.

[43] Fjelde translates this as "O hide me, hide me within," while Mansfield (or Archer?) prudishly adds "thy love" as a qualifier: "In thy love — oh, there hide me, hide me!"

[44] Günther Rühle, *Frankfurter Allgemeine Zeitung,* April 26, 1972. Quoted by Patterson, 86.

[45] Peter Stein, interview with Bernard Dort, *Travail théâtral* (1972): 34–34. Quoted by Patterson, 74.

[46] Rustom Bharucha, "Under the Sign of the Onion: Intracultural Negotiations in Theatre," *New Theatre Quarterly* 12 (May 1996), 121–122. Subsequent references to this article will be indicated by page number in the body of the text.

[47] Bharucha, *Theatre of the World: Performance and the Politics of Culture.* (New York and London: Routledge, 1993).

[48] See note 44, above.

[49] Bharucha quotes Patrice Pavis from the latter's *Theatre at the Crossroads of Culture* (London and New York: Routledge, 1992), 20. Bharucha also takes issue with Pavis's notion of intercultural exchange as the uncomplicated passage from a "source culture" to a "target culture," and with his failure to recognize the difficult negotiation of differences and power imbalance involved in actual transcultural borrowing. In the above work Pavis simplifies both non-Western "source cultures" and his own French "target culture" but tends to universalize the latter. In his recent anthology, *The Intercultural Performance Reader* (London and New York: Routledge, 1996), Pavis, as editor, responds to these concerns in his introduction and has even included an essay by Bharucha, although he is still somewhat suspicious of the latter's politicized perspective.

[50] It is important to note that Stein's *Peer Gynt* critically *exposed* the link between miniaturization and bourgeois self-identity as owner. In the essay "Toys" in *Mythologies,* trans. Annette Lavers (New York: Hill and Wang, 1980), 53–55, Barthes comments that most French toys are miniature versions of adult objects, and do not teach the child to create but only to be an owner and user. With a simple set of blocks, however, the child *"creates life, not property: objects now act by themselves, they are no longer an inert and complicated material in the palm of his hand."* Barthes's observations also apply to naturalistic representations of time and space.

[51] Bharucha takes the term *intersemiotic* from Roman Jakobsen's classification of translation, as discussed in Susan Bassnett, *Translation Studies* (New York and London: Routledge, 1991). The concept of the "intersemiotic" is applicable to the various sign systems of the stage as they are used in several productions of the same play.

[52] See Rolf Fjelde, note 2 above, and Brian Johnston, note 17 above.

Peer Gynt, as a "philosopher-historian," meets the Sphinx. Peter Stein's production of Peer Gynt, Schaubühne am Hallischen Ufer, Berlin, 1973. Photo © and courtesy of Helga Kneidl.

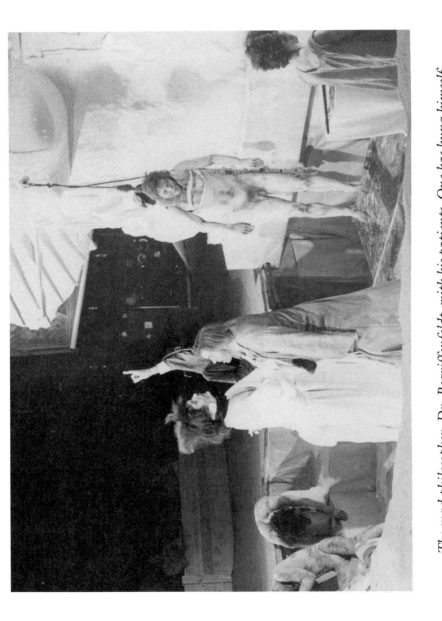

The mad philosopher, Dr. Begriffenfeldt, with his patients. One has hung himself.
From Peter Stein's production of Peer Gynt, *1972. Photo © and courtesy of Helga Kneidl.*

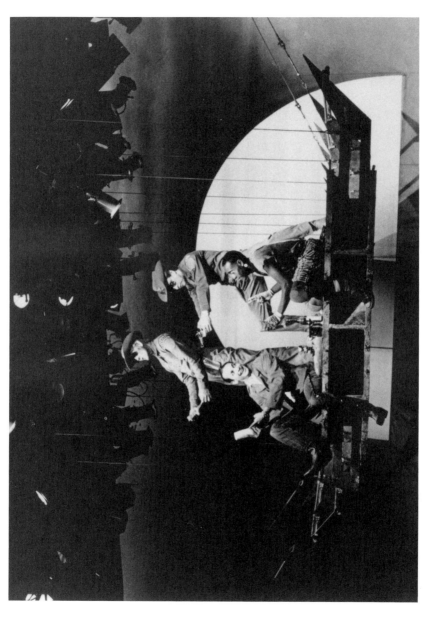

Leon and Val are chased by two Texas Rangers. Leon and Lena (& Lenz), 1987, directed by Joanne Akalaitis. By permission of the Guthrie Theatre, Minneapolis. Photo by Joe Gianetti.

5: JoAnne Akalaitis's Postmodern Epic Staging of Leon and Lena (& lenz)

The poor people tamely haul the cart on which the princes and liberals act out their ludicrous comedy.[1]

I've no time now to write you a political treatise, anyway it wouldn't be worth the effort, the whole thing after all is just a comedy. The king and his councils rule, the people applaud and pay. . . .[2]

The dramatist is in my view nothing other than a historian, but is *superior* to the latter in that he *re-creates* history: instead of offering us a bare narrative, he transports us directly into the life of an age; . . . His play must be neither more *moral* nor more *immoral* than *history itself.*[3]

— Georg Büchner

Reality, History, Aesthetics

GEORGE BÜCHNER WAS A PHILOSOPHER who rejected the idealism prevalent in his own time, a physician who foresaw the dehumanizing power of medical science, a political organizer whose revolutionary manifesto *The Hessian Messenger*[4] is considered second in power only to Marx's *Communist Manifesto*, and a novelist and playwright who demonstrated qualities that would be associated with naturalism, expressionism, epic theater, existentialism, and, indeed, postmodernism a century or more before these movements emerged. Büchner saw an unbridgeable gulf between the rich and the poor, the educated and the uneducated; and he saw historical events as the playing and replaying of these class relationships, an ironic comedy run through with tragedy. His aesthetic was based on a concept of reality that had much in common with Brecht's and that rejected both illusionistic art, which attempts to reproduce reality, and idealistic art, which presumes to transform it. Ostensibly quoting from the *Sturm und Drang* playwright J. M. R. Lenz, Büchner articulates his own concept of realism: human existence should define art, not vice versa. Therefore, the artist should not attempt to contain experience within a conventional dramatic form. Even time and space could not be taken for granted as fixed ontological givens but were as fluid as the mind perceiving them. The following passage from *Lenz,* the novella that Büchner left unfinished when he died of typhus at twenty-three in 1837, articulates Büchner's concept of an artistic representation so true to life that it would avoid surrendering human nature to idealistic categories, and would penetrate beneath the surface of objective phenomena to the experiential universe.

> Even the poets of whom we say that they reproduce reality have no conception of what reality is, but they're a good deal more bearable than those who wish to transform reality. . . . This idealism is the most shameful contempt for human nature. If only artists would try to submerge themselves into the life of the very humblest person and to reproduce it with all its faint agitations, hints of experience, . . . the emotional vein is identical in almost every individual. . . .One must love human nature in order to penetrate [it] . . . nobody, however insignificant . . . should be despised; only then can one understand humankind as a whole.[5]

As Büchner scholar and translator John Reddick notes, the idealism that Büchner detested in the arts was "the same reductivism that he saw in philosophy and the new sciences, and above all in society," the reduction of life itself to "mechanical processes": "the ridiculous puppets of the contemporary stage; the *homme machine* of Cartesian rationalism; the body as functional . . . mechanism in the new sciences; the peasantry as work-machines and money-machines" for the ruling class.[6]

Büchner was nearly forgotten for fifty years after his premature death, but on being rediscovered he would inspire the naturalist playwright Gerhardt Hauptmann and succeeding generations of dramatists. In his own era, however, Büchner had no parallel. He shared the early realists' interest in the urgent issues that arose out of the French Revolution: Could economic misery be eliminated by political change, assuming that such change would be allowed? Could science and education really throw light on the human condition, and, if so, would that knowledge be used wisely and for the common good? Could humanity control its own fate? Was nature, including human nature, good, evil, or indifferent? Like Emile Augier and Alexandre Dumas *fils*, Büchner scorned the idealistic brand of Romanticism that dominated his era, and he sided with history's pawns rather than its leaders. Büchner, unlike his contemporaries, despaired that human reason, least of all in its reductivist, mechanistic form, could ever redress injustice. Accordingly, whereas the mainstream realist playwrights adapted their new content to the forms of the melodrama or the well-made play, Büchner reached back to the *Sturm und Drang* dramatists of the 1770s, particularly Lenz and Goethe, and ultimately back to Shakespeare. Both J. M. R. Lenz and Büchner rejected Hegel's notion of history as a rational development guided by the movement of the World Spirit, and they often parodied this notion through their plays. Büchner's parodies entailed a radical change in the dramatic form itself, while Lenz's are presented more often as characters' discussions and monologues. Likewise, Lenz's plays, as iconoclastic as they were, end with a reestablishment of order and Enlightenment values, whereas Büchner's do not. A few early critics dismissed Büchner's parody or outright rejection of the old dramatic unities that supported these values as naive clumsiness, arguing that he had no practical theater experience.[7] But out of what once seemed formless a unique and complex vision of reality and history has emerged, with new dimensions continually being discovered.

In November 1987 at the Guthrie Theatre in Minneapolis a production was presented that took up the challenge of Büchner's revolutionary vision of reality and history. Avant-garde director JoAnne Akalaitis, one of the founders of the Mabou Mines troupe, collaborated with actors, designers, musicians, and dramaturg to develop a performance that incorporated into the text of *Leonce and Lena* much of the novella *Lenz,* as well as passages from *Danton's Death* and *Woyzeck.* The resulting work was titled *Leon and Lena (& lenz)*[8] and shifted from the original nineteenth-century European fairytale kingdoms of Popo and Pipi to the Corporate Kingdom of Moneywell in the American sunbelt, with a landscape resembling the high plains of Texas.[9] Büchner's comedy played on a white stage lit in neon colors, while the documentary of Lenz's mental breakdown was produced as a black-and-white, expressionist-style silent film that was projected intermittently throughout the production on three large screens.[10] The action shifted back and forth between these two narratives and media. Unlike an antihistorical postmodernist performance, which would merely proliferate the media in order to fragment the historical dimensions in an anachronistic manner, Akalaitis had only two dominant media — the live stage and the film — to juxtapose past with present systematically throughout the performance. The same Chicano actor-singer, an intense, pony-tailed Jesse Borrego, played both Lenz and Leon, who were not separate individual characters but a split subjectivity existing on two spatio-temporal planes. All three protagonists were played by young actors of minority races — Val by an African-American and Lena by a Korean-American — thus paralleling the original Lenz's outsider status with the new social context of the multi-racial United States.

Akalaitis and her collaborators believed that setting the play in the American Southwest could accommodate both the Leonce and Lena play and the story of Lenz. It was not to be the literal geography of that region but the legendary one of our imagination: the Big Sky, blazing yellow sun, endless plains and rolling hills, cut through only with a system of wide highways and remote roadside motels and cafes. This, notes dramaturg Mark Bly, was "a major transcultural leap for a nineteenth-century Germany set in an imaginary European kingdom"(Bly, 81). Further, the company decided that, since there is no royalty in contemporary America, the closest comparable moneyed realms would be the "corporate kingdoms." One other element that served as inspiration for the new setting was the group of "Cadillac Ranch" sculptures located outside Amarillo, Texas. This element of Southwestern pop culture developed into the idea of a ghostly, driverless 1950s car appearing mysteriously and ominously on the "Highway in the Sky," evoking the myth of the "ghost riders in the sky." The cultural icon of the highway, so powerful in the American imagination, was materialized in the form of a huge chunk of freeway suspended above the stage, complete with yellow and white painted lines and apparently torn up out of the ground. "Christine the Mystery Car," as it was nicknamed by Akalaitis and the set designer, appeared only once, just before Leon and Lena's wedding, but the chunk of freeway remained throughout the production. This set was intended to serve as an equivalent to Büchner's original landscape of mountains, forests, valleys, "endless sky and road on an empty plain, . . . moving clouds, where all is vast and brilliant,"[11] or, by turns, dark and frightening in a storm — the wild Nature which held so much meaning for the Romantic imagination of Büchner, Lenz, and their contemporaries.

Music, as a third medium, also helped connect the two narratives: New Wave composer Terry Allen, a Texan himself, adapted or wrote new Country and Western songs that commented on the events in the play. Sometimes the music ironically extolled born-again American consumerism and corporate conformity, and at other times it rang out sadly, as if from the lonely honkytonks, cafes, and small-town main streets, expressing the pain of those "very humblest persons" for whom Büchner reserved his deepest compassion. The music also periodically soared into dancing, hand-clapping rhythms that seemed to transport actors and audience away from the stage events altogether.

The combining of the two works into one is not an arbitrary pastiche in the antihistorical postmodernist sense, as it might seem at first glance. Underneath the ironic comic fairytale of *Leonce and Lena* we see the same oppressive historical process as in *Woyzeck, Danton's Death,* and *Lenz.* No one is able to lead this history; instead, it threatens to draw Prince Leonce, as he himself is aware, into his institutional role as king, into the public theater of politics. Because Akalaitis uses *Lenz* to break into the fairy-tale play, a few critics quickly concluded that this was just another self-indulgent invasion of a classic by a pop culture alien to it. But in fact, Büchner's text is already multilayered:

echoes of Lenz's anguished ordeal reverberate through the text of the comedy in dialectical opposition to the actions of its gossamer-thin plot. The production *materializes* the questions that Büchner already implies in the original *Leonce and Lena:* do we play our roles in the theater of history, do they play us, or is history nothing but a set of props on a stage after all? The Guthrie production brought these questions to the fore without definitively answering them.

Even though the company chose to emphasize an existential cultural critique rather than a specific critique of class, the latter was still strongly present, and the staging itself was far more epic than absurdist in its practical execution. Above all, its passionate attempt to bring Büchner's social vision of his world to bear on our own was historically critical in the epic sense, but effected this critique through a representation of time and space that was postmodern. As such it was at odds with the antihistorical postmodernist theater whose aesthetic aim is to arouse and then thwart the spectator's attempt to unify the meaning of the performance. A typical production of this kind overtly questions the integrity of the author's vision, impedes the identification of actor with character, provides so many foci that no resolution can be reached, and, in general, brings to the fore the idea that theatrical performance is an arbitrary mechanism wherein all meanings are equally valid — and thus quite possibly irrelevant. The postmodernist approach of the Guthrie staging, by contrast, was historically "responsible" in Büchner and Brecht's sense.[12]

As many scholars have noted, the names Leonce and Lena sound like variations of Lenz — which lends weight to the argument that this pair are not to be taken at face value as autonomous "well-rounded characters," but as two dimensions of the Lenzian consciousness. This consciousness, however, which is the real dramatic subject, encompasses more than the stage characters. In the Guthrie montage, as in both the comedy and novella, the subject does not hold itself intact. Instead, it is dispersed between stage and film, thus fragmenting into what Julia Kristeva calls a *subjectivity in process,*[13] which relinquishes sovereign control over language and can no longer be contained within rigid spatial and temporal bounds.

A sense of "traveling" between the two dimensions of consciousness was effected whenever the stage action stopped, the lights dimmed, and the film was projected. Leon, Lena, and other characters took turns reading passages from *Lenz* into a microphone as they watched his story unfolding on the screen. The spectators were not sure which of the two stories to take as the "real" one: was it the "live" events on stage or those recorded on the film? Was reality the bright neon-lit Moneywell in the country of Poopoo with its bored young protagonist Leon and outrageous caricatures such as King Peter in his neon-green, gold-fringed Las Vegas cowboy costume and his "court" of gray-flannel-suited, fawning mannequins? Or was reality the silent black-and-white film of Lenz in his eighteenth-century dress, desperately fighting to retain his hold on sanity among the barren mountains, lonely forests, and white walls?

The production did not privilege one reality and time dimension over the other: the world-weary, hedonistic Leon of the present, holding a small volume of *Lenz* in his hand, might have been reading about his "alter ego." He appeared to be more absorbed in his forebear's world than in his own. Or, in a more profound sense, perhaps the stage events that seemed so real to us were shadow plays in Lenz's mind. If this were so, the neon fairy-tale world of Moneywell would be a nightmare answer to Leon's question about the meaning of existence.

Since the Renaissance the conventional stage picture within the proscenium arch has re-created the visual perspective of one observer in measurable space. By the fifteenth century this perception of "reality" had begun to erode the medieval principle of simultaneity, wherein one performance and its site could represent several dimensions of historical time and geographical space. The drama unfolding on this site comprised the image of the cosmos itself as the *theatrum mundi*. With the Renaissance, unity of action came to mean a time *line*. In accordance with linear spatial perspective, the stage set was like an official painting of a historical event, framed by the proscenium and focusing the spectators' attention on famous and powerful human figures rather than lowly, anonymous ones. By contrast, Büchner, like Shakespeare before him, drew on the medieval concept of unity wherein contiguous scenes are presented that do not necessarily grow out of each other causally but are often juxtaposed as aspects of a theme, "stations" in an allegorical journey of the soul.[14] The spatial perspective of this theater is not limited to the viewpoint and portrayal of kings and generals but also includes that of fools, soldiers, peasants, and supernatural beings, and time is not linear and teleological but simultaneous and circular.

In Büchner "history" itself is exposed as an arbitrary theatrical production, but its material effects, especially on the powerless, are very real. This is also what Brecht meant by the "dialectical" production of historical reality on the stage, and what attracted him to Büchner. In the wake of the French Revolution the Romantic idealists saw history as a progression toward an ideal state led by guiding spirits exemplified, above all, in the heroic figure of Napoleon. Indeed, Büchner himself, like his father, had once invested great hope in Napoleonic reforms for

his own German state, but this optimism gradually gave way to the disillusionment evident in *Danton's Death* and *Leonce and Lena*. Accordingly, the only great leaders Leonce can think of are the bloody tyrants
Caligula and Nero. The Guthrie production underlined this bitterly
anti-idealist irony in Büchner's lines through *gestic* physical means: at
certain moments in the play the actors' naturalistic movement was suspended, and expressionistically choreographed gestic movement and
expression ensued. As Leon began to speak of these two tyrant emper-
ors, he moved like a robot, saying with his puppetlike body that he
would be moved into his father's position and would not be able to de-
viate from his role as oppressor.

Büchner refutes idealism not by arguing in its own terms of philosophical discourse but by quoting it in ludicrous dramatic contexts. In
the text we first see King Peter running about in his chamber nearly
naked, trying to find him*self* as well as his clothing. "Where are my
trousers? . . . You've left my free will quite exposed in front. Where's
morality? Where are my cuffs?" (I: 2, p. 6). He remembers his subjects
by tying a knot in his handkerchief — they have reality for him only via
his costume. In the Guthrie production Peter was being made ready for
a photography session. In his lime-green cowboy suit with its huge up-
holstered shoulders hung with gold braid and wearing six-inch elevator
cowboy boots, he was rolled by his Executive Secretaries around the
stage on a saddle attached to a wheeled stand. To the tune of "Happy
Trails to You" he sang a paraphrase of Büchner's words:

> I am I. I am he. I am you. But you're not me.

Audiences laughed at this song, and the whole scene was a popular tour
de force. The members of the Corporate Kingdom were dressed in gray
suits, and attached to each actor's back were two clonelike mannequins
set on wheels who, in effect, "followed" the actors everywhere with
perfect synchronization and tripled the population of the Moneywell
Corporate Court. But amid the satiric comedy the underlying tragedy
of this situation was discernible. So long trapped in the role of king,
with only sycophants to anticipate and echo his statements, Peter has
lost the ability to distinguish between the simplest cause and effect: he
decrees that the kingdom rejoice, even though the prince and princess
have not yet appeared for the wedding. In other words, he supplies the
theatrical effect before there is a cause. Yet even Peter is more than a
figure of ridicule: in the midst of inanity we hear the disoriented isolation of a man effaced by his own kingly persona:

> I am always so embarrassed when I have to speak in public. . . . When I speak so loud I don't know who is in fact speaking, myself or another man; this worries me. (I: 2, p. 7)

As heir to Peter's kingdom, Leonce has his existence — his time — preset along the same track. This sense of isolation and imprisonment is spatial, temporal, and existential, echoes through all the characters in the comedy, and is the whole focus of *Lenz,* as the Guthrie film made clear. So that we could hear the lonely voice of King Peter as one of the "faint agitations, hints of experience common to us all," Akalaitis stopped the flow of the plot, introduced abstract, sometimes almost autistic movements and gestures, and often altered the actors' voices mechanically by magnifying, echoing, or setting them into the "dead space" of a vacuum through the use of the microphone.

Büchner gives us a clue to the design of the victims' time in the textual images of the dead child, the unborn child, the sleeping child, the frightened child hiding in its cradle afraid of the fleeting spirits passing above it. The Guthrie production began the play with a visual stage image of birth: the nude young body of Jesse Borrego as Leon, with his back to the spectators, rose slowly out of a steaming jacuzzi, holding an old volume of *Lenz.* In the novella and film, Lenz becomes obsessed with bringing a dead child back to life. He calls for her to arise and walk,

> but soberly the walls echoed his voice, as though to mock him, and the corpse remained cold. Half-mad, he collapsed on the floor; then terror seized him (53).

Leonce, on the other hand, wills his love for Rosetta to remain a dead child inside his head, an embryo he does not want to disturb. By contrast, when he later falls in love with Lena — or, rather, with her *voice* — he describes it as an orgasmic birth:

> My whole being is concentrated in this one moment. Now die! More there could never be. How freshly breathing, gleaming with beauty, creation surges towards me out of chaos (II: 4, p. 23).

At this point in the production Leon was standing on the edge of the elevated chunk of freeway as if to jump from it — in lieu of the riverbank in the original text. Below Leon, Lena knelt with praying hands, eyes closed, and face turned upward, in what appeared to be a golden wheatfield, an ironic stage materialization of the amber-waves-of-grain image from the song "America the Beautiful." She was on an island of light on the darkened, starlit stage and suddenly gestured as if she were preparing to drink poison. These parallel suicide rituals of Leon and Lena again drew them together on stage into one subjectivity. But Leon was physically held back from jumping to his death by his ever practical companion Val, and Lena, to her frustration, could not get the top off of her child-proof poison bottle. In counterpoint to these comic-melodramatic suicide attempts, we saw on the large screens the tortured Lenz jump out of the window and heard his body crash onto the courtyard below. Lenz also failed, like the others, and his attempt to die became yet another stillbirth — the pain made meaningless without removing it. These spatial and existential juxtapositions of high and low, birth and death, earth and sky were gestic sequences in the epic sense, serving as a nexus where several spatio-temporal dimensions and conflicting ideological discourses intersect without ever melting into a homogeneous whole.

The characters in Büchner's play and novella never experience time as a harmonious pattern: only in rare moments do they feel at ease in the present. On what is described in the original text as an idyllic hill-top, Leonce is suddenly terrified by a revelation of time as relative and space as an illusion disguising nothingness: in the valley below time seems to stand still, but as he looks up, he sees the clouds racing through a sky too cold, clear, and high — the sun appears and disappears, and everything is whirling by in confusion. When he subsequently falls in love with Lena, he is relieved because the "sky has been lowered," and the terrifying speed of the clouds is obscured. The painted Southwestern landscape evoked the same great expanse as the original Hartz mountains and could be transformed in an instant from an image of freedom to that of cosmic terror.

Leon/Leonce's fear of time and space is paralleled everywhere in *Lenz:*

> He stretched himself out and lay on the earth, dug his way into the All. . . . But these were only moments. . . as though a shadow play had passed before his eyes — he remembered nothing. . . .
>
> Toward evening he came to the highest point of the mountain range. . . . the clouds, constant and motionless, hung in the sky; as far as the eyes could reach, nothing but summits . . . and everything so still, so gray, lost in twilight. He experienced a feeling of terrible loneliness; . . . he was seized with a nameless terror in this nothingness: he was in the void! (38)

Every aspect of the Guthrie production — set, lighting, music, sound, and choreographed movement — was turned to the service of the central image of unending space and multidimensional time: while the vast expanses of mountain and forest alternately terrify and empower Lenz, the modern characters Leon and Val ran from the neon city of Moneywell via the chunk of floating freeway into a wide, pink Texan landscape with a dusty town painted into the far distance. This landscape, where they met Lena and her governess, Laverne, seemed to promise them a great escape, but from the beginning it suspiciously resembled the colorized, slightly garish set of a Hollywood Western. In mute, film-like slow motion, two Texas Rangers pursued Leon and Val. Thus, in Akalaitis's staging the Romantics' old dream of escaping into the space of Nature was transformed into the particularly American dream of Manifest Destiny — the myth that if we only keep moving (preferably westward) we will outrun despair and find meaning, happiness, and material prosperity.

This myth was materialized in one spectacular moment on stage. During the wedding celebration in the final scene — at which Leon and Lena had not yet actually arrived — the celebrants looked upward from their barbecue/dance as the jubilant Western song "Texas Tears Falling Down" dissolved into a chorus of piercing sirens. An apocalypse seemed to be at hand. Then, high above the heads of the people, out of a cloud of stage fog on the chunk of freeway, and glowing mysteriously from its empty interior, the wheelless, driverless body of a 1950s white Studebaker floated out to the edge of the pavement. A weather bulletin over the loudspeaker announced a tornado watch, the wind rose, and lightning and thunder emanated from the car's interior, lighting up the dark sky around it. It hovered, illuminating the night sky for a long moment, as the people, struck silent, looked upward, and then it receded. This scene was intended to represent an apocalypse that was awaited but never happened and to evoke the mood of a "pentecostal" revival meeting, where wonder and awe are generated. The people sang the "Tornado Song" in anticipation of a great historic event:

> Well it came in from the southwest
> In the middle of the night
> Loomed over the Kingdom
> What a God Almighty sight
> It dipped down into the darkness
> All crazy out of control
> An' tossed around the panhandle town
> 'Til it couldn't throw it around no more
> Some blamed secret government projects
> Some blamed it on the president
> One blamed wind from the wings of Jesus
> Just flappin' 'round heaven sent . . .
> An' some blamed Communist sabotage
> Some blamed rednecks on the right
> Some blamed teenage restlessness
> Rock n' Roll goin' berserk in the night
> Yeah but I don't know
> (It's a UFO)

I don't know
(It's a UFO)
They don't know . . .
Some said it was the ghost of Buddy
Some said the ghost of Cain
Some said the soul of the prodigal son
Is just stumblin' back home again
Yeah but I don't know
(It's a tornado)
I don't know
(It's a tornado)
Maybe so. . . .[15]

This scene caused the company and some reviewers concern that the inventive attempts to bring Büchner into the American cultural and sociohistorical context were in danger of obscuring him. In her importation of the contemporary American culture and historical imagination Akalaitis was not playing false to that of Büchner — or Brecht, for that matter — however, but was working in their spirit of ironic intervention. Where she did betray the tenets of this interventionist theater was in confining such satiric portrayal of the American myths of its own historical existence to the blue-collar class. In rehearsal she referred to the common citizens of Poopoo as "the K-Mart People," a far cry, from Büchner's passionate championing of "the very humblest persons....One must love human nature in order to penetrate [it]."[16] Akalaitis's condescension, as epitomized in the term "K-Mart People," came to the fore again in the scene that, in Büchner's original, depicts a group of poor peasants being given new clothes and lined up along the route that the royal couple will travel, holding trees in their hands to make it seem as if the drought-stricken countryside is blooming with vegetation. This sequence was the least clear in the production: the same K-Mart people held small evergreen trees before their faces, obscuring Büchner's political critique and puzzling the audience, who could not connect it to the barbeque/wedding context. What happened, on the most serious level, is that the original sense of these scenes as a political theatrical spectacle *orchestrated for the sole benefit of and by the ruling class* had been lost. Indeed, the miraculous car appeared to have no director or producer at all — leaving the responsibility for this myth entirely on the heads of the common people, as if it were their own invention and, thus, their own fault if they were deluded by it.

Akalaitis, while politically astute and engaged, in fact has shown a seeming lack of understanding of the type of theatrical political critique carried out by Büchner and Brecht and even a hostility toward the latter, although, ironically, all of her stage work with actors, space, and time is epic and *gestic* in the deepest sense. In an interview about her work in 1997 she confesses that she "has not figured out who Brecht is in our theatrical lives." She recalls that she saw and was awed by the masterpieces of the Berliner Ensemble but now finds him too clear in his political agenda and even naive in his staging principles:

> There's no way to ignore the fact that Brecht had a very clear political agenda which to many of us, at this time, is abhorrent. It's almost a Stalinist thing. And in some plays — like *Arturo Ui* which is a delightful play — the level of the polemic is so naive, I wouldn't even know how to direct those plays. . . . Other plays like *Galileo* and *Mother Courage* . . . are basically Broadway hits, . . . commercial, . . . written for some kind of star. . . . But . . . for us to say, well, we can do [his plays] without dealing with his politics, in some way seems ignorant.[17]

To which the interviewer replies, "It seems naive of *us*."[18] Indeed, Akalaitis articulates a much more superficial notion of the *Verfremdungseffekt* than is demonstrated in Brecht's stagings or writings or, most significantly, in her own markedly epic work in the theater:

> Alienation — it is basically a Greek idea. To see this as *only* the seeing of *oneself* doing something and putting it out into space to communicate something . . . that seems extraordinarily naive on his part. It's a great acting idea, but to use it politically is very very naïve. . . . But if you're not working with people for whom the bottom line is some kind of social reality, then you're not working.[19]

In fact, Akalaitis's modes of working with actors' bodies in space and time, as well as her use of multiple, juxtaposed media, owe a great debt to epic practice and are often identical to Brecht's and Piscator's methods.

There is no doubt, however, in either the original works or the Guthrie adaptation, that space and time terrify in a gestic manner — or, rather, the recurrent half-realization that they are nothing but a kind of theatrical illusion is what terrifies. In the text Leonce, in his flight with Valerio, is at first glad to have escaped the palace to a lovely field; but suddenly he becomes afraid to stretch out his hand for fear that the scene will be a mirror and that he will shatter it, revealing "bare walls" — or, even worse, behind the walls, nothingness. But Valerio, like his modern stage counterpart, the breakdancing, streetwise Val, has the ancient wisdom of the clown. Unlike his superiors, he keeps himself intact by refusing to advance beyond a medieval concept of time and space. He sees in nature only the signs of a gigantic power game: the sun is a sign for the tavern, he and Leonce are cards with which God and Satan are playing, and the seas are wine spilled on their table.

All the characters experience time and space diversely: Leonce trustingly follows what he calls the "closer," warmer path of falling in love with Lena, but the clairvoyant Valerio watches him and sees a mad prince walking a broad road lined with bare trees, not feeling the cold winter day but wiping his face with his handkerchief, strongly recalling Lenz's schizophrenic state. Unfortunately, the visual imagery and music of the Guthrie staging drowned out this momentary glimpse into another temporal dimension.

Time shrinks and expands. Leonce laments: "Oh, every way is long . . . every drop of blood takes its time . . . ," and when Lena speaks out the rest of this thought, he falls in love with her, and the emptiness of the universe recedes, as the sky, like a stage backdrop, descends and glows as if the soft candlelight or gaslight of the stage had replaced the bright sun:

> The air's no longer so bright and cold, the sky descends, glowing, close to me, and wraps me up. . . . oh that voice . . . is the way so long then? So many voices talk on the earth, . . . but I've understood *this* one. . . . how that voice is suffused in space! (II: 3, p. 21).

The voice of Lena seems to cohere, fill, and warm the space for him as his voice does for her. Lena, likewise, loves Leonce because she can recognize that time tortures him: he has "spring on his cheeks" but "winter in his heart." Their only escape is to unite through suffering.

Valerio fears that if he is reflected in mirrors or in the eyes of the crowd, he will lose his sense of authenticity. In the production Leon was also threatened in this way by the apparatus of mimetic representation. Rather than indicating superstition or ignorance, this fear indicates a presciently modern or even postmodern realization of the power of representation to constitute and dissolve the human subject as a historical agent. In Büchner's terms, Leonce is afraid of becoming a puppet, an "automaton." On stage, Leon rebelled by trying to catch the obsequious mannequins off guard as they mimicked every move he made: if they were to succeed in mirroring him, he would lose himself. Taking his "historical role" means that he will wither like a fragile plant and be blinded in the constant glare of representation. Likewise, Valerio says to King Peter:

> Turn the mirrors to the wall . . . and don't look at me so that I have to see my reflection in your eyes, or I shall really no longer know who I am (III: 3, p. 29).

Val wore no masks, but the spirit of the famous scene in which Valerio takes off one mask after another was preserved in the Guthrie staging. By a wizardly hand gesture, he froze the members of court and delivered his soliloquy while circling around them; then, when he had finished it, he puffed life back into them, as if he were reinflating balloons.

Lena also fears being turned into a mirror in her impending arranged marriage:

> Am I then no more than the poor, helpless stream forced to reflect every image that bends over its untroubled bed? (I:15, p. 13)

At this moment in the staging Lauren Thom as Lena was imprisoned inside a triangular glass box like an exotic Asian butterfly. In her ragged white wedding dress she pressed her long-gloved, bloody hands against the panes of her glass prison. Her voice, when she was in the box, was magnified by a microphone and given a metallic, echoing quality.

For a night Leonce and Lena seem to escape time, and, without revealing their true identities to each other, they decide, independently of each other, to present themselves as wedding dolls at the next day's long-dreaded marriage celebration. Evoking a lividly tinted and slightly off-track video of Prince Charles and Princess Diana at their famous wedding, Leon and Lena, pretending to be life-size dolls, mechanically went through the motions of marrying, dancing, and waving and smiling to the crowd. But when they kissed, they were dismayed to learn each other's true identity. They now recognized this happy ending as the contrived climax of the comedy, the historical fate from which they had been running. The crowd froze in time lapse as Leon silently "exploded": his face twisted, his body convulsed, and his hands fluttered in a strange out-of-control dance. He was repeating precisely the same symptoms of madness just seen in the film of Lenz. The filmic closeups lingered in the mind's eye and were, thus, superimposed on the live actor: through this Eisensteinian montage effect the actor playing Leon was literally cut apart from the rest of the stage picture and blown up — in both senses of this term.

The original *Leonce and Lena* ends on an ironic note as Leonce gives his first inflated speech as the new king of Popo, assuming with theatrical flourish the role that King Peter is happy to be escaping as he passes the kingdom on to its proper heir. Leonce decrees that the reflection of the sun itself will be captured in a magnifying glass and a tropical climate created for his kingdom. Thus, the characters' space will be marked off as in theater: they will escape from winter, work, pain, and death — from all the effects of time. In the production all on stage applauded this speech and walked slowly to the rear of the Guthrie's thrust stage in a farewell movement. Lena, at this moment, slowly separated herself from the others and deliberately closed herself into her glass box again — and forever.

The Guthrie performance did not end here but gave the final word to Lenz. The stage darkened, and on the screen the moon appeared from behind flying clouds as Lena narrated the last passages of *Lenz* from her eerily lit glass prison, her voice reverberating through the theater with a mechanical echo of itself. In the growing darkness this moon became the only thing visible, as the audience heard the end of the novella *Lenz*:

> He seemed quite reasonable and . . . did everything just as the others did, but there was a terrible emptiness inside him, he no longer felt any fear, any desire, his existence was a burden to him, a burden he must bear.
> So he lived on. . . .[20]

But the play did not. It ended here with a slow hissing sound — its life breath pouring out as the moon shrank to a point of light and then disappeared into darkness.

The Guthrie production was controversial. Most spectators were unfamiliar with Büchner, and a few were annoyed at not finding a plot line, while others — especially young people who had grown up with music videos — enjoyed it most as an amusing, ironic musical spectacle. Some, especially those who did not know Büchner well, too quickly assumed that the production had betrayed him by overpowering the subtleties of the text with contemporary references. But ultimately, in spite of its excessive moments and Akalaitis's emphasis on the existential, to the detriment of the political reading of Büchner's works, the interweaving of texts with each other and with textual, visual, and aural signs from our own era did not betray the author's concept of reality. Instead, the *iridescence* of that reality became even more apparent: a brightly colored, patterned veil of sights and sounds that floats over but does not conceal the abyss behind it. Finally, Büchner still lingers in the mind like the inarticulate flutelike sound that Lenz makes up in his lonely room.

Notes

[1] Georg Büchner, letter to August Stöber, Darmstadt, December 1833, in *Georg Büchner: The Complete Plays, Lenz and Other Writings*, ed. John Reddick (London: Penguin, 1993), 192.

[2] Büchner, letter to his family, Strasbourg, December 1832, idem., 190.

[3] Büchner, letter to his family, Strasbourg, July 28, 1835, idem., 201–202.

[4] Büchner, *The Hessian Messenger,* idem., 165–179.

[5] Georg Büchner, *Lenz,* in *Leonce and Lena. Lenz. Woyzeck,* trans. Michael Hamburger (Chicago: U of Chicago P, 1972), 45–47. Büchner began work on *Lenz* in 1835, and wrote *Leonce und Lena* in 1836. They were first published in 1850. The definitive German edition is *Georg Büchner: Sämtliche Werke und Briefe: Historische-Kritische Ausgabe mit Kommentar,* ed. Werner R. Lehmann, 2 vols. (Hamburg: Christian Wegner, 1967–71).

[6] John Reddick, "Notes to *Lenz,*" in *Georg Büchner: The Complete Plays, Lenz and Other Writings,* 269.

[7] John Reddick sees Büchner's "systematic discontinuity" as a key quality that must be taken seriously but that has eluded even many modern critics: "The most unsubtle way of not taking it seriously is that favoured by certain critics in the English tradition, who have patronizingly applied the yardstick of good old English common sense, and declared Büchner to be insufficiently mature," lacking in "practical dramatic sense" and exhibiting "philosophical and . . . poetic-dramatic immaturity." *Georg Büchner: The Shattered Whole* (Oxford: Clarendon P/ Oxford UP, 1994), 5.

[8] The Guthrie production used a translation by Henry J. Schmidt, in *Georg Büchner: Complete Works and Letters,* trans. Henry J. Schmidt, ed. Walter Hinderer and Schmidt (New York: Continuum, 1986). A number of changes were made in Schmidt's translation of the text, including the use of contemporary language in some passages, all of which were approved by the translator.

[9] "Moneywell" is a direct play on the name Honeywell, a multinational company based in Minneapolis, and was immediately recognizable to the Twin City audiences.

[10] Akalaitis had the film of *Lenz* modeled specifically on the Danish director Carl Dreyer's works, including *The Passion of Joan of Arc,* whose look, in Akalaitis's words, was created though "silent, meditative, and romantic images." Mark Bly, "JoAnne Akalaitis's *Leon and Lena (and lenz):* A Log from the Dramaturg," *Yale Theater* (1989): 81–95.

[11] Mark Bly, quoting JoAnne Akalaitis, 82.

[12] Philip Auslander's chapter "Boal, Blau, Brecht: the body," in his *From Acting to Performance: Essays in Modernism and Postmodernism* (London and New York: Routledge, 1997), illuminates the use of the actor's body in the theater of Brecht compared and contrasted to that of Augusto Boal. Auslander explores the practices and ideological values of modernist versus postmodernist theater. Akalaitis's theater draws from both.

[13] Julia Kristeva, "The True-Real," in *The Kristeva Reader,* ed. Toril Moi (New York: Columbia UP, 1976), 214–237.

[14] *Woyzeck,* to present the medieval oppression in which the victim-protagonist lives in this age of science, returns to the station drama in its structure, and interweaves the objective with the subjective. Woyzeck does not see the sun rising, but the earth going down. Far from opening the way for humane enlightenment, scientific rationality becomes a vicious tool by which Woyzeck's social superiors torture him. His mystical perception of nature is akin to an earlier radical, non-sentimental Romanticism that saw in nature a demonic power, with destruction as the other side of creation, and that had not yet subjugated this dialectic to idealism.

[15] Terry Allen, "Tornado Song," copyright Green Shoes Publishing Company, 1980. Quoted by Mark Bly, 91.

[16] See note 1.

[17] "JoAnne Akalaitis Interviewed by Deborah Saivetz: Releasing the 'Profound Physicality of Performance,'" *New Theatre Quarterly* 13 (November 1997), 333–334.

[18] Ibid., 334.

[19] Akalaitis, ibid.

[20] Büchner, in *Lenz,* Henry Schmidt translation, 62. See note 8, above.

Leon and Lena discover each other for the first time.
Leon and Lena (& Lenz), *by permission of the Guthrie*
Theatre, Minneapolis. Photo by Joe Gianetti.

Agamemnon and Clytemnestra, in Agamemnon, *from* Les Atrides, *1991, directed by Ariane Mnouchkine. By permission of the Théâtre du Soleil, © Michèle Laurent, CNDF.*

6: Gender, Empire and Body Politic: Ariane Mnouchkine's *Les Atrides*

"The end of history?" That amuses me. Saying this, one risks the loss of language and the loss of the possibility of thinking, one risks becoming more and more passive, able to be bought and sold. . . . Theater is doubtless the most fragile of the arts . . . the theater public is now really a very small group . . . but the theater keeps reminding us of the possibility to collectively seek the history of the people and to tell it. The contradictions, the battles of power, and the split in ourselves will always exist. I think the theater best tells us of the enemy in ourselves. Yes, theater is a grain of sand in the works.

— Ariane Mnouchkine[1]

It is in giving the *Oresteia* its exact figure, not archaeological but historical, that we manifest the tie that unites us to this work. Represented in its particularity, its monolithic aspect, progressive in relation to its own past but barbaric in relation to our present, the antique tragedy concerns us in the measure that it gives us to understand *clearly*, by all the prestige of theater, that history is plastic, fluid, at the service of men, not the least because they want to master it with lucidity. To seize the historical specificity of the *Oresteia*, its exact *originality*, is the only way for us to make dynamic, responsible use of it.

— Roland Barthes[2]

We must take seriously Vico's great observation that men make their own history, that what they can know is what they have made, and [that they] extend it to geographical, . . . cultural, . . . and historical entities . . . such as "Orient" and "Occident."

— Edward Said[3]

Historically Responsible Theater: Mnouchkine and Brecht / Barrault and Artaud

IN 1955 ROLAND BARTHES witnessed Jean-Louis Barrault's production of *L'Orestie* at the Marigny Theater. In the review quoted above he ironically comments on what he saw as a misguided attempt to wrest the work loose from the academic rhetorical tradition in France by presenting it as "Artaudian trance theater" in the style of African mask ceremony. Barthes describes it as an impossible combination of partici-patory theater in which no one really wanted to participate, with a "bourgeois-psychological" acting style full of secretive nuances, and costumes and decor that exuded Greco-Parisian elegance. Yet he most seriously criticizes Barrault not for aiming at the exotic but for lacking historical responsibility. It is important to note that Barthes's remarks were made during a highly charged moment for French theater, an era of retrenchment and polarization that had begun in 1954 with the guest appearance of the Berliner Ensemble's *Mother Courage* at the Théâtre des Nations. By the following year Barthes had become an out-spoken proponent of Brechtian theater and he seems to be judging Bar-rault's *Oresteia* as its antithesis.[4] By contrast, Mnouchkine's 1991–1992 *Les Atrides* at the Théâtre du Soleil demonstrates, despite its exotic elements borrowed from Asia, a historical responsibility of which Bar-thes would surely approve.

Inspired by Brecht's example, as were directors Roger Planchon, Antoine Vitez, Patrice Chéreau, Giorgio Strehler, and many others who began their careers in the 1960s, Mnouchkine has based more than thirty years of work on the principle of historical responsibility. Her leftist politics and collaborative rehearsal and management practices have been constant since she cofounded the Théâtre du Soleil in 1964, even as her aesthetic and political vision has continued to evolve. Ac-cording to Bernard Dort, Mnouchkine is the only one from her gen-eration of directors who has, without fanfare, never stopped working in the critical spirit of Brecht, using theater to interrogate the making of history. In order to venerate her, Dort believes, the French press has consistently ignored this fact.[5] Unlike Giorgio Strehler, whose produc-tions of Brecht sometimes too successfully followed the letter of the master in staging and, thus, failed to be historically relevant, Mnouch-kine has confronted new issues arising in a changed historical situation. Characteristically, she describes Brecht as a master with whom one must be careful: "I like him when he searches, but I don't like him when he legislates."[6] Yet her commitment to a historically responsible theater has taken her along a Brechtian route through a *Verfremdung* achieved by borrowing from Asian theater. She explains that she can only seize the historical import of a work — i.e., its relevance for our time — by creating a distance. For *Les Atrides,* a cycle of four plays that adds Euripides' *Iphigenia at Aulis* to Aeschylus's *Oresteia,* this distanc-ing is achieved through the filter of an imaginative context inspired mainly by Kathakali dance, makeup, and costumes, and the colors and fabrics of India. The Atreus cycle is part of a long series of "Orientalist" projects for which the Théâtre du Soleil has adapted Asian theater conventions to stage Western texts or created new works that depict the colonization of the Third World more directly. The productions have alternated between classical plays such as *Les Atrides* and the Shakespeare cycle — *Richard II, Twelfth Night,* and *Henry IV* — and new creations such as *L'Indiade* and *L'Histoire terrible mais inachevée de Norodom Sihanouk, roi du Cambodge* (The Terrible but Unfinished History of Norodom Sihanouk, King of Cambodia). As Mnouchkine is well aware, the canonical works are sure to receive a warmer critical reception and more box-office success than the contemporary ones. However, both serve a necessary function in the Théâtre du Soleil's ongoing political and cultural critique, a dialogical engagement against and with the Western and specifically the French theatrical tradition.

Like Brecht, Artaud, Barrault, Peter Brook, or anyone else who appropriates the art of a different culture, Mnouchkine risks practicing cultural hegemony.[7] In *Orientalism* Edward Said warns of enervating the traditions and colonizing the people from whom one borrows, of positioning oneself as the primary and knowing subject and the other as the secondary object to be known — the medium through which the subject gains self-knowledge. Said defines Orientalism as a manifold discourse enmeshed deeply in politics, art, philosophy, religion, the social sciences, the physical sciences, and every other area, "a style of thought based upon an ontological and epistemological distinction made between 'the Orient' and . . . 'the Occident.' . . . European culture gained in strength and identity by setting itself off against the Orient as a sort of surrogate and even underground self."[8] I hope to show that while *Les Atrides* may not escape producing hegemonous effects with its own orientalist project, it nevertheless historically contextualizes the *cultural production* of orientalism as a semiotic process in the way that epic theater has taught. Brecht admired and borrowed from Asian theater without yet realizing its implications in postcolonialist political terms — even though, from today's perspective, his *Lehrstück, The Exception and the Rule,* is clearly a postcolonialist critique. Mnouchkine is understandably more aware of postcolonial politics than was Brecht. *Les Atrides* stages as historical the verbal, visual, and aural discourses through which the West *embodies* the multiple Other as a non-Western, nonmasculine, ultimately nonhuman "oriental" whose language is barbaric, at best strange music, and at worst demonic noise. But because this is the *Oresteia,* the pillar of the Western theatrical canon, the Western spectator perforce hears it as more than music or noise. The historical responsibility taken on by Mnouchkine is an elucidation through theatrical means, above all that of *l'écriture corporelle,* or writing by the actors' bodies, of the fateful intersection between the discourses of gender and empire in this founding myth of the West, setting forth power relations that remain in force today.

In recent years Said himself has refuted the growing oversimplification of the concept of Orientalism as a one-directional hegemony. In *Orientalism,* in fact, he notes its capacity for a productive interrogation of the "idea of the West" and the power relations that this idea has entailed. Precisely because Orientalism is "a grid for filtering through the Orient into Western consciousness," he believes that it is "valuable more . . . as a sign of European-Atlantic power over the Orient than it is as a veridic discourse about the Orient."[9] Since classical antiquity the idea of the oriental exotic has been used in the embodiment of private and public power relations, or, as Foucault might put it, the deployment of power through institutionally staged discourses or "technologies" involving the human body. The colonizer often imagines the colonized as an other by feminizing, demonizing, and depriving the other of language. The outlines of this corporate image of the other are already evident in the first extant Greek play, Aeschylus's *The Persians.* The feminine in ancient Greece was equated not only with irrational nature but, especially in times of crisis, with the "barbarians" (literally, non-Greeks) to the east, whom Athens feared and had been trying to fend off or colonize for nearly a thousand years, ever since the wars with Persia and later with Troy in Asia Minor (present-day Turkey). In *Les Atrides* the discourses of Orientalism are deployed through theatrical signifiers, and in the process women, eastern barbarians, ill winds, and other threats to the rising patriarchal Greek empire are condensed, expanded, or diffused into a *bodied other* that can be followed in the texts and production.

For Mnouchkine, as for Brecht, the historically responsible theater does not aim to *reproduce* a context outside itself. In *Les Atrides* neither ancient Greece nor India is imitated realistically. Any attempted reproduction would imply that history flows along everywhere but on stage, unless theater is forcibly transformed into history's channel. Instead, theater is both a producer and a staging of historical consciousness, and Greece, Asia, and, implicitly, France and Europe are shown as floating cultural signs. In short the mise en scène is *semiotic,* not as a formalistic structure but as a site where historical signs are produced. It is more than a theater aware of itself, or a theater with direct speeches to the audience, "nonlinear" time, montage space, separation of elements, and songs and dancing interrupting dialogue. Above all, *Les Atrides* is a staging not of a tragedy that was inevitable but of *a history that did not have to be.*

Gender and Empire:
Feminism and the Critical Tradition

The Oresteia has become so encased in canonical production styles and receptions that it appears to be suspended in a world sealed off from time. It is often claimed as the founding text not only of Western drama but of Western culture and usually interpreted as the defeat of the old barbaric tribal law of revenge and the victory of the new rule of democratic law. Yet a historical inscription of gender, race, and empire underlies this idealized mythic reading. Mnouchkine's prefacing of the trilogy with the rarely staged *Iphigenia at Aulis* strongly foregrounds the ambition, violence, misogyny, and sheer political expediency of the militaristic patriarchy.[10] While Mnouchkine shares with Brecht and Barthes an insistence on historical responsibility and a resolute rejection of psychologizing, naturalism, and universalism, her politics also includes feminism, although she is aware that this is a red-flag "label" to many, an automatic synonym for dogmatism. As a long-time collaborator with Hélène Cixous, who has authored a number of scripts for the Théâtre du Soleil and is a major theorist of *l'écriture féminine,* Mnouchkine has been part of the feminist movement for two decades, and has often lashed out against the sexism and misogyny she has witnessed as a female director in a field dominated by men.[11] By simply prefacing the *Oresteia* with *Iphigenia at Aulis,* Mnouchkine opens the work to a feminist perspective. Indeed, she sees sympathy for Clytemnestra and a critique of the patriarchal Greek empire as already inherent not only in Euripides but even in Aeschylus — with the work of *Les Atrides* being to strip away the layers of time and convention and "let the text speak for itself." Barthes and many others have also found it significant that the old matriarchal gods are defeated by the new patriarchal state, but they have fallen back on essentialist poles of gender in place of historical explanations. Barthes, writing in 1955, and theater historian David Grene in 1987 both call for a historical outlook yet uncritically accept the polarities of masculine and feminine, patriarchy and matriarchy, not recognizing — though Barthes seems very near to it — that this gender inscription itself is the myth that naturalizes specific power arrangements:

> Antique tragedy . . . makes sense only if we . . . clearly respond to two questions: what exactly was the *Oresteia* for contemporaries of Aeschylus? And what have we, *men of the twentieth century,* to do with the antique sense of the work? . . . *The Oresteia* was a progressive work [testifying] to *the passage from a matriarchal society,* represented by the Furies, *to a patriarchal society,* represented by Apollo and Athena.

... [T]he *Oresteia* is a profoundly politicized work [that] ... unites a precise historical structure and a particular myth. Let others ... discover an eternal problem of evil and judgment. ... That will never prevent the *Oresteia* from being above all a work of a precise epoch, of a socially defined state and a contingent moral debate. ... *Men of that era tried to pass from obscurantism to enlightenment.* ... They tried to *lift away barbarism* [italics mine].[12]

Grene seems to agree:

There is ... Athena, unmothered, all father. Against these [qualities] ... the terrifying element of Clytemnestra's sexual drive, twisted, perverse, but deeply recognizable. ... the wolfish Electra, driven by her intense love of her dead father to the enjoyment of the murder of her mother and Aegisthus. ... Did Aeschylus feel that ... there was a *moment* when Attic human society shifted its emphasis ... from female to male, and that the true image of [the shift] was ... the trial of Orestes? ... The Furies ... stand for something frightening in *femaleness.* ... They are the exaggerated ... nightmare expression of what is terrifying in Clytemnestra herself.[13]

Staging Social Constructs

The mise en scène, whether historically responsible or not, is fundamentally signified through culturally constructed human bodies. These bodies are materially anchored in the actors on stage but touch every other element of the production. The bodies of actors and characters belong to two discrete yet interweaving sign systems; the bodies are both real and fictional as a primary nexus where signs of gender, race, and political power intersect and seem to be generated. The actors' bodies in *Les Atrides* are most heavily marked by the signs of the exotic and of gender, yet the gendered and "oriented" bodies are not limited to actors or characters but dispersed throughout the mise en scène, marking its boundaries, shapes, and rhythms. Moreover, the body-assign is not simply *in* the theatrical time and space of the production but constitutes it, mapping out the Greek imaginary as a geopsychic territorial body to be defended and contested. The semiotic processes of the historical mise en scène outlined here can also be elucidated in the terms of feminist Judith Butler, who uses theatrical images to theorize the gendered body as actor and stage in the social and political performance of real life.

For Butler, as for Foucault, ideology is "inscribed" through human bodies to support particular "technologies," arrangements of social and political power.[14] That is, the human body is a primary space upon which ideological schema are projected. This ideological inscription is materialized especially clearly in theater, and in the productions of Mnouchkine it is the conscious purpose. Four terms employed by Judith Butler are relevant here: *embodiment, impersonation,* the *performative,* and *mise en scène.*[15] These concepts relate directly to theater and can be used to analyze how all elements of the staging — the casting; the actors' gestures, costumes, and makeup; their movement and placement; and the scenography — participate in inscribing power. Butler defines *impersonation* and *embodiment* as processes by which discourses of gender, class, and race are signified through and on the human body to privilege some groups and marginalize others. Such semiotic operations regulate cultural signs and meaning, promoting some and suppressing others. Impersonation and embodiment in the staging of *Les Atrides* construct social positions marked by gender and race, and also foreground that construction. Gender identity is an "imitative structure," and impersonation and embodiment help construct it. Whereas impersonation implies a mirroring, a pretended sameness that stays on the surface, embodiment goes beneath the mirrored surface, marking out human bodies as positions in a social hierarchy. In postcolonialist terms, embodiment is used to imagine oneself or one's group as a complex interior territory of the same, set apart from an undifferentiated exterior territory as other. The *performative* is defined as *acts* by which identities are constructed. We are all actors and spectators who use available scripts, roles, and costumes to perform real social exchanges with real effects. For Butler, the *mise en scène* is the *site* of this performance where identities are constructed. Yet precisely because the mise en scène is a "construction site" of multiple identities, it can also be the site of historical agency and historical change.

Embodiment as sociosemiotic construction often involves the hypostasized feminine body, making of it the so-called *ground* of representation itself, as Teresa de Lauretis has also noted.[16] Historically, the concept of "grounding" has a mythical past, an old association with the masculine as sky and the feminine as earth, energetic but chaotic subterranean matter that threatens to rise up and displace the order above it. In *The Oresteia* this myth is connected to the Furies, matriarchal goddesses who literally go underground at the end of the trilogy to become the Eumenides, benign guardians of reproduction within lawful marriage, and give up their old power, which terrified, challenged, and sometimes even checked the patriarchy. David Grene's reading of Clytemnestra and the Furies as demonic forces of female sexuality reproduces this mythic view. But *Les Atrides* strongly implicates the myth as a self-serving invention of the Greek patriarchy, a way to naturalize the politics of an empire trying to establish itself. Mythic embodiment of this Idea of the West is exposed as politically expedient and juxtaposed again and again with a social G*estus* that says: in this moment the sign of gender determines a specific power arrangement, *but it need not be so.*

Construction Sites and Performative Acts

The concept of the mise en scène as a historical construction site is evidenced in the theatrical space as soon as the spectators enter the building of the Théâtre du Soleil. On the back wall of the spacious *salle d'acceuille,* or reception hall, and illuminated as the focal point of the whole hall is a large political map of the ancient Mediterranean world, with a red line representing the voyages of Agamemnon. Around the room on the walls, stands, and tables are photos, artifacts, and books on Greek history and culture. At a long counter and on small carts Greek food is prepared, sold, and eaten on site. Mnouchkine herself is often seen clearing tables and chatting with the "guests," and all company members take a turn mingling and working during the breaks between plays (in addition to the two hours daily of cleaning, mending, and other chores). On their way to the performance in the adjoining hangar, spectators must walk along a path above what resembles excavation sites filled with life-size terra-cotta statues of people wearing the same costumes as the actors, facing in one direction and either standing alone or leading horses, recalling for many the famous army of ancient Chinese warriors. Sculpted by Erhard Stiefel, the statues have been affectionately nicknamed "the crowd" by the theater company and seem to be frozen in the moment of walking up out of the earth. After the spectators cross this "excavated" transition space and take their seats in the steep bleachers, the lights dim as the sound of a kettledrum rises to a thunderous roar, and suddenly the dancers of the chorus rush on with exuberant shouts in a whirling blaze of red, black, and yellow costumes, as if the crowd of statues had returned to life and found their way to the stage.

According to Mnouchkine, the chorus is the key to achieving a historical perspective, of distancing what is too near and recalling the past to life. The stage-filling energy of the dancers, with their bounding leaps, cries, richly elaborate Kathakali-like costumes, their faces an expressive circle of white makeup, black-lined eyes, and curved red lips, is the most startling departure from conventional stagings of Greek plays. The physical presence of twelve to fifteen men and women of the chorus accompanied by the live percussive music of Jean-Jacques Lemêtre electrifies the theater. Because it was crucial for Mnouchkine that the audience hear the text clearly, it was never sung; only chorus leader Catherine Schaub or other single voices spoke the chorus's lines. Moreover, the chorus never danced while dialogue was being spoken. The principal actors often joined them, either as characters or as anonymous chorus members. Convinced of the importance of the choral dance to ancient tragedy, Mnouchkine aimed to restore its vital role — not by reconstructing it from iconic or textual evidence but by imbuing it with the still-living energy of the Kathakali and Bharata Natyam dance theaters, whose forerunners almost surely had confluence with those of Greek theater.[17]

The space mobilized by the decor, music and light, and the voices, gestures, and movements of the actors sets up a historical writing — above all what Mnouchkine calls an *écriture corporelle,* a writing with the body, a *gestic* vocabulary of signs that reappear throughout the plays, not just delineating a style or illustrating the text but haunting the action so that there can never be the sense of a pure present. The performance is the discovery site of a buried story. The bare simplicity of the set and scenography expresses this site as a cosmos waiting to be historically specified. The playing space has no curtains, flies, or wings but is a wide expanse of terra-cotta-colored floor surrounded by a wall of the same material and color, crumbling in spots and broken by several recesses and by a double-doored gate in the upstage center. The space of the Greek cosmos is defined as enclosure within enclosure: the terra-cotta wall encloses the stage, and this inner wall, in turn, is enclosed by a high wooden wall painted the bright blue of sky and sea, in the middle of which is a second large gate that opens at times to reveal darkness beyond. Suspended above the stage is a white canvas "tent" roof decorated with Greek designs, through which bright sunlight (actually fluorescent) seems to shine. Several spectators have compared the playing space to a sun-baked bullfighting arena, connecting it to the matadorlike costumes worn by Iphigenia, Clytemnestra, and Orestes. For portentous entrances or exits, large box-shaped gliding platforms on hidden wheels carry the main characters and define the locale. In *Iphigenia at Aulis* a glide brings Iphigenia, Clytemnestra, and Orestes to Aulis; a second becomes the altar of Iphigenia's sacrifice; and a third carries Agamemnon to war. In *Agamemnon* it brings Cassandra and Agamemnon to Argos. Finally, in *The Libation Bearers* it is the tomb of Agamemnon. Only these platforms, pulled by ropes that have no visible operators, pass through the outer wooden doors beyond the blue wall. Thus they alone seem able to traverse the space between life and death, the known and the unknown worlds. In the course of the productions the gliding platforms come to signify the movement of time, of a fate whose drivers remain a mystery.

The psychic and social space of the Greek world is also related by other scenographic signs. The sound of vicious dogs is heard at the end of three plays, and in two of them it is accompanied by a tableau of the murder that has just taken place. Each tableau is a mattress with life-sized mannequins of the murdered couple lying together as if caught in sexual embrace, and each time it is dragged with increasing difficulty on and off the stage by actors. Whereas the platforms glide seemingly without effort through the two sets of gates, the mattresses are always dragged through a central vomitorium from under the audience, emphasizing their significance as deathbeds, all-too-human *vehicles of fate* connected expressly to sexual relations. The mattresses visibly replace the *ekkyklema* used in Greek theater for such violent and fateful tableaux, but their difficult maneuverability contrasts with our image of the rolling ekkyklema, as it does with the gliding platforms.

Throughout the plays the wind is a less obvious but important sign of moving time, a poetic index tracing the plot and the movement of the gliding platforms. Wind functions as a signifier of a history-bound phallic power, "phallic" because it is connected to male agents (above all Agamemnon, but also Menelaus, Achilles, Orestes, and Apollo) who are marked for power and whose acts of expediency are justified as a force of nature. Even though the winds are often *embodied* by the feminine, they coincide with operations of male power. They are nearly always marked by a struggle involving gender and sexuality: Artemis avenging pregnant animals or the "truth-bearing" winds of Apollo piercing the unwilling body of his priestess Cassandra. Whenever wind appears, it is connected with "fate" but coincides with some "necessary" act, such as waging war or committing murder:

> I am slain, I perish, foully slaughtered by a godless father. I wish that Aulis had never received . . . the fleet that speeds the host to Troy. Why should Zeus raise winds on the Euripus to bar *our* voyage? He sends pleasant winds to other men, for happy sailing. Many are his winds: winds of sorrow and winds of hardship, winds to set sail in and winds to drop sail in, and winds of waiting.
>
> — Iphigenia, *Iphigenia at Aulis*, 368[18]

> I call on Apollo the Healer / to keep [Artemis] from setting against the Greeks / those contrary winds, winds that hold ships / staying winds, winds that stop sailing altogether.
>
> — Chorus, *Agamemnon*, lines 146–149[19]

The hurricane that came from Strymon, / breeding deadly delays, starvation, lost anchorages, / driving crews to aimless wanderings, / . . . wore down the flower of the Argives. . .

> — Chorus, *Agamemnon*, lines 190–194

Helen means death, and death indeed she was, /. . .as she sailed out of the delicate fabrics of her curtained room,/ fanned by the breeze of giant Zephyr. . . . [She] came to the city of Ilium/ a spirit of windless calm.

> — Chorus, *Agamemnon*, lines 736–737

Now my prophecy [from Apollo] shall no longer peer from behind veils / like a newly married bride. / No, it will rush on, a wind brightly blowing / into the sun's rising, / to send disaster surging like a wave to meet the sunbeams. . . .

> — Cassandra, *Agamemnon*, lines 1178–1182

May Hermes . . . help [Orestes]; / may he give him a fair wind for what he does! . . . Then for the deliverance of the house's wealth / we shall raise the shout of female voices; we shall strike up the magic cry, "She sails well!"

> — Chorus, *The Libation Bearers*, lines 813–822

On the stage this "wind of fate" is represented by sound, music, and, above all, by the fluttering of drapery that covers the gliding platforms. Significantly, wind is created not by any offstage machines but by the movement of these gliding platforms, which are maneuvered by visible ropes and invisible hands. In sum, the stage becomes a site on which the actors and a few stage *machinae* write the sharp, clear lines of the story.

The concept of the mise en scène as a site where identities and scripts can be tried out is concretely applied in a rehearsal practice shared by Brecht and Mnouchkine. All the costumes from the company's past productions are laid out together, and the actors browse at will, choosing their own costumes, like the bit player in *The Threepenny Opera* who, after two days of searching and weighing every possibility, finally decided on the perfect hat. Mnouchkine goes further, not only encouraging the actors to improvise their own costumes (the chosen articles serve as the basis for the final costumes), but allowing them to choose the roles they will rehearse. The final casting is gradually and collectively decided, often with one actor taking more than one role, as in *Les Atrides*. This practice of actors' trying on roles and costumes to generate the mise en scène is also a way of turning identifications to *agency:* not essentialist identity as a unity of character with actor or spectator but identification as a *performative social act* in Butler's sense. This is especially important for the spectator watching Clytemnestra, Iphigenia, Electra, Cassandra, and Athena through the plays, aware that these characters are not autonomous subjects with whom one can simply identify or not, but subject positions constructed through gender and placed strategically to mark out a progressively cohering ideological system combining patriarchy with imperial hegemony. Not despite but *because of* this, the mise en scène is a site where roles and costumes can proliferate, and, thus, a site of potential agency. Historical agency is claimed by the actors in choosing their own costumes and roles and by the spectators in reading meanings that go "out of bounds" to reflect on, rather than accept as fate, the dominant social system being presented on stage. As is shown in the comments of Mnouchkine and costume designer Natalie Thomas, the company tries in many ways to facilitate such agency for the spectators but never to dictate the form that it takes:

> In the theater it isn't the same as in the cinema, where the spectators don't work but [are] bottle fed; in the warmth and dark one lets oneself be fed. In theater one is much less in the dark . . . and one works. The public peoples the stage. Thus I believe that the stage should be as empty as possible, so that the spectators can people it with the pictures they expect. . . . My dream would be to photograph the 600 stagings that the public produces in one evening!
>
> — Ariane Mnouchkine[20]

> The spectator sees in the appearance of the actor the evocation of an Assyrian frieze. . . . For another spectator, a hairstyle carries a reminiscence of Crete. . . . That is the richness of a mise en scène, the capacity to set the imagination of the spectator into play.
>
> — Nathalie Thomas[21]

In studying Mnouchkine's work one becomes aware of a distinction between her depiction of feminine and masculine gender (and even of sexuality itself) as something often destructive that is imposed by a power structure, in contrast to Cixous's rather more universalizing feminism that claims female sexuality as a repressed natural power potentially liberating for women. Unlike the proponents of *l'écriture féminine* and others, Mnouchkine does not propose a "femimesis" to replace Platonic-Aristotelian mimesis, but, through stage practice, she systematically revises the major assumptions of traditional mimesis.[22] The idea of tragic catharsis remains, but it is not reached through the spectator's "identification" with the individual character as an uncovering of a hidden mirror reflecting back the secrets of the spectator's own interior psyche. Rather, as Mnouchkine explains, the actors plunge into the interior of the work and of their characters and then express every emotional state *in the most exterior manner possible*. In contrast to psychological naturalism, which blends the actor's emotions together in a smooth, causal "motivated" development, the Théâtre du Soleil aims to represent one fully explored and *exteriorized* emotional *state* after another. The *états*, as they are called, are as separate from each other as the *mudras* of classical Indian theater and present the spectator with the elements and the freedom to join them into a history. A parallel to Mnouchkine's theory of catharsis is found in Brecht, although he did not call it "catharsis." The point for both of them is not that the actor and spectator should feel no emotional empathy for the character. The actor certainly must explore the psychological states of his or her character. Empathy and catharsis are not ends in themselves, however, but steps, pieces of a *montage* for the spectator to connect, on the way to illuminating the story. Whereas in "dramatic theater" the emotions of the characters are *expressed* only with "suggestions" of a deep *interior,* the epic theater *exteriorizes* them as fully legible *signification,* so that they are not kept in the *secret* interior of the individual but are out in the open, connecting with others to reveal *social relationships*. Brecht explains:

> [Empathy in epic theater] is a *rehearsal* measure. . . . Whatever empathy is achieved should incorporate no element of suggestion, i.e., the audience is not to be induced to empathise too. . . . For an actor in the present theater empathising himself and inducing the audience to empathise (suggestive empathy) are of course identical. . . . In reality the two . . . occur separately, and combining them is an art in itself, not *the* art. [artists of comedy often produce effects without suggestion.] it takes an artist to be effective without suggestion. Suggestive acting is something quite artificial. tension in certain parts of the muscular system, head movements executed as if pulling on an elastic band, the feet as if wading in tar, intermittent stiffness, sudden changes, moments of restraint, also monotony of voice, remembered from church responses, all this induces hypnosis, and it can be said that snakes, tigers, hawks and actors rival one another in this art.[23]

For *Les Atrides,* as for all of Mnouchkine's productions, the actors work closely with the musicians in creating a distinctive *écriture corporelle,* in this case inspired by the Kathakali yet unlike it in that a new corporal vocabulary is created with Western audiences in mind — although certain elements in this vocabulary are always passed on from one production to the next. Mnouchkine has deeply explored the *emotional athleticism* that Artaud could only invoke and that does not lead to hidden psychological depths but to the clarity of the epic *Verfrem-dungseffekt*. In Odette Aslan's words, the Théâtre du Soleil has evolved a mode of "recounting a history with the body, constantly addressing that narrative to the public, a way of speaking the text . . . that has nothing to do with the actor's . . . simply playing a situation with a partner. . . . [The theater has evolved] a mode of narrating founded on the body, a vocal expression wrested from the text to become a pure rhetoric. Body and voice are transposed, elevated in a gigantic effort of generosity."[24] Mnouchkine explains further:

> For *Les Atrides,* except for Catherine Schaub who had learned it in India [and Franco-Indian Nirupama Nityanandan, who had spent twenty years training as a Madras dancer], Kathakali is a source of inspiration but completely imaginary. *It isn't the techniques that are important for us, but the demands of clarity, of form, of minutia of detail.* In certain rehearsals, I sensed the bodies shaken, aggressed by the feelings unleashed; the dances, like chills or frictions, were liberating. We felt them like a vital, necessary element. . . . The tragic characters are in anguish to their entrails, the chorus of *Les Choéphores* [*The Libation Bearers*] is full of hatred and cries of vengeance. One must take the works head on and go to their depths. *Push to the depths the interior feeling and the exterior form.* Thus the emotion is born and the catharsis produces itself. [25]

Aslan and Mnouchkine explain, for example, that Simon Abkarian's tall, statuesque, straight-backed posture was particularly effective for embodying, after the manner of the gods and heroes of Kathakali, an almost superhuman masculinity. He becomes even more imposing through the voluminous black costume, stylized beard and wig, and white face with red mouth and black eyeliner magnifying the slightest change of expression. With his body and face weighed down and encased in the signs of his powerful status, he seems not simply unwilling but unable to bend. Standing beside Agamemnon, Clytemnestra, and especially Iphigenia, look tiny and vulnerable, but far more mobile. Their makeup is also white with black and red lines but more transparent, while their clothing is lighter in weight: Iphigenia, as played by Nirupama Nityanandan, looks like a fourteen-year-old in black knee pants and a white shirt, while Clytemnestra wears a matron's black dress. As Clytemnestra, Brazilian actor Juliana Carneiro da Cunha has the same white makeup and red lips but without the heavy eyeliner of the rest of the cast. She thus seems more fragile and exposed, inviting greater empathy. Everything about the mother and daughter emphasizes their vulnerability and naïveté (qualities that will mark the feminine as powerless), in contrast to the unbending, massive quality of Agamemnon (which defines masculine power). Clytemnestra will not wear a dress again in the following plays, but matadorlike trousers reminiscent of Iphigenia's. While masculinity is magnified, there are no magnified representations of femininity until the Furies appear at the end of *The Eumenides,* but they are demonic and bestial rather than outsized.

The Politics of Gender and Empire:
Iphigenia at Aulis

With Euripides' *Iphigenia at Aulis,* Mnouchkine brings new historical evidence to an old crime case. The recovery and playing out of Iphigenia's death, the murder of a virgin daughter by the sword of her father, becomes a historical mise en scène that will never go away. Whereas Aeschylus has the chorus in *Agamemnon* open the play with a narration that includes Iphigenia's sacrifice, Euripides' play gives a different account of this event, opening the *Oresteia* to new readings. In Aeschylus, Iphigenia is depicted as struggling against her sacrifice, while in Euripides she chooses to accept it. To use Butler's sense of the term, this creates a new mise en scène that in turn allows a proliferation of meanings that further undermine the trilogy's unequivocal idealistic interpretation as the victory of democratic law over blood revenge and civilization over barbarism. After *Iphigenia at Aulis,* where we witness Clytemnestra's trust shattered and her fight for her daughter's life defeated, she can no longer so easily embody the patriarchal fear of women's power. Stranded at Aulis with the whole Greek fleet, which cannot sail to attack Troy because the winds of Thrace have died, Agamemnon, as commander, hears from his priest that Artemis is angry: his "winged hounds" have killed a pregnant hare, and since the goddess protects wild mothers and their young, she will restore the winds only if he sacrifices Iphigenia. He vacillates but finally is persuaded by his brother Menelaus. Their reasons are political fears of looking unmanly and indecisive before the army and giving advantage to their rivals in Athens. Here Achilles is comically vain and not very bright — not his usual heroic self. Agamemnon has written for Iphigenia to come to Aulis to marry Achilles, and a pleased Clytemnestra soon arrives with her daughter and baby son Orestes to arrange the joyful celebration.

The first meeting of this family, as played out in the corporal writing of the actors, illuminates the interlocking politics of gender and empire. After entering on a gliding platform Clytemnestra and Iphigenia are helped down by the chorus of excited young women of Aulis who have traveled here to see the glorious Greek fleet. Simon Abkarian, as Aga-

memnon, enters and sits cross-legged on a low stool, spreading his voluminous black robes, facing forward as Iphigenia runs to him impul-
sively, dances around him, and embraces him. Clytemnestra pauses
from across the stage to greet him formally, then goes smiling to him
and sits on the floor before him, taking one of his arms and putting it
across her breast. Both are facing forward in the iconic family pose.
Later, in *Agamemnon,* she will go through the same ceremonious
greeting, running to take her wifely position at his feet — but this time
with a forced smile and at a faster, almost frantic pace. She will place his
hand across her breast as before, but he will soon take it away. Standing
up abruptly, he will inform her that he has brought his mistress Cassandra to the palace, and sweep his hand down over his genitals in a
gesture of disdain. This "genital sweep" is repeated throughout the
plays by other characters, including Clytemnestra and Cassandra, but
with different meanings. These gestured *states* one after the other
"write" the sign of gender as it intersects with social power.

In *Iphigenia at Aulis,* as Agamemnon's plan to sacrifice Iphigenia
becomes known, both wife and daughter plead with him not to do it.
Ironically, he argues that Iphigenia would die to save Greek women
from barbarians:

> There rages a passion in the Hellene host to sail with all speed to the
> barbarian land and to put an end to the rape of Hellene wives. They
> will kill my daughters in Argos, they will kill you, and me, if I break
> the gods' oracles. . . . It is Hellas for whom I must, whether I wish or
> not, offer you as sacrifice. . . . We are Hellenes; we must not allow our
> women to be violated and carried off by barbarians.
>
> — Agamemnon, *Iphigenia at Aulis,* 345

Agamemnon's decision unearths Clytemnestra's memory of the
past, and she reveals the violent prehistory of their marriage: Agamemnon killed her first husband, raped her, and crushed her baby to death
for fear he would grow up to avenge the father's murder. Clytemnestra's father then married her to Agamemnon against her will.
(Clytemnestra's father was also the father of the famous Helen, and had
made her suitors pledge to defend the honor of her chosen husband.
Thus, when Paris abducted Helen, her former suitors mobilized the
entire army to defend a Greek husband's honor — in a war for which
Helen was blamed.) Thus Clytemnestra connects past to present: men's
acts have determined her history. In the production the mother and
daughter crawl on their knees like children before the unbending figure
of Agamemnon. But Iphigenia, hearing her mother's outrage at her

father, unexpectedly decides to accept her death, the war, and all their spurious justifications:

> The whole might of Hellas depends on me. . . . Shall my single life be a hindrance to all this? . . . It is not right that [Achilles] die for a woman's sake [hers]. One man is worthier to look upon the light than ten thousand women. If Artemis has willed to take my body, shall I, a mortal woman, thwart the goddess? . . . I give my body to Hellas. . . . That will be my monument, . . . my children, my marriage. . . . It is natural for Hellenes to rule barbarians, and not, mother, for barbarians to rule Hellenes. They are a slave race, Hellenes are free.
>
> — Iphigenia, *Iphigenia at Aulis,* 348

To this speech Achilles admiringly replies, "Noble were your words, and a credit to your fatherland," and offers to marry her, now that it is too late. Clytemnestra gives way to grief, but Iphigenia suddenly breaks away with a defiant cry to join the chorus in a frenzied, exultant dance. Carneiro da Cunha, as Clytemnestra, crawls to her knees to stop them, grasps at their flying feet, and is nearly trampled. As the dance ends, the chorus recedes along the walls, the great outer doors open, and a platform-altar rolls in silently, its white drape fluttering gently as an ominous sign that the winds are beginning to stir. As Iphigenia walks toward the platform Clytemnestra rises to stop her but is held back by Achilles, who puts his hand over her mouth. She faints and falls backward, and is caught by two chorus women, as Iphigenia stands on the white-draped platform and calls out the single word "Père!" All exit but the mother and daughter, with Clytemnestra left lying on her side on the floor in the peaceful pose of a sleeping child or an unarmed protester in front of a tank. High on the altar, Iphigenia also lies down as if to sleep, taking the same position as her mother but with her head pointed in the opposite direction. The platform glides out into the darkness as the gates close behind it. Clytemnestra lies in her sleeping position throughout the speech of the Messenger, who narrates the scene of Iphigenia's death: how the girl expressed her love of her father and "the Greek fatherland" and offered her throat to the sword "with courage, without a cry." All closed their eyes "médusés" (literally, *medusa-ed;* figuratively, turned to stone) as they heard the sword descend and strike its target.[26] When they looked up again the next moment, the blood was spurting up from a wild deer's throat onto the altar of Artemis. Kneeling on the floor in a white robe and headdress spattered with blood, Georges Bigot as the Messenger delivers Agamemnon's news in a cold ringing voice: "I tell you what fortune he receives from the gods, and what *imperishable glory* he has won in Greece." A few lines later, on the words "This day has seen your child dead and alive,"

Clytemnestra finally opens her eyes. Agamemnon is rolled in, standing proudly on a platform, and orders her to return home and be joyful because Iphigenia has had "commerce with the gods," then he rolls away to war. As the great vehicle exits, Clytemnestra is left alone on stage. The drums begin as the lights dim except for the fluorescent "sun" above the tented ceiling; she begins to move slowly; the lights go dark, and the sound of vicious attacking dogs rises louder and louder and then blends into the audience's applause.

Thus the stage and actors are mobilized for a historical writing, a vocabulary of stage signs and relationships that will continue through the coming plays, mirrored and recast but with traces of the same, a construction, deconstruction, and reconstruction of the forms this history has adapted. The two conflicting versions of Iphigenia's sacrifice do not cancel out but instead proliferate its significance, which from the start cannot be confined to memorializing Agamemnon's glory and the rightness of the Greek war. Indeed, these meanings intended to serve the patriarchal empire were already being undermined at the "original scene" of sacrifice, which no one dared to witness but only represented.

The Casting of Actors:
Gendered Boundary Markers

The characters in the plays and the actors on stage defend, challenge, and progressively delineate the boundaries of the *Athenian body politic as mise en scène*. The actors' reappearance in more than one role emphasizes the functionality of the roles within the history being written. The materialist feminist distinction of gender as social construct and sex as biological is not quite sufficient here, because sexuality also involves a performance of power.[27] Juliana Carneiro da Cunha first appears in *Iphigenia at Aulis* as a woman content and proud in her place as a king's wife and loving mother to their children. When this idyll is shattered she discards her subservience and confronts Agamemnon and the army to save her daughter. She returns in *Agamemnon* as the worldly, embittered ruler of Argos, sarcastic and defiant against patriarchal disapproval, her blood-spattered face at the end grimly and sensually satisfied as she stands over the corpses of Agamemnon and Cassandra. She continues on this defiant course through the *The Libation Bearers,* her unnatural power signified by her unlawful sexual pleasure with Aegisthus, alienated from Electra and the chorus of harpylike slave women zealously loyal to the patriarchy. And Carneiro da Cunha appears twice more in *The Eumenides,* first as Clytemnestra's ghost still in the bloody clothes in which she was murdered, and finally as the goddess Athena. The last role becomes an ironic sequel to all preceding it, and a symmetry becomes apparent with the obedient wife at one end and the divine mouthpiece of the patriarchy at the other: one woman, the exchanged, is passed through the system challenging and defining its positions and borders along the way. Likewise the roles of Iphigenia, Cassandra, Electra, and finally a leader of the defeated Furies are played by Nirupama Nityanandan, underscoring their function as daughter roles within the patriarchy. The overall pattern that emerges for women is one of suffering, betrayal, rape, sacrifice, infanticide, matricide, and separation from each other, with daughters repeating the experience of mothers. There is no escaping the story.

The costumes of Clytemnestra and Iphigenia also reflect the performance of gender and their attempts to perform *against* it: Clytemnestra first appears in a matron's dress in *Iphigenia at Aulis* while Iphigenia wears matadorlike knee breeches. When Clytemnestra next appears, in *Agamemnon,* she wears similar breeches, while Nityanandan as Cassandra wears a heavy white Asian robe. This repetition-with-variation suggests a flight not to "freedom of gender identity" but from one constructed position to another, creating a sense of narrative displacement, of *a history rolling past to expose a social landscape.* Iphigenia's boylike costume ironically "fits" her decision to die, like a male hero, by the sword for "father and fatherland." After the death of Iphigenia, with similarly "masculine" decisiveness, Clytemnestra discards her feminine subservience and takes over the rule of Argos. Both women shift positions within, and challenge the limits of, the gendered political system even as they reaffirm it. Likewise, Simon Abkarian plays the father, son, and military men — Agamemnon, Achilles, the Emissary, Orestes, and even the drag role of Orestes' old nurse. As Orestes, Abkarian shows that his inherited role as champion of the patriarchy is difficult for him. This attitude is clear when Abkarian hides behind his father's tomb, the same platform that carried his father to war and Iphigenia to death.

In a sense the platform, too, appears as the same "actor" in different dress — its human (and sexual) quality is evoked by a tail of long black hair that hangs down over it (Orestes'? Electra's? Agamemnon's? The whole family has such hair). The chorus includes both men and women, but for each of the plays they all take on either the male or female gender. Although their dances retain the same basic moves, signs of gender, age, and class are added, emphasizing the "added on" quality of identity itself as theatrical. The positionality of their group identity is evident in the chesslike spatial patterns of the dancers, the red-black-gold "exotic" costumes worn by all, and the false beards of the old men of Argos—who perform the dances dutifully but in stiff and lumbering fashion, collapsing somewhat comically on the floor in exhaustion after each is completed, especially the one led by Clytemnestra.

Women also deceive, betray, and murder, but unlike the men they never carry these acts off with success. *They are what is trafficked in the exchange of power between men, and their flight or challenge is stopped by the limits of the system:* Clytemnestra is passed from father to husband, dares while in power to take Aegisthus as a "woman," only to be murdered by her son; still resisting even as a ghost, she is finally stopped by Apollo and, in a more profound way, by Athena. Iphigenia is passed from her father to Hades, her choice being to trade children for the fame of patriotic sacrifice. Electra repudiates her "female half" and marriage but submits her life to her dead father and then to her brother: she thinks Orestes' hair is her own, walks in his footprints, and is in effect absorbed by him. Cassandra is forced to be Apollo's prophet and "birth" his visions, then is captured and enslaved to Agamemnon. Yet there is a counterdiscourse created by the movement of these characters within the power structure, a movement illuminated by the multiple casting.

Speaking through Death

Nicole Loraux contends in *Tragic Ways of Killing a Woman* that the scenes of women being sacrificed are sites of unstable social meaning, because this death could be a way for them to speak, to condemn the patriarchy even as they submit to it.[28] In Gayatri Spivak's sense, Iphigenia is a subaltern who, like Kattrin in *Mother Courage,* speaks through her manner of death, in the very act of being silenced. Although real women in ancient Greece were allowed no social definition outside of the household of their fathers, husbands, brothers, and sons, in myth and tragedy they attain a certain subjecthood. To be sure, this subject is a fictional construct, yet historical agency for the character and the spectator is generated in their *mises en scène.* The discrepancy between Euripides' and Aeschylus's versions of the sacrifice opens the way for a counterdiscourse. Through the old men of Argos, Aeschylus tells a much more brutal tale than we have heard in Euripides:

Her prayers, and her cries of "Father," and her maiden life
they set at nothing, those military umpires. Her father
ordered his servants to lift her carefully over the altar
after the prayer, swooning, her clothes all round her,
like a young goat, and with a gag on her beautiful lips
to restrain the cry that would curse his house.
Constrained to voicelessness by the violence of the bit, . . .
She stood out, like a figure in a picture, struggling to speak. . . .
What happened after that I neither saw nor tell.

> — Chorus, *Agamemnon,* lines 230–245 [Italics mine.]

Because this narrative is told by men loyal to Agamemnon, it casts more doubt on the one in Euripides, which the Messenger delivered at Agamemnon's command.[29] In *Iphigenia at Aulis* the Messenger describes the scene as follows:

Every man clearly heard the sound of the stroke, but no one saw where in the world the maiden vanished. The priest cried out and the whole army echoed his shout as they saw an amazing prodigy from some god, incredible even if they saw it. *A deer was lying on the ground, gasping: she was very large and handsome to see, and the goddess's altar was thoroughly sprinkled with blood* . . . Calchas said with joy: "Do you see this victim which the goddess has laid before her altar, this *deer of the mountains?* More acceptable than the maid by far she welcomes this offering, that she may not stain her altar with noble blood."

> — Messenger, *Iphigenia at Aulis,* p. 353 [Italics mine.]

Loraux explains that Iphigenia's sacrifice violated the law and would have shocked Athenians. In Aeschylus she is hoisted upside down "like a goat" while in Euripides she is replaced by a deer. It was not only illegal to sacrifice humans, but also an abomination to sacrifice a wild animal or any animal that fought back. Only a "willing" offering was proper (32). In either case, the manner of Iphigenia's death proclaims that a murder has been committed under the guise of sacrifice — the crime of a father's murdering his own daughter is *reenacted* in Euripides by cutting the throat of a wild animal. The death means that a virgin's blood is exchanged for that of warriors. But another exchange also occurs, as Loraux explains: when Iphigenia is transformed into a deer "the savagery of the victim takes over from the savagery of the act. . . . When Artemis substitutes a mountain hind to die, untamed nature is now in the sacrifice" (35). The sacrifice is also a kind of reverse marriage and deflowerment by the father:

Sacrifices in tragedy illuminate the ritual in marriage where the virgin passes from one . . . guardian to another, from the father who "gives her away" to the bridegroom, who "leads her off." Hence the tragic irony of those funeral processions that ought to have been wedding processions. . . . They are weddings in reverse in that they lead toward a sacrificer, who is often the father, and . . . toward the home of a bridegroom called Hades. . . . The sacrifice . . . resembles, all too closely, a marriage. (36–37)

Iphigenia seizes for herself a heroic death reserved only for men, yet in doing so she also proclaims its savagery. In tragedy and in real life, the proper death for Greek women was strangulation, poison, or hanging. Electra takes a sword to guard the palace while Clytemnestra is being slain, and she stands ready to kill herself with it. Taking the prop of the male gender becomes a performative act. Orestes kills Clytemnestra with a sword in the text, but uses a long theatrical wooden dagger in the production, underlining the murder itself as a gender-sex performance. Cassandra is the subaltern subject par excellence: she manages to speak through her "barbarian" sounds and through her death to condemn her violators. As the visions from Apollo penetrate her, she screams out and, through the downward motion of her hand over her body in the "genital sweep," we witness a rape. Foreseeing her own violent death, she throws her prophet's scepter to the ground and spins screaming with her white robe flying outward in a circle. Significantly, her costume is a white embroidered robe of Noh theater, as befits her position of exotic foreign woman captured from the enemy land to the east.

Even though the chorus leader in *Agamemnon* describes Iphigenia's murder in brutal detail, the chorus refuses to credit this act as Clytemnestra's reason for murdering Agamemnon. They ascribe her act to two paradoxical qualities: her masculine greed for power and her feminine sexual passion. They believe that her usurpation of male rule will destroy Argos. A long tradition of critics has accepted the chorus's demonizing, misogynist view of Clytemnestra, and judged the sacrificial infanticide as an irrelevant excuse, not a credible motivation for murder. For these critics, as for the Argos elders, her crime is not only murder but proclaiming her female sexuality openly during the act of *impersonating* the male. Significantly, the chorus scornfully calls Aegisthus a "woman" because he lets Clytemnestra take responsibility for the murders. The Greek audience would also have recognized scandalous dishonor in Agamemnon's murder itself: to be killed with a sword was a proper hero's death, but death at the hands of a woman, even one who used a sword, signified social descent (Loraux, 10–11). In contrast to Aeschylus and the staging by Mnouchkine, iconic depictions of the myth show Aegisthus killing Agamemnon with a sword while Clytemnestra kills Cassandra with an ax, indicating an impulsive act and a domestic setting. In playing a role not assigned to women, Clytemnestra violates the patriarchal order of the state. Her murder of Agamemnon is the climax of her crime and brings her sexual enjoyment:

> (Clytemnestra to the Chorus:)
> Now it's against me that you proclaim banishment
> but in the old days you brought nothing against that man,
> who . . . had no care for the death of a lamb.
> He sacrificed his own daughter,
> dearest pain of my womb,
> to charm the contrariness of Thracian winds. . . .
> By the justice due to my child, and now perfected,
> by the Spirit of Destruction and the Fury,
> in whose honor I cut this man's throat. . . .
> There lies Agamemnon, this girl's [Cassandra's] seducer —
> he was the darling of all the women of Troy —
> and there she is, our prophet, prisoner of war,
> that shared his bed, a faithful whore that spoke her auguries for him.
>   . . .
> He died as I said, and she has sung her swan song in death,
> and lies with him, her lover.
> But to me she has brought an additional side dish
> to my pleasure in bed.
>
> — *Agamemnon*, 1413–1417, 1431–1446

Her sexual enjoyment of the revenge is taken as proof of her demonism and far outweighs Iphigenia's death. The politics of gender and empire are ironically complicit in this act: in obtaining justice for Iphigenia's death, she punishes the Trojan Cassandra, who is as innocent as her daughter. And whereas Iphigenia died to protect *Greek* women from being taken by Trojan men, here the Greek man has taken a Trojan woman.

The production of *Les Atrides* underscores in several ways the sad irony of Clytemnestra's murder of Cassandra: most important, Cassandra, Iphigenia, Electra, and a leader of the Furies are played by the same actress. In *Agamemnon* the chorus has just described the death of Iphigenia: how she struggled and tried to cling to the ground but was tied, hoisted up, held face down "like a goat," and gagged and silenced; then her throat was cut with a sword. Listening to this account, Clytemnestra is doubled over, a signal gesture for pain that will be repeated by several characters. Just at this moment, Cassandra appears upstage at the outer gateway on a chariot-platform, and Clytemnestra hesitantly takes a few steps towards her as if she recognized her; but the chorus blocks her path and the moment is gone. Later the same platform is taken into what seems to be the palace grounds, and the two women have a moment alone. Clytemnestra tears down the red cloth behind which Cassandra is sitting with her back turned, unwilling to come out. Clytemnestra tries to speak to her, asks her to use sign language, and even climbs up on the platform with her, but finally gives up. Recognizing the actress, we sense that somehow it *is* Iphigenia, and that if she only turned around or spoke, she and Clytemnestra would see it too.

Embodying the Foreign

As characters, all these women are "foreign" in their personal histories, having been taken by force or lured by deception from their native cities. In having the women embody foreignness and then display silence or submission, the threat of the foreign is *contained,* at least momentarily. The chorus of young women in *Iphigenia at Aulis* are the first foreigners we see, and after their initial dance they remark excitedly on the "foreign women," Iphigenia and Clytemnestra, whom they are eager to meet. The sisters Clytemnestra and Helen are foreign in their new cities, and Cassandra is captured by the Greeks from the "barbarian" Troy to the east and brought back to Argos. Cassandra is marked as the most oriental by her white robe from the Noh theater, the only "authentic" Asian costume: *she is a nexus where signs of empire, gender, class, and race intersect.* Most tragic is the foreignness of women to each other; this aspect is played out many times in the encounters between Clytemnestra and the daughter figures, first Cassandra and then Electra. Indeed, the women's failure to recognize each other is part of the whole avoidable history that feminism — and this production — tries to show us. In *The Eumenides,* the problem of foreignness is settled by divine decree: Athena forbids the Greeks to fight each other, but sanctions their communal hatred of others because (as the Furies now agree) this sort of hatred is good for the City. The trial scene officially celebrates the colonization of women, barbarian cultures, and all else that is a *useful* threat to the patriarchal Athenian city-state.

In both Aeschylus and Euripides, we see a radical but productive split in the author's positions vis-à-vis women: as usual, women serve an anchoring and embodying role in structuring the sociopolitical ideology into the image of a male-dominated body politic. But both authors are critical of militarism and war, and set Iphigenia's innocence against it. In Euripides, her selflessness and patriotism contrast sharply with the men's brutality in the name of saving civilization. Their specious argument that the sacrifice will save thousands of Greek women from the barbarians makes it plain that to the men who deal in military, political, and colonial power the world is a game board divided into territories, and women are dispensable objects who can be moved into any position — other or same, familiar or foreign — that suits their immediate quests for power.

Aeschylus has traditionally been thought less sympathetic than Euripides to Clytemnestra, though this picture might have been different if his play *Iphigenia* had not been lost. In any case, in *Agamemnon* the arrogant machismo of war leaders comes under bitter attack in the first speech of the chorus, and then in that of the exhausted Emissary, who recounts the great losses (the lowly Emissary and the powerful Agamemnon and Achilles are all played by Simon Abkarian). The brutal murder of Iphigenia and the war's devastation of the lives of ordinary people are thus the immediate frame of reference through which Clytemnestra's own bitterness is presented. This context undercuts the chorus's later misogynist depiction of Clytemnestra as a power-hungry sexual demon usurping the role of a worthy husband and ruler.

Mnouchkine's production of *The Eumenides* strongly historicizes the text's depiction of the feminine Furies/Eumenides and by implication of women themselves as elemental irrational forces that must be tamed and submerged by rational male forces. Although the preceding plays are epic in their practice of *Verfremdung, The Eumenides* becomes overtly so, even "quoting" Brechtian details of production. Through the striking addition of contemporary costume elements, the Furies are exposed as an embodiment of demonic femininity, a monstrous foreign other, a *construction* against which the patriarchal state defines itself. When the Furies finally appear, they are revealed as the "real" source of the sound of raging dogs we heard at the close of each of the preceding plays. As the Furies, the chorus now wear fierce dog-ape masks, snarl, and move with an apelike gait, and whereas the choruses in the preceding plays were free to climb over, sit on, or stand behind the inner wall, to retreat to its recesses, and go in and out of its entrances, all the openings are now blocked by metal grates behind which the Furies are trapped. The quality of anachronistic pastiche in the costumes is verified by critics' comparison of the Furies to creatures from *2001: A Space Odyssey* or *Planet of the Apes*.[30] The three Leaders of the Furies, by contrast, wear tennis shoes and the earth-toned, rough-spun, ragged clothing of Brechtian characters — or, in the words of one critic, "Brechtian bag ladies,"[31] with Nirupama Nityanandan dressed and posed like Mother Courage. The ghost of Clytemnestra appears, still blood-spattered and wearing the same red cloak and black knee pants in which she died, whereas Apollo wears a white robe that evokes both Louis XIV and an oriental potentate, but that also recalls the white robe of the Messenger who narrated the death of Iphigenia — except that the blood is now gone. As in other instances, the repetition in costumes and multiple casting creates its own historicizing comment. Carneiro da Cunha soon returns as Athena to address Nirupama Nityanandan, who is now a Leader of the Furies. Through this *counternarrative* created by the repetitions in casting and costume, and the anachronisms of the final scene, the unified image of the Greek cosmos is shattered, and, along with it, the discursive unity of the myth itself.

We recall that two of the preceding plays ended with a violent tableau of two mannequin corpses lying in sexual embrace on a bloody mattress. In this context, the voices of attacking dogs gave a sense of recurrent *human* brutality in which both sexes participate. With all this preceding *The Eumenides,* we literally cannot believe our eyes when all the violence is attributed to the feminine elements gathered here, represented by Clytemnestra and the Furies. Textually, the winged hounds of Agamemnon are never quite forgotten even though the Furies are set up as the apparent source of the violent sound. As increasingly contemporary embodiments of violent feminine forces they expose their semiotic function of *grounding* the patriarchal Greek state. Athena herself, recognizable as the same actress who played Clytemnestra, ironically stands on yet another white mattress, a clean one this time, as if it were a throne or pedestal. When the Furies finally accept their new role as guardians of the hearth, Athena confers upon them the privilege of standing on it as well. The stage narrative of the mattresses culminates in this last play. We recall that Aegisthus and Clytemnestra managed only with difficulty to drag the mattress off by themselves, whereas Electra and Orestes had to be assisted by the chorus. But at the end of *The Eumenides* not even the combined forces of humans, gods, and Furies can drag it off. And in contrast to all the preceding plays, the gliding platforms of "inevitable fate" never reappear here at all.

This staging of the women's final defeat does not totally serve the patriarchy, however, nor erase the threat it feels. The barring of the performance space by metal grates is only the final concretization of a long historical process, the open, flagrant admission of what the signs have been telling us all along: that Greece is a militaristic, racist, patriarchal empire, and Athens a city-state and an Idea whose borders must be policed. Athena, standing on her white mattress, notes that the site of the trial that will soon exonerate Orestes and disempower the Furies was also the spot where the Amazons fought against Theseus, legendary founder of Athens. Here where the iron gates stand was a *city within the City.*

ATHENA [to the assembled men of Athens, who are about to vote]
For this is Ares' hill, place of the Amazons;
here their tents stood when they came here campaigning
in hatred against Theseus; here they built
tower against tower, *a new city against the City.*
                            — *The Eumenides*, lines 684–687 [Italics mine.]

It is my task to render final judgment:
this vote which I possess
I will give on Orestes' side.
For no mother had a part in *my* birth;
I am entirely for the male, with all my heart,
except in marriage; I am entirely my father's.
I will never give precedence in honor
to a woman who killed her man, the guardian of her house.
                    — Athena, *The Eumenides*, lines 733–740; 161–162

This city within the City has never disappeared from the Greek state as a mental territory in the Western imagination because the threats to that territory — its *others* — are still perceived. In the text the threat literally goes underground, as the Eumenides are escorted to their subterranean home by a crowd of Athenian women and girls, by association joining the Amazons. In the production, however, the bars are lifted and the Furies are "freed" only to enter the performance arena, where they first rush toward the audience in their apelike gait, screaming and gesturing from the edge of the stage, then gradually take on human posture, as they end the play with a dance that little by little comes to resemble those in the preceding plays. Then they are forced back behind the gates. In the final image of *The Eumenides,* Athena/da Cunha stands in her white judolike costume, conspicuously clean of blood spots in contrast to the blood-spattered white costumes of characters in earlier scenes in the plays. In this closing moment of the tetralogy, da Cunha is left alone on stage, turns her back to the audience, and raises her trembling arms as if to hold back some invisible force. Thus a kind of terrible peace is reached.

Strangely, few reviewers or ordinary spectators mention or even seem to have noticed the Guards of Apollo who appeared briefly at the end and beginning of *The Eumenides,* even though they were in plain view and were listed in the program. They stood face out forming a barrier between the stage and spectators, dressed in black uniforms and opaque black net headgear recalling that of beekeepers, carrying cellular phones and watching the spectators silently. Those who saw them were truly frightened — even when they realized that it was all part of the performance. Even at the Cartoucherie, where it is unheard of to have police in the theater, almost no one saw the Guards, and no one in the New York audience mentions them, so well did they blend into what has become an ordinary scene of security police controlling the crowd. This in itself is an eloquent *Gestus*, a proof of the unbroken legacy of state terror from past to present times.

Thus the mise en scène is a *body politic* closing in just as it becomes visible. When Athena embraces the Leader of the Furies, who is about to be led away, it is one more ironic sealing of the women's defeat. The painful irony of mother set against daughter, goddess against demon, trapped forever as *positions* within the patriarchal system, becomes even sharper. However, since the spectators know that these two actresses also played Clytemnestra and Iphigenia, the Gestus of their closing embrace has multiple meanings. The embrace is also quite moving, because we have watched these two since they were a mother and daughter torn apart in the first play, and later have seen them pass by each other, each fighting her battle alone, needing and yet failing to recognize the other. Thus there is also a joy that they are finally reunited, because this moment has been so long in coming. In fact, the stage image of ragged women embracing each other has recurred at the end of many Théâtre du Soleil productions over the years, and has become a kind of signature of Mnouchkine herself, both epic and feminist at once. The spectator's *identification* of these small signs of women's solidarity has become a performative act in itself, a counterdiscourse to the master narrative, even in the moment it inscribes defeat. As a whole, the mise en scène illuminates the violent story through which the City still inscribes itself as the dawn of democracy and the victory of civilization, law, and rationality over barbarism, revenge, and irrationality.

Yet Aeschylus, in identifying the site of this inscription as the very site where the Amazons also fought, enables another story and space to be constructed, a hidden city in the shadow of the patriarchal one.

The Critical Reception

Although the critical and public reception of *Les Atrides* was in general overwhelmingly positive, the response to it, as to other Mnouchkine productions, often mirrors the very mindsets that the work tries to theatrically expose and interrogate: bourgeois universalism, an obliviousness to colonialism, and a hatred and fear of women in power. The addition of *Iphigenia at Aulis,* the seemingly abrupt shift to modern times in *The Eumenides,* and the illumination of sexual politics in *Les Atrides* as a whole has caused divided reactions among the critics: some think that this has "distorted" the plays (from what norm is not stated).[32] Some think a feminist interpretation is long overdue; others see it pragmatically as "good theater and good feminism,"[33] and still others believe that the performance succeeds in spite of Mnouchkine's feminist outlook because *good theater overcomes feminist dogma*.[34] True to her materialist principles, she barely conceals her exasperation with those who still manage, despite all evidence to the contrary, to see *Les Atrides* as an ahistorical, apolitical, archetypal struggle between Man and Woman. In several interviews such as the one below for *Theater Heute,* she takes the historicizing stance of materialist feminism without calling attention to it as such:

> EBERHART SPRENGE: Agamemnon seemed to lean towards his right side in *Iphigenia,* as if leaning towards the rational: was this meant to indicate the battle between reason and feeling, and the battle of the sexes?
>
> ARIANE MNOUCHKINE: [reacts with amusement to the notion of the actor leaning to the right] . . . The battle of the sexes was not a theme for me in rehearsal. Naturally it is an important motif in the plays. Most tragedy again and again reports murders of women. When one produces *Iphigenia* and the *Oresteia,* naturally one notices that in the first play a woman [Iphigenia] is murdered, in the second Agamemnon and Cassandra, in *The Libation Bearers* Clytemnestra, and in the *Eumenides* it is the absolute defeat of the Furies that is shown. With this one doesn't need to put a special emphasis on it. *Iphigenia* tells of the battle of a woman, Clytemnestra, for the life of her daughter, and against the greed for power, fame, dominance, and the leadership of an army.[35]

Sprenge's linking of the "battle of the sexes" to the polarity of "reason versus feeling" through the familiar equation of men with reason and women with feeling is exactly the kind of essentializing that Mnouchkine aims to deconstruct. Sprenge's formula comes from the same patriarchal discourse of gender that has been used to naturalize historically contingent political and social relations from ancient Greece until today, and which *Les Atrides* tries to illuminate by theatrical means — obviously not with total success for every spectator.

Mnouchkine's adaptations of Asian theater forms, her periodic return to Western classics, and her insistence that the mise en scène retain an imaginative distance and a fantastic theatricality have led some to accuse her of abandoning her leftist ideals in favor of an escapist, decorative, irresponsible, ultimately safe high-art theater. Nothing could be farther from the truth, and the practices for which she is criticized are precisely those of epic theater. A comparison of her work and its reception with that of Peter Brook is instructive on this question. On the surface her work parallels Brook's: he too has been on an "orientalist" quest for over a decade (with Africa added to Asia). However, while critics often fault Mnouchkine with being an ideologue, Brook is perceived as non-ideological. Patrice Pavis, for instance, calls Mnouchkine's *L'Indiade* a dry, didactic "exercise" in historicization to which it was impossible to relate, while he unconditionally praises Brook's adaptation of *The Mahabharata* as "charming" and universal. Of *L'Indiade* he writes: "All the formal theatre research has given way to a rather sterile exercise in imitation . . . of historical figures and ethnic groups"; and of *The Mahabharata:* "For Brook, the actors are involved in . . . almost a ritual search for authenticity . . . they do not attempt to imitate the world [of India], but try to preserve the sacred quality of their performance."[36] Striking also is Pavis's language which colors Mnouchkine as a tyrant and Brook as a liberator: while Mnouchkine "*delegates* a member of the [Indian] lower classes . . . to comment on the action," Brook "*gave* two French actors the roles of narrator and intermediary between myth and audience."[37] In describing this use of mediators between the "source culture" and the "target culture" in the two productions, Pavis overlooks the privileging, even unintentionally colonialist effect of Brook's using two white, French-speaking men as narrators while the other actors were nearly all people of color from non-Western countries. This casting pattern was repeated in the English-language production and in the subsequent film by placing two white British men in these positions. *Les Atrides* has more in common with Brook's *Marat/Sade* than with *The Mahabharata,* because the first two expose to historical critique ideological constructs and power relations formative of our own society. Thus the difference between Brook and Mnouchkine is analogous to that between Barrault and Brecht: one approach wants to stage a universalizing, dehistoricized, "history of humanity," while the other disavows universality and tries to historicize "humanity on stage."

The playing out of historical power relations through embodiment and impersonation even went beyond the limits of the performance itself. The Théâtre de Soleil's production toured internationally, appearing in the English milltown of Bradford, and in New York, Berlin, and Montreal, each time in widely different physical spaces and environments.[38] Though, as stated, the overall critical response was quite positive, whenever negative criticism did appear a distinct pattern was discernible in many of the (male) critics' reports from the various sites of the tour: they tended to experience the staging, the performance area, the theater building, and even the outside environment as a *pro-*

jected embodiment of the female persona of Ariane Mnouchkine herself. The most striking reviews were those that sensed in the whole event the displaced but ominous qualities of a controlling feminine (and foreign) ideologue, a "forbidding French intellectual,"[39] who forced the audience to endure "punishing bleacher seats" in an "airless" atmosphere on stage and in the auditorium.[40] Their perception of the performance seemed to involve being enveloped in a woman's presence that was diffused throughout the theater space — at worst a hostile, foreign, militant atmosphere, and at best a cozy maternal one. The director herself is thus conflated with the theater space — just as the chorus attributed the still air of Aulis and the oppressive atmosphere of Argos to the fact that a woman was in power. *Plus ça change, plus c'est la même chose.*

In summary, through the signs of a fantasized Asian theater, *Les Atrides* sets a double *Verfremdungseffekt* into dialectical motion: in attempting to keep the text "as we know it" from dissolving into its new "oriental" setting, we can hear it with new clarity. At the same time, the interlocking sexual and imperial politics are brought to light through many nonverbal stage discourses, so that we can retrace the familiar *Oresteia* story as a playing out and legitimization of a set of power relations that we recognize all too well because they still exist today. Although the multiracial cast and the Kathakali-inspired dances, costumes, make-up, and bodily language of Gestus in *Les Atrides* do make the performance appear exotic, the East becomes a stage sign that is exposed as such, as a repertoire of images used to write a story in the space/time of a theatrical arena. But in being written the unity of the myth is not shored up but visibly disintegrates. Signs of the East share this arena with signs from the West, from Greek theater to contemporary film. In its cumulative effect, the borrowing does not *reproduce* and perpetuate the reduction of India or Asia to a colonized other, but illuminates this orientalism as a borrowing of living traditions in order to retell and interrogate a founding story of the West. Wherever the colorful figures originated, and whatever their proportion of Eastern and Western ingredients, the abiding memory is that they unearthed themselves to walk up from the past, dance for us, and rewrite the old yet new story of the House of Atreus.

Notes

[1] Ariane Mnouchkine, interview with Eberhard Sprenge, *Theater Heute* 6 (June 1991), 9. See also Peter von Becker in "Die Inszenierung: 'Les Atrides,'" 1–10, in the same issue. All translations from German and French sources are mine, unless otherwise indicated.

[2] Roland Barthes, "Comment représenter l'Antique?" *Théâtre Aujourd'hui No.1. La Tragédie Grecque. Les Atrides au Théâtre du Soleil* (Paris: CNDP, 1992), 48–51. Originally in *Théâtre Populaire* (1955); reprinted in *Les essais critiques* (Paris: Éditions de Seuil, 1964).

[3] Edward Said, *Orientalism* (New York: Vintage, 1979), 4–5. See also Hayden White, *Tropics of Discourse* (Baltimore: Johns Hopkins UP, 1978); and Gayatri Chakravorty Spivak, "Can the Subaltern Speak?", in *Marxism and the Interpretation of Culture*, eds. C. Nelson and L. Grossberg (Urbana and Chicago: U of Illinois P, 1988), 271–313. Spivak is the preeminent postcolonialist, deconstructive feminist critic.

[4] Barthes, ibid., 51.

[5] Bernard Dort, Lecture at Université de Paris VIII, June 15, 1986.

[6] Ariane Mnouchkine, interview with Adrian Kiernander, in Kiernander, *Ariane Mnouchkine and the Théâtre du Soleil* (Cambridge: Cambridge UP, 1993), 142.

[7] Artaud's influential view of Balinese theater as an exotic, opaque, and thus universal language is opposed to that of Brecht who admired Chinese theater because he thought it allowed an escape from the trance effect and universalizing of Western naturalism. Artaud, to a lesser extent, and Brecht misunderstood the Asian theaters' meaning to their own cultures and imagined them as all that Western theater was not. An informative article on Western borrowing from Indian theater is Rustom Bharucha's "A Collision of Cultures: Some Western Interpretations of the Indian Theatre," *Asian Theatre Journal* 1 (Spring 1984), 1–20.

[8] Said, ibid., 2–3.

[9] Said, ibid., 6–7.

[10] Sue-Ellen Case, in her *Feminism and Theatre* (London: Routledge, 1988), includes an influential chapter, "Deconstructing the Canon," which points out the sexist violence of the *Oresteia* and the myths of Athena and the Amazons.

[11] Disaffected company members, critics, and others have sometimes criticized Mnouchkine for being authoritarian and thus betraying the company's collectivist ideals, to which she replies that authoritarianism is never perceived as a fault in male directors. In *Ariane Mnouchkine and the Théâtre du Soleil*, Adrian Kiernander quotes Mnouchkine in a revealing remark: "A man who knows that he is double [part feminine] is a complete man. The men I work with have overcome the misogyny which permeates our society. They are, I would say, more civilized. The boys of the Soleil are very careful not to let themselves fall back into misogynist reflexes" (131).

[12] Barthes, ibid., 51.

[13] David Grene, "Introduction," *The Oresteia by Aeschylus*, trans. David Grene and Wendy Doniger O'Flaherty (Chicago and London: U of Chicago P, 1989), 15.

[14] Foucault, *The History of Sexuality,* trans. Robert Hurley (New York: Vintage, 1980).

[15] Butler theorizes these terms in *Gender Trouble: Feminism and the Subversion of Identity* (New York and London: Routledge, 1990); and "Performative Acts and Gender Constitution: An Essay in Phenomenology and Feminist Theory," in *Performing Feminisms: Feminist Critical Theory and Theatre,* ed. Sue-Ellen Case (Baltimore: Johns Hopkins UP, 1990): 270–284.

[16] Teresa de Lauretis, *Technologies of Gender: Essays on Theory, Film, and Fiction* (Bloomington: Indiana UP, 1987); and *Alice Doesn't: Feminism, Semiotics, Cinema* (Bloomington: Indiana UP, 1984).

[17] V. P. Dhananjayan, *A Dancer on Dance* (Madras, India: Bharata Kalanjaali, 1991). Dhananjayan, head of a national dance institute at Madras, writes: "Kathakali is an indigenous . . . dance drama from Kerala in the south west of India. Kerala, situated as it is on the coast of the Arabian Sea, claims ancient contact with countries like Egypt, Syria, Rome and Greece and to a certain extent, these contacts are reflected in the art, literature and society of that area. It is said that even Kathakali shows traces of the influence of other countries" (26). Of course, there is also the opposite possibility: that the Indian influence made its way to Greece, as it did to all of Asia.

[18] *Iphigenia at Aulis,* in *Euripides: Ten Plays,* trans. Moses Hadas and John McLean (New York: Bantam, 1960), 354. Subsequent passages from this volume will be referenced by character, play, and page numbers in the body of the essay.

[19] Aeschylus, *Agamemnon,* in *The Oresteia: Agamemnon, the Libation Bearers, the Eumenides,* trans. David Grene and Wendy Doniger O'Flaherty (Chicago and London: U of Chicago P, 1989), 368. Subsequent passages from this volume will be referenced by character, play, and line numbers in the body of the essay.

[20] Ariane Mnouchkine, *Theater Heute,* 7.

[21] Natalie Thomas, "Les Costumes et les Maquillages," *Théâtre Aujourd'hui 1: La Tragédie Grecque. Les Atrides au Théâtre du Soleil.* Paris: CNDP, 1992, 32. Thomas has designed for the Théâtre du Soleil for more than a decade, from the Shakespeares onward. She also designed for Mnouchkine's film *Molière* and the staging of *Mephisto* before coming permanently to the theater.

[22] See Elin Diamond, "Mimesis, Mimicry, and the True-Real," in *Modern Drama* 32 (March 1989): 58–72.

[23] Bertolt Brecht, diary entries January 11 and 14, 1941, in *Bertolt Brecht: Plays, Poetry and Prose,* eds. John Willett and Ralph Manheim (New York: Routledge, 1996), 124–126.

[24] Odette Aslan, "Au Théâtre du Soleil les acteurs ecrivent avec leur corps" (At the Théâtre du Soleil the actors write with their bodies), in *LE CORPS EN JEU,* ed. Aslan (Paris: C.N.R.S. Éditions, 1993), 294.

[25] Ariane Mnouchkine, "Écorchement et Catharsis" (Flaying and Catharsis), in *LE CORPS EN JEU*, 296.

[26] The Messenger quotes Iphigenia during his account: "'Sans cri, j'offrirai mon cou, avec courage.' Voilà ce qu'elle a dit. Tous était médusés en entendant." From the translation commissioned by Mnouchkine: Euripides, *Iphigénie à Aulis*, trans. Jean and Mayotte Bollack (Paris: Les Editions de Minuit, 1990), 91. For this essay I also consulted Mnouchkine's own translation of Aeschylus's *L'Orestie. Agamemnon. Les Choéphores, Les Eumènides* (Paris: Théâtre du Soleil, 1990). She translated *Les Choéphores* as well. She and the Bollacks, who are classics scholars, consulted the earliest versions of the play from the ninth century. These translations contain excellent critical notes.

[27] See Judith Butler's essay "Bodies That Matter," in her *Bodies That Matter: On the Discursive Limits of "Sex,"* ed. Butler (New York and London: Routledge, 1993).

[28] Nicole Loraux, *Tragic Ways of Killing a Woman*, trans. Anthony Forster (Cambridge and London: Harvard UP, 1987), 10–11.

[29] Some scholars point to evidence that in Euripides' original version Artemis spoke directly to Clytemnestra, saying: "I shall put a horned deer into the Achaeans' dear hands, and they shall imagine, as they sacrifice it, that they are sacrificing your daughter." *Iphigenia at Aulis*, 354.

[30] Linda Winer, in "The Splendid Pageantry of Greek Tragedy, *New York Newsday,* October 6, 1991, 11, compares the Furies to "goofy ghouls [who] seem a bit too much like something from Oz or 'The Planet of the Apes.'" Frank Rich thinks they look like creatures from Kubrick's *2001: A Space Odyssey*. In "Taking the Stage to Some of Its Extremes," *The New York Times,* October 6, 1992, B1 and B4.

[31] See Jack Kroll, "Blood and Bones of Tragedy," *Newsweek* (October 5, 1992): 51: "Mnouchkine turns the three chief Furies into bag ladies, dressed in tattered duds and sneakers." John Rockwell describes them as "three harpies straight from a Brechtian proletarian netherworld," in "Behind the Masks of a Moralist," *New York Times,* September 27, 1991, 5.

[32] Benedict Nightingale, in "Epic Rewoven in Human Terms," *Life and Times* (London), July 20, 1992, reviews the *Les Atrides* production at Bradford, England, and writes: "When Simon Abkarian's Agamemnon trundles back from Troy like some pristine Nazi, his smug face just visible above the red drapery of his moving platform — well, what decent mother would not stick a spear into him? That is a distortion and causes some awkwardness in this all-French *Oresteia*." As Marvin Carlson notes, Nightingale is so influenced by being in Bradford, a milltown, that he uses language such as "the original story has been lovingly reknit by one of the world's great directors." I would only add that Nightingale uses distinctly maternal imagery.

[33] The exact line is: "Her grief at the sacrifice of her daughter makes her murder of her husband more understandable. It's better theater and better feminism." John Rockwell, "Behind the Masks of a Moralist,"5.

[34] Linda Winer, in "The Splendid Pageantry of Greek Tragedy," writes: "This is not to suggest that Mnouchkine has reduced the works to anything as one dimensional as dogmatic sexual politics."

[35] Ariane Mnouchkine, interview with Eberhard Sprenge, *Theater Heute,* 10.

[36] Patrice Pavis, *Theatre at the Crossroads of Culture* (London and New York: Routledge, 1992), 198, 202. The generally useful concepts of a "source culture" and a "target culture" are difficult to apply to a performance like *Les Atrides.* First, there are at least two "source cultures," India and Greece. More important, from a postcolonialist standpoint, these ostensibly neutral terms imply equal status of two cultures while the critic actually centers on his own "target culture" and marginalizes the other. What is called the target is the critic's source position. Because these terms are already polar, they cannot remain neutral.

[37] Pavis, ibid., 202. Italics mine.

[38] My thanks to Marvin Carlson for sharing his documentary material on *Les Atrides* and for his useful essay "*Accueil* on the Road: Mnouchkine's *Les Atrides* in Context," in *Assaph* C 8:1992: 153–160, which concerns the diverse reception of the work by critics reacting to the different physical and social environments at various cities where the production toured.

[39] John Rockwell, in "Behind the Masks of a Moralist," writes: "She combines the images of a . . . nurturing mother and forbidding French intellectual,"5.

[40] Frank Rich, in "Taking the Stage to Some of Its Extremes," B1 and B4, projects misogynist hostility toward Mnouchkine onto the theater environment and vice versa: he calls her a "champion control freak" with "strict rules to be obeyed." He feels a "militaristic atmosphere" in her theater "which even extends to the director's choices of venue, whether an armory in Brooklyn or a former munitions factory outside Paris — it is easy to imagine the chilling authenticity she will bring to [her next project]." Rich was misinformed about the Théâtre du Soleil's aims, methods, and home venue in the Cartoucherie, which is without doubt one of the warmest, most welcoming, and least stuffy in Europe, if not in the world.

The messenger from Troy, with the Chorus of Elders. Agamemnon, 1990–91.
By permission of the Théâtre du Soleil. © Michèle Laurent, CNDP.

Iphigenia dances before her execution. Iphigenia at Aulis,
1990–91. By permission of the Théâtre du Soleil.
© Michèle Laurent, CNDP.

Afterword: Epic Theater and the Imagination of History

WHAT CAN BE LEARNED from the epic theater's stage critique of the representation of space, time, and history? It is, above all, the lesson that history is written and perceived in spatial and temporal images specific to each era and culture. In the twentieth century, epic theater originated during a crisis of representation wherein the old set of images of space, time, and history became irreconcilable with the new. For Brecht and Piscator's generation in the 1920s new mass media and technology offered hope in that they registered the multiple human perspectives of the metropolis but also despair in that they made mass warfare more efficient. Earlier crises in representation were confronted by the *Sturm und Drang* playwrights on the eve of the French Revolution and by Georg Büchner one generation afterward, with all of them disillusioned by the Revolution's failure to eliminate oppression and Büchner horrified by science's reduction of all life to a mechanical process. Our own era has seen the rise of postmodern distrust, passivity, and relativism toward all media of communication; and with the fall of the Berlin Wall the map of the planet has changed from its old division into First, Second, and Third Worlds, while multinational economic alliances render national borders obsolete. The search for insights from epic theater and its legacy is an attempt to face this crisis.

What lessons from epic theater can help us face the present situation? One important lesson, disseminated far beyond the theater, is how to intervene critically as spectators of mass media that represent war and other complex and fateful events in sound bites and rapid images on the video or movie screen, rather than passively acquiescing to the play of images. The other lesson, related to the first, is that theater can still be used as a forum to stage and critique the crises of our own era, to help us see the images we have constructed of our own historical existence, constructions that have real-life consequences.

The lessons of epic theater have not been taken up everywhere simultaneously, as Marc Silberman notes in an essay written just after the fall of the Berlin Wall.[1] In the U.S. and Europe of the 1960s the antiwar, civil rights, women's liberation, gay rights, and farm workers' movements rediscovered the practices of Piscator, Brecht, and the agitprop troupes of the 1920s, and used them as models in creating an activist theater to mobilize their public. Also in the 1960s came a need to confront what Marshall McLuhan exposed as the "massage" of the media. Responding to this need, John Berger's *Ways of Seeing* draws the strength of its interventionist critique of old and new visual media directly from Walter Benjamin's profound insights as a fellow traveler of Brecht and Piscator in the 1920s and 1930s.[2] Beginning in the 1970s the struggles in Latin America, Africa, and Asia for liberation from neocolonialism and state oppression have engaged epic practice in an activist theater that promotes social consciousness, incorporating this practice with indigenous theater forms and content. In the West at the end of the twentieth century new insights are being sought not only in relation to the mass media but also to a theater that is no longer the broad public forum it was in the past.

One way to marshal the strength of theater as a social forum is to reexamine the relationships among the practices of theater artists, historians, and theorists, and try to discern the common aims that transcend their different methods and training. The attempt to examine our habits of thinking about history is one such aim. Theater historian Thomas Postlewait argues that these habits have led to such widely accepted oversimplifications as the reduction of Renaissance theater to a polar struggle between the sacred and the secular.[3] Important research into our habits of imagining history has been done not only by historiographers but also by socially committed theater artists, especially those who have continued to develop the practices of epic theater, including the directors Joan Littlewood, Ariane Mnouchkine, Peter Stein, Rustom Bharucha, JoAnne Akalaitis, and Tina Landau, who work with actors to create *a critical writing of and by the human body in the time and space of performance.*[4] Through this work the actors and spectators become increasingly aware, as individuals living in a specific culture, that we have developed certain modes of perceiving ourselves in relation to the real space that we inhabit; likewise, our ways of perceiving time prescribe and limit how we imagine our movement from past to present to future. Postlewait has discerned a number of these habitual ways of imagining history:

— looking for chains of cause and effect,
— following arcs to their projected endpoint even after they have dropped out of their expected path,
— equating cause with intention,
— equating effect with anything that happens to follow,
— rigidly separating event from context,
— projecting the pattern of inside-versus-outside onto all phenomena,
— adhering to this pattern even when relationships have shifted,
— and, most crucially, following an *oppositional mandate.*

This mandate is the organizing of historical data, including our day-to-day personal experience, into oppositional polar structures that we attempt to retain, even to the point of emptying them of specific historical material. These modes of imagining past and present experience, in turn, help perpetuate oppressive and often destructive arrangements of power in the social and political spheres. In short, we apply preordained unities to *make sense* of a world that is too various for us. This making sense is circumscribed by our own naturalized perceptions of ourselves and our physical presence in the world. While they articulate the problem differently, the historian and the historically critical theater artist struggle equally to become aware of these habits. The struggle waged by artists is located at what I will term the *ground zero of historical consciousness,* as they try to illuminate the experiential, corporal norms through which we construct, map out, destroy, and reconstruct our space and time — our own historical *sites.*

The reversibility of the values of spatio-temporal signs is what makes epic theater's dialectical contradiction possible. Indeed, the historicizing of spatio-temporal signs is at the heart of the work of all the artists discussed in this book. It is important to note that the gradual rejection over the past four centuries of the absolute opposition of space and time and the other opposite pairings, such as interior and exterior, backward and forward, horizontal and vertical, beginning and end, and history and nature, has also irrevocably undermined the long-unquestioned theological oppositions of body and soul, and body and mind. Now we conceive of a theater in which *the human body may speak and write* through movement and words. This is possible because the body is no longer considered a separate entity from the mind, spirit, and soul; all are incorporated into one whole. The same shift is also seen in Foucault's contention that the *soul* may act as *a prison of the body,* in the sense that the concept of Soul, like that of Hegel's History as Spirit, does not necessarily set human subjects free but may tyrannically define, control, and, thus, enslave them.

The *Gestus* is the main organizing principle of epic spatio-temporality, both as an aesthetic structure and as a sociohistorical signifier of ideology. The relationship among the actors is presented as a stage constellation that *materializes* the characters' social relationships in the separate scenes and for the work as a whole. The Gestus is also a nexus where spatio-temporal dimensions and their ideological values converge in one material object. Objects may be props, parts of the set, or isolated parts of an actor's body. They pass from character to character and connect one scene to another, marking out certain rhythms. In appearing and disappearing they give the sense of traveling between visible and invisible space and of gradual or sudden transformation. When actors handle them, objects *anchor* the Gestus. Thus epic theater rejects the old dichotomy between, on one side, human consciousness as the *interior time of the spirit of history;* and, on the other side, the world, including the human body, as the *exterior space and matter of nature.*

In epic theatrical practice spatio-temporality is signified through culturally constructed and ideologically marked human bodies. The real bodies of actors and fictional bodies of characters belong to two discrete sign systems that never merge with each other, as seems to occur when spectators uncritically identify with characters and forget the actors. Epic actors' bodies are always *present,* both physically and historically. They are the nexus where signs of gender, class, race, and political power intersect — and are generated. The resulting *constructed* bodies may be dispersed throughout the mise en scène or condensed as one prevailing image of a body, which unites all signs. Building on the *Sturm und Drang* playwright J. M. R. Lenz's prescient revolutionary concept of the human subject as victim of a historical process driven blindly by those in power, Büchner, then Brecht, Piscator and those following, stage the construction of the human body by science, law, religion, the military, and politics. The *abject* body serves as the outer boundary of these ideological systems, as when the bodies of Woyzeck and Marie are literally drawn and quartered on the doctor's autopsy table.[5]

The body of contemporary Chicano performance artist Guillermo Gomez-Peña also becomes abject in this sense: the sight of Gomez-Peña tied to a wooden cross in the desert landscape of the Mexican-U.S. border, dressed as an Anglo cliche of Ché Guevara or the sombreroed *bandito,* makes it impossible for the spectator to "go home again" to the image of America as an integrated social space with freedom for all. Gomez-Peña performs with his body on this site the split self-image of America. As postcolonialist critic Homi Bhabha notes, Gomez-Peña exposes both the inside and outside of this image simultaneously.[6] Like Brecht's Tutor and Mother Courage, Mnouchkine's Iphigenia, Büchner's Leonce and Lenz, and Gomez-Peña's Chicano, the American feminist performance artist Karen Finley also represents the *abject of society.* Dressed as a strip-tease artist, she speaks to unseen oppressors who would turn her into a silent object. She also voices their degrading thoughts about her. Thus she is a subject-as-object who performs both the oppressor and the victim, embodying another epic *contradiction,* with her body a single site that is violently split.

Similarly, playwright Caryl Churchill's Dull Gret in *Top Girls* speaks from within a misogynist construct of the female body. Dull Gret recounts her life struggle inside the hellish landscape of Pieter Bruegel's painting *Dulle Griet:*

> DULL GRET: We come to hell through a big mouth. Hell's black and red. It's . . . like the village where I come from. There's a river and a bridge and houses. There's places on fire like when the soldiers come. There's a big devil sat on a roof with a big hole in his arse and he's scooping [money] out of it . . . and it's falling down on us. . . . But most of us [women] is fighting the devils . . . our size. . . . My big son die on a wheel. Birds eat him. My baby, a soldier run her through with a sword. I'd had enough, *I was mad,* I hate the bastards. I come out of my front door . . . and I said [to the other peasant housewives], "Come on, we're going where the evil come from and pay the bastards out." And . . . we push down the street and the ground opens up and we go through a big mouth into a street just like ours but in hell. I've got a sword in my hand from somewhere. . . . You . . . keep running on and fighting, you didn't stop for nothing.[7]

Ironically, in *Top Girls* Dull Gret is still only a servant at this banquet table honoring other mythic-historical women heroes. She speaks from within the alienated body of an object bought and sold in Marx's sense, circulating endlessly in the marketplace of culture, like Bruegel's painting itself, which was the inspiration of Helene Weigel's costume and the set design for Brecht's production. In *Top Girls* a historical parallel is evoked by the fact that the actress playing Dull Gret is the same who plays Angie, the neglected and abandoned daughter of the new-age "feminist heroine" of the play, a Thatcherite capitalist climber.

Likewise, one actress in Mnouchkine's *Les Atrides* plays all the alienated daughters who are passed from one man to another among their fathers, husbands, masters, and brothers: Iphigenia, Cassandra, and Electra. At the Théâtre du Soleil socioscapes of alienated bodies are represented by actors in mobile relation to each other, plunging into one separate and independent *état,* or "state," after another, with each state becoming an element of a unique stage language that the spectators can connect into meaningful sequences. Mnouchkine's use of the actors' bodies as principal conveyer of signs stands in contrast to the work of Peter Stein, whose representation of historical spaces and times is just as dependent on stage objects and architectural constructions as it is on the actors' bodies.

American director Tina Landau, like Mnouchkine, asks that the actors neither anticipate a future state nor linger in the one that has passed. She insists on the actor's being *present,* versus being a *presence,* because presence implies wholeness and permanence, and allows only identification of actor with character and spectator with actor. Landau's and Mnouchkine's actors give *present after present,* and these present states are elements not drawn into a narrowly aimed "through line" but left as montage elements for the spectators to connect.

In a series of Greek tragedies rewritten and staged as collage, the director Landau, in collaboration with historian-turned-playwright Charles Mee, juxtaposes textual passages with modern music, contemporary clichés, and performance venues from television, popular films, nightclubs, health spas, and karaoke bars. In *The Trojan Women a Love Story* the historical events of the Trojan War and Aeneas's quest to establish Rome become apparent as an avoidable tragedy.[8] At the same time, our familiar unified image of the Greek and Roman civic edifice — the city-state as reflected by the theater edifice itself — is shattered, as well as the discursive unity of our own civilization, since the myth of our origin has been *contained* in the Greco-Roman site. History becomes tragedy as one city after another is built up, destroyed, and rebuilt elsewhere. The destruction of cities in the classical epic and tragedy represents that of whole civilizations, and *The Trojan Women a Love Story,* like many productions discussed in this book, draws a clear parallel between those societies and ours, because the old habit of destroying, abandoning, and seeking new sites on which to build is still with us.

Landau's Viewpoints, an approach she developed in collaboration with director Anne Bogart, seek to awaken actors and spectators alike to the fact that we build our social space and time, or "architecture," *on a contingency basis.* This is also historian Thomas Postlewait's message. The Viewpoints heighten the actors' and spectators' awareness of how our bodies exist and move in relation to the world around us by *isolating the ways we habitually use time and space.* This is the development of historical consciousness at ground zero.

— A separate movement track not motivated by psychology must be created in the performance space.
— This movement track is created through spatial relationships among bodies and between bodies and objects.
— Extreme distances and proximities must be created.
— Architecture is created through solid mass, color patterns, light, and textures.
— Gestures are created that are both behavioral (everyday, idiosyncratic) and expressive (archetypal, social, communal).
— Large shapes must be created by the body: geometrical curves, positive and negative spaces. The body is not accustomed to this but must become so.

— Some tempos must be created that are not comfortable.
— An awareness of duration and pauses must be cultivated.
— Kinesthetic responses are encouraged and examined: the response of movement as well as the response of stillness.
— Repetitions cohere all the above.
— The repeating of one viewpoint by another builds the architecture, including the architecture of the actor's dialogue.[9]

For Part One of the Seattle production of *The Trojan Women a Love Story,* based on Euripides' play, the spectators enter a dark, close blackbox room piled with hundreds of shoes of women, men, children, and babies; a mannequin of a corpse; and the women of Troy sitting at computer-like machines in a sweatshop atmosphere suddenly invaded by Greek men with microphones and machine guns, who arrive in a thundering helicopter surrounded by heroic music and billows of smoke. The floor and wall are filled with random objects as if after a bombing. By contrast, the large room used for Part Two, based on Berlioz's opera, *The Trojans,* becomes a clean, cool, expensive spa, devoid of random objects. The same actresses who were the defeated Trojan women in Part One are now not even touching the floor but swinging in white body suits from exercise trapezes. This cool haven is the new city of Carthage built by Dido and her followers, but it too is soon to be invaded: by Aeneas and the ragged remnants of the Trojan army — played by the same actors who just played the invading Greeks — except for Aeneas, who continues through both plays, first as a conquered war victim and now as a conqueror.

The corporeal writing of this story is brought into sharp, violent focus in the last moment of the play when the lights go off, the actors exit, the lights come back up, and the actors return for the final bows and an enthusiastic standing ovation. Here the music suddenly comes back on, and the actors go into a "rehearsal-recital" of all the corporeal vocabulary they have used throughout the performance, now set to loud hard-rock music with a staccato rhythm, as they defiantly and aggressively face the audience on all four sides. The lives they have performed in this site are now stripped to the basic material that they — and we — have available: our own bodies. The message here is that we have the power to make a social site of every material object and space we find, but also the power to destroy it — and ourselves — if we repeat the past.

JoAnne Akalaitis's adaptation of Büchner's play *Leonce and Lena* and his novella *Lenz* also presents the historical imagination as a stage construction in which the actors' bodies write and are written upon —

and finally written out — by juxtaposing old and new, organic and mechanical media in counterpoint throughout the production: *Leonce and Lena* on an ultramodern set in a live theater of many colors, and *Lenz* as a black-and-white expressionistic film of the same actor in a bleak, nineteenth-century mountain landscape. The two spatio-temporal dimensions are dialectically separated and united by one actor's body. The production thus materially stages and historicizes Büchner's view that philosophical idealism, medical science, and political tyranny reduce life to "mechanical processes" and people to "ridiculous puppets."[10] Likewise, Brecht shows Lenz's Tutor as such a puppet.

Before concluding this study, it must be said that the preceding analyses of these productions do not escape from the habit of stopping and framing the action, which in itself is an imposition of an already constructed historical order. Perhaps, like other rituals, the stop-and-frame action of the performance analyst is necessary so that we may seem to hold off death — and, thus, the passage of time in the world. It is surprising that, contrary to the prevailing collective memory of Brecht's *Mother Courage* as a series of still pictures, each obediently standing still for the critic Roland Barthes, and even for Brecht himself, as a quotable Gestus, the seldom-seen film of this famous production shocks the spectator with the realization that the action of the play, like that of the war it depicts, *never stops but is absolutely relentless.*[11] As in Walter Benjamin's vision of Paul Klee's painting *Angelus Novus,*[12] we must, it seems, be blown into the future of history, and must also, perhaps as a tactic of survival, keep ourselves turned backwards looking at the images in the memories behind us.

Notes

[1] Marc Silberman, "A Postmodernized Brecht?" *Theatre Journal* 45 (March 1993): 1–20. Special issue titled *German Theatre after the F/Wall.*

[2] John Berger, *Ways of Seeing* (London and Harmondsworth: British Broadcasting Corporation and Penguin, 1972).

[3] Thomas Postlewait, "The Sacred and the Secular: Reflections on the Writing of Renaissance Theater History," was a keynote speech at the International Federation for Theatre Research Congress in Tel Aviv, Israel, June 1996, and appeared as an article in *Assaph* C 12 (1997): 1–32.

[4] Philip Auslander usefully compares the politicization of the body in Brecht's modernist and Boal's postmodernist theater practice in the essay "Boal, Blau, Brecht: the body," in his *From Acting to Performance: Essays in Modernism and Postmodernism* (London and New York: Routledge, 1997), 98–107.

[5] Judith Butler, *Gender Trouble: Feminism and the Subversion of Identity* (New York and London, Routledge, 1990), 147. Julia Kristeva, "The True-Real," *The Kristeva Reader,* ed. Toril Moi (New York: Columbia UP, 1988), 214–237.

[6] Homi Bhabha, *The Location of Culture* (New York and London: Routledge, 1997).

[7] Caryl Churchill, *Top Girls* (London: Methuen, 1982), I:i.

[8] Charles Mee, *The Trojan Women a Love Story,* in *History Plays* (Baltimore and London: Johns Hopkins UP, 1998), 159–250.

[9] Tina Landau, symposium at University of Washington in Seattle, April 1, 1996. Landau stresses that the Viewpoints are continually being expanded and refined in exploratory research with actors in workshops and rehearsals.

[10] Georg Büchner, Letter to August Stöber, Darmstadt, December 1833, in *Georg Büchner: The Complete Plays, Lenz and Other Writings,* ed. John Reddick (London: Penguin, 1993), 192.

[11] Bertolt Brecht, *Mutter Courage und ihre Kinder,* film of the Berliner Ensemble production with Helene Weigel, directed by Peter Palitzch and Manfred Wekwerth (East Berlin: DEFA, 1961).

[12] Walter Benjamin, "Theses on the Philosophy of History," in *Illuminations,* ed. Hannah Arendt, trans. Harry Zohn (New York: Schocken, 1969), 257–258.

Works Consulted

Aeschylus. *The Oresteia: Agamemnon, The Libation Bearers, The Eumenides*. Translated by David Grene and Wendy Doniger O'Flaherty. Chicago and London: U of Chicago P, 1989.

———. *L'Orestie: Agamemnon. Les Choéphores. Les Eumènides*. Translated by Ariane Mnouchkine. Paris: Théâtre du Soleil, 1990.

Akalaitis, JoAnne. "JoAnne Akalaitis Interviewed by Deborah Saivetz: Releasing the 'Profound Physicality of Performance.'" In *New Theatre Quarterly* 13 (November 1997): 329–338.

Allen, Terry. "Tornado Song." Copyright Green Shoes Publishing Company, 1980.

Althusser, Louis. "Piccolo Teatro: Bertolazzi and Brecht. Notes on a Materialist Theatre." In his *For Marx*. Translated by Ben Brewster. New York: Pantheon, 1969.

Aslan, Odette. "Au Théâtre du Soleil les acteurs écrivent avec leur corps" [At the Théâtre du Soleil the actors write with their bodies]. In *LE CORPS EN JEU*, edited by Aslan, 294. Paris: CNRS Éditions, 1993.

"Aufführung des Jahres: Peer Gynt" [Premiere of the year: Peer Gynt]. Peter Stein's production at the Berlin Schaubühne am Hallischen Ufer. *Theater Heute* 13 (1971): 18–39 and 70–71.

Auslander, Philip. "Boal, Blau, Brecht: the body." In his *From Acting to Performance: Essays in Modernism and Postmodernism*. London and New York: Routledge, 1997, 98–107.

Bachelard, Gaston. *Le Nouvel esprit scientifique* [The new scientific spirit] (1934). Paris: Presses Universitaires de France, 1963.

———. *The Poetics of Space* (1958). Translated by Maria Jolas. Boston: Beacon, 1994.

Bakhtin, Mikhail. "Forms of Time and of the Chronotope in the Novel: Notes Toward a Historical Poetics." In his *The Dialogic Imagination*. Translated by Michael Holquist, 84–258. Austin: U of Texas P, 1981.

———. *Rabelais and His World*. Translated by H. Iswolsky. Cambridge, Mass.: M.I.T. P, 1968.

Bang-Hanson, Kjetil; Tormod Skagestad; and Helge Hoff Monsen. Interview with three Norwegian directors of Peer Gynt. February 16, 1983, U of Minnesota, Minneapolis.

Banu, Georges. *Bertolt Brecht*. Paris: Subier Montaigne, 1981.

Barthes, Roland. *Camera Lucida: Reflections on Photography*. Translated by Richard Howard. New York: Hill and Wang, 1981.

———. "Comment représenter l'Antique?" (How to represent antiquity?) *Théâtre Aujourd'hui 1: La Tragédie Grecque. Les Atrides au Théâtre du Soleil*. Paris: CNDP (Centre National de Documentation Pédagogique), 1992: 48–51. Originally in *Théâtre populaire* (scholarly theatre journal published 1949–1960), 1955. Reprinted in Barthes, *Les Essais critiques*. Paris: Éditions de Seuil, 1964.

———. *Critical Essays*. Translated by Richard Howard. Evanston: Northwestern UP, 1972.

———. *The Eiffel Tower and Other Mythologies*. Translated by Richard Howard. New York: Hill and Wang, 1979.

———. *Image – Music – Text*. Translated by Stephen Heath. New York: Hill and Wang, 1977.

———. *Mythologies*. Translated by Annette Lavers. New York: Hill and Wang, 1980.

———. *On Racine*. Translated by Richard Howard. New York: Hill and Wang, 1964.

———. *Roland Barthes by Roland Barthes*. Translated by Richard Howard. New York: Hill and Wang, 1977.

———. *The Rustle of Language*. Translated by Richard Howard. Berkeley and Los Angeles: U of California P, 1989.

Bassnett, Susan. *Translation Studies*. New York and London: Routledge, 1991.

Baudrillard, Jean. *The Gulf War did not take place*. Translated by Paul Patton. Bloomington and Indianapolis: Indiana UP, 1995. Originally published as three essays in the newspaper *Libération* on January 4, February 4, and March 29, 1991.

———. "Simulacrum and Simulacrae." *The Baudrillard Reader*. Translated by Sheila Glaser. Ann Arbor: U of Michigan P, 1994.

Beauvoir, Simone de. *The Second Sex*. Translated by H. M. Parshley. New York: Vintage, 1952.

Becker, Peter von. "Die Inszenierung: 'Les Atrides'" [The staging: *Les Atrides*]. *Theater Heute* 6 (June 1991): 1–10.

———. "So schnell, so falsch vergeht das Leben. Wie Patrice Chéreau inszeniert Ibsen's Peer Gynt in Villeurbanne" [So quickly, so falsely life goes by. How Patrice Chéreau stages Ibsen's Peer Gynt in Villeurbanne]. *Theater Heute* 7 (1981): 11.

Benjamin, Walter. *Illuminations*. Translated by Harry Zohn, edited by Hannah Arendt. New York: Schocken, 1969.

———. *The Origins of German Tragic Drama*. Translated by John Osborne. London: NLB, 1977.

———. *Reflections*. Translated by Edmund Jephcott, edited by Peter Demetz. New York: Harcourt Brace Jovanovich, 1978.

Bensmaïa, Réda. *The Barthes Effect*. Translated by Pat Fedkiew. Minneapolis: U of Minnesota P, 1986.

Berger, John. *Ways of Seeing*. London and Harmondsworth: British Broadcasting Corporation and Penguin, 1972.

Bhabha, Homi. *The Location of Culture*. New York and London: Routledge, 1997.

Bharucha, Rustom. "A Collision of Cultures: Some Western Interpretations of the Indian Theatre." *Asian Theatre Journal* 1 (Spring 1984): 1–20.

———. *Theatre of the World: Performance and the Politics of Culture*. New York and London: Routledge, 1993.

———. "Under the Sign of the Onion: Intracultural Negotiations in Theatre." *New Theatre Quarterly* 12 (May 1996):116–129.

Blau, Herbert. "Ideology and Performance." *Theatre Journal* 35 (December 1983): 441–459.

Bly, Mark. Interview with Bly as dramaturg of the Guthrie Theatre's *Leon and Lena (& lenz)*. October 1991, U of Washington, Seattle.

———. Interview with Bly as dramaturg of the Guthrie Theatre's *Peer Gynt*. February 16, 1983, U of Minnesota, Minneapolis.

———. "JoAnne Akalaitis's *Leon and Lena (and lenz):* A Log from the Dramaturg." *Yale Theater* 3 (1989): 81–95.

Bogatyrev, Petr. "Signs in the Theater." In *Sign, Sound, and Meaning. Quinquagenary of the Prague Linguistic Circle*. Ann Arbor: U of Michigan P, 1976.

Brecht, Bertolt. Adaptation of J. M. R. Lenz's *Der Hofmeister* [The Tutor], Berliner Ensemble, 1950. Manuscript 539/575, in the Bertolt-Brecht-Archiv in Berlin.

———. *Bertolt Brecht: Plays, Poetry and Prose*. Edited by John Willet and Ralph Manheim. New York: Routledge, 1996.

———. "An Expression of Faith in Wedekind." Eulogy first published in the *Augsburger Neueste Nachrichten,* March 1918. Translated by Erich Albrecht, in *The Tulane Drama Review* 6 (September 1961): 26–27.

———. *Bertolt Brecht Werke,* volumes 1–30. Edited by Werner Hecht, Jan Knopf, Werner Mittenzwei, Klaus Detlef Müller, et al. Berlin and Weimar: Aufbau/ Frankfurt am Main: Suhrkamp, 1989.

———. *"Hofmeister" Material.* In the Bertolt-Brecht-Archiv, Berlin. Includes the typescript of the play, director's log, director's diaries, actors' logs, stage manager's log, set designer's log, letters, program, reviews, photographs, and drawings.

———. *Bertolt Brecht Journals 1934–1955.* Edited by John Willett and Ralph Manheim, translated by Hugh Rorrison. New York and London: Routledge, 1993.

———. *Materialien zu Brechts "Mutter Courage und ihre Kinder."* Frankfurt am Main: Suhrkamp, 1964.

———. Material on *Der brave Soldaten Schwejk* and *Schwejk im zweiten Weltkrieg* [Schwejk in the Second World War]. In the Erwin-Piscator-Center, Akademie der Künste, West Berlin. Includes Brecht's annotated copy of Hašek's novel *Der brave Soldaten Schwejk,* as well as Herbert Knust's publication of Brecht's annotated typescript of *Der brave Soldaten Schwejk,* and Brecht's play *Schwejk im zweiten Weltkrieg.*

———. *Brecht on Theatre: The Development of an Aesthetic.* Edited and translated by John Willett. London: Methuen, 1986.

———. *Mother Courage and Her Children: A Chronicle of the Thirty Years' War.* Translated by Eric Bentley. In *Masters of Modern Drama,* edited by Haskell Block and Robert Shedd, 843–890. New York: Random House, 1962.

———. *Mutter Courage und ihre Kinder: Eine Chronik aus dem Dreißigjährigen Krieg* [Mother Courage and Her Children: A Chronicle of the Thirty Years' War]. Berlin: Suhrkamp, 1949.

———. *Mutter Courage und ihre Kinder.* Film adapted from Brecht's Berliner Ensemble staging, directed by Peter Palitzch and Manfred Wekwerth. East Berlin: DEFA, 1961. A video of this film is located at the Goethe Institute.

———. *The Tutor: An Adaptation of the Play by J. M. R. Lenz.* Translated by Pipi Broughton. New York: Applause Theatre Book Publishers, 1988.

Brecht, Bertolt, et al. *Theaterarbeit: 6 Aufführungen des Berliner Ensembles* [Theater work: 6 productions of the Berliner Ensemble]. Dresden: VVV Dresdner Verlag, 1952.

Brecht in Asia and Africa. Brecht Yearbook 14. Edited by John Fuegi, Renata Voris, Carl Weber, and Marc Silberman. College Park, Md.: International Brecht Society, 1989.

Brecht in Afrika, Asien und Lateinamerika. Brecht Tage 1980 proceedings, edited by Werner Hecht, Karl-Claus Hahn, and Elifius Paffrath. Berlin: Henschelverlag Kunst und Gesellschaft, 1980.

Brecht: Women and Politics/Frauen und Politik. Brecht Yearbook 12. Edited by John Fuegi, Gisela Bahr, and John Willett. Detroit: Wayne State UP, 1983.

Bryant-Bertail, Sarah. "Courage Recovered: Grimmelshausen, Brecht, and the Pícara." *Assaph* C 8 (1992): 177–190.

————. *"Écriture corporelle* and the Body Politic: *Les Atrides."* In *Collaborative Theatre: The Théâtre du Soleil Sourcebook.* Edited by David Williams, translated by Eric Prenowitz and David Williams, 179–185. London and New York: Routledge, 1999.

————. "Gender, Empire, and Body Politic as *Mise en Scène:* Mnouchkine's *Les Atrides."* In *Theatre Journal* 46 (March 1994), 1–30.

————. *"The Good Soldier Schwejk* as Dialectical Theater." In *The Performance of Power: Theatrical Discourse and Politics.* Edited by Sue-Ellen Case and Janelle Reinelt, 19–40. Iowa City: U of Iowa P, 1991.

————. *"Leon and Lena (& lenz):* Iridescent Reality." In *Text and Presentation.* Edited by K. Hartigan, 1–12. Lanham, Md. and London: UP of America, 1989.

————. "Moving Piscator Out of Context." In *Paradigm Exchange.* Edited by René Jara and Jochen Schulte-Sasse, 32–51. Minneapolis: U of Minnesota, 1987.

————. "Spatio-Temporality as Theater Performance." In *Text and Presentation.* Edited by K. Hartigan, 120–135. Lanham, Md. and London: UP of America, 1990.

————. "Women, Space, Ideology: Mutter Courage und ihre Kinder." In *Brecht: Women and Politics/Frauen und Politik. Brecht Yearbook 12.* Edited by John Fuegi, Gisela Bahr, and John Willett, 43–61. Detroit: Wayne State UP, 1983.

———— and Frank Hirschbach. "Theater in the Weimar Republic." In *Germany in the Twenties: The Artist as Social Critic.* Edited by Frank Hirschbach, Sarah Bryant-Bertail et al, 48–61. U of Minnesota, 1980. Republished Berlin: Text und Kritik/ Detroit: Wayne State UP, 1984.

Büchner, Georg. *Georg Büchner: The Complete Plays, Lenz and Other Writings.* Edited by John Reddick. London: Penguin, 1993.

————. *Georg Büchner: Complete Plays and Prose.* Translated by Carl Richard Miller. New York: Hill and Wang, 1963.

————. *Georg Büchner: Complete Works and Letters.* Translated by Henry J. Schmidt, edited by Walter Hinderer and Henry J. Schmidt. New York: Continuum, 1986.

————. *Leonce and Lena. Lenz. Woyzeck.* Translated by Michael Hamburger. Chicago: U of Chicago P, 1972.

————. *Georg Büchner: Sämtliche Werke und Briefe. Historische-kritische Ausgabe mit Kommentar.* Edited by Werner R. Lehmann. 2 vols. Hamburg: Christian Wegner, 1967-71.

Butler, Judith. *Bodies That Matter: On the Discursive Limits of "Sex."* London and New York: Routledge, 1993.

———. *Gender Trouble: Feminism and the Subversion of Identity.* New York and London: Routledge, 1990.

———. "Performative Acts and Gender Constitution: An Essay in Phenomenology and Feminist Theory." In *Performing Feminisms: Feminist Critical Theory and Theatre,* ed. Sue–Ellen Case, 270–285. Baltimore: Johns Hopkins UP, 1990.

Carlson, Marvin. *"Accueil* on the Road: Mnouchkine's *Les Atrides* in Context." *Assaph* C 8 (1992): 153–160.

———. "Brook and Mnouchkine: Passages to India?" In *The Intercultural Performance Reader.* Edited by Patrice Pavis, 79–92. London and New York: Routledge, 1996.

———. *Places of Performance: The Semiotics of Theatre Architecture.* Ithaca, N.Y., and London: Cornell UP, 1989.

———. *Signs of Life: Theater Semiotics.* Ithaca, N.Y. and London: Cornell UP, 1993.

Case, Sue-Ellen. *Feminism and Theatre.* London and New York: Routledge, 1988.

———, ed. *Performing Feminisms: Feminist Critical Theory and Theatre.* Ann Arbor: U of Michigan P, 1990.

Certeau, Michel de. *Heterologies: Discourse on the Other.* Translated by Brian Massumi. Minneapolis: U of Minnesota P, 1986.

———. *The Practice of Everyday Life.* Translated by Steven Rendall. Berkeley, Los Angeles, and London: U of California P, 1984.

Churchill, Caryl. *Top Girls.* London: Methuen, 1982.

Cima, Gay Gibson. *Performing Women: Female Characters, Male Playwrights, and the Modern Stage.* Ithaca, N. Y., and London: Cornell UP, 1993.

Colapietro, Vincent M. *Glossary of Semiotics.* New York: Paragon, 1993.

Davidson, H. R. Ellis. *Gods and Myths of Northern Europe.* Harmondsworth, England: Penguin, 1964.

Derrida, Jacques. "The Theatre of Cruelty." In his *Writing and Difference.* Translated by A. Bass. Chicago: U of Chicago P/ Ithaca, N.Y. and London: Cornell UP, 1989.

———. *Of Grammatology.* Translated by Gayatri Chakravorty Spivak. Baltimore and London: Johns Hopkins UP, 1974.

Dhananjayan, V. P. *A Dancer on Dance.* Madras: Bharata Kalanjaali, 1991.

Diamond, Elin. "Brechtian Theory/Feminist Theory: Toward a Gestic Feminist Criticism." In *A Sourcebook of Feminist Theatre and Performance,* edited by Carol Martin, 120–135. London and New York: Routledge, 1996.

————. "Mimicry, Mimesis, and the True Real." In *Modern Drama* 32 (March 1989): 58–72.

Dolan, Jill. *The Feminist Spectator as Critic.* Ann Arbor: UMI Research P, 1988.

Dort, Bernard. Lecture at Université de Paris VIII, June 15, 1986.

————. *Lecture de Brecht* [Reading Brecht]. Paris: Éditions du Seuil, 1960.

————. *Théâtre en jeu* [Theater in play]. Paris: Éditions du Seuil, 1979.

————. *Théâtre public.* Paris: Éditions du Seuil, 1967.

————. *Théâtre réel* [Real theater]. Paris: Éditions du Seuil, 1971.

Dumar, Guy. "Le Norvégien volant" [The flying Norwegian]. Review of Patrice Chéreau's production of *Peer Gynt,* at the Théâtre national populaire in Villeurbanne. *Le Nouvel Observateur,* May 24, 1981, 11.

Eco, Umberto. "Semiotics of Performance." *The Drama Review* 21 (1977): 51–58.

————. *A Theory of Semiotics.* Bloomington and London: Indiana UP, 1976.

Eddershaw, Margaret. *Performing Brecht: Forty Years of British Performances.* London and New York: Routledge, 1996.

Eisenstein, Sergei. "A Dialectical Approach to Film Form" (1929). In his *Film Form.* Edited and translated by Jay Leyda, 101–122. New York: Harcourt Brace Jovanovich, 1949.

Ellis, Lorena B. *Brecht's Reception in Brazil.* New York: Peter Lang, 1995.

Erwin-Piscator-Center. This archive in Berlin's Akademie der Künste has organized world exhibitions and produced catalogues and other publications on Piscator. It contains Piscator's published and unpublished plays, books, essays, letters, director's logs, diaries, and notes; the logs of actors, designers, and other collaborators; production photos, drawings, press releases, reviews, programs, telegrams, and letters; and other authors' works on Piscator from several countries.

Essays on Brecht/Versuche über Brecht. Brecht Yearbook 15. Edited by Marc Silberman, John Fuegi, Renata Voris, and Carl Weber. College Park, Md.: International Brecht Society, 1990.

Euripides. *Iphigénie à Aulis.* Translated by Jean and Mayotte Bollack. Paris: Éditions de Minuit, 1990.

————. *Iphigenia at Aulis.* In *Euripides: Ten Plays.* Translated by Moses Hadas and John McLean. New York: Bantam, 1960.

Fenton, James. "James Fenton Reports from Paris." Review of Patrice Chéreau's 1981 production of *Peer Gynt* at the Théâtre National Populaire in Villeurbanne-Lyon. *Sunday Times* (London), December 27 , 1981.

Féral, Josette. "Brecht Inverted: Alienation Effect and Multimedia Performance." *Theatre Journal* 39 (issue "Distancing Brecht") (December 1987): 461–472.

———. "Building up the Muscle of the Imagination." In *Collaborative Theatre: The Théâtre du Soleil Sourcebook*. Edited by David Williams, translations by Williams and Eric Prenowitz, 169–173. London and New York: Routledge, 1999.

———. moderator. "Des Dinosaures à Contre-Courant: Rencontre avec Ariane Mnouchkine sur la formation de l'acteur" [From dinosaurs to counter-current: discussion with Ariane Mnouchkine on the actor's training]. Transcription of the discussion at the University of Quebec in Montreal, November 6, 1992, in connection with the *Les Atrides* touring production in Montreal.

Fischer-Lichte, Erika. *The Semiotics of Theater*. Translated by Jeremy Gaines and Doris J. Jones. Bloomington: Indiana UP, 1992.

Fjelde, Rolf. "Appendix I: Text/Translation/Script." In Henrik Ibsen, *Peer Gynt*. Translated by Fjelde. Minneapolis: U of Minnesota P, 1980.

———. "Peer Gynt, Naturalism, and the Dissolving Self." *The Drama Review* 13 (Winter 1969): 28–43.

Foucault, Michel. Essays from *Discipline and Punish: The Birth of the Prison*. In *The Foucault Reader*. Edited by Paul Rabinow, translated by Alan Sheridan, 169–256. New York: Pantheon, 1984.

———. *The History of Sexuality*. Translated by Robert Hurley. New York: New Random House, 1978.

Frank, Joseph. *The Widening Gyre*. New Brunswick, N.J.: Rutgers UP, 1963.

Fuegi, John. *The Essential Brecht*. Los Angeles: Hennessey and Ingalls, 1972.

———. *Brecht and Company: Sex, Politics and the Making of the Modern Drama*. New York: Grove, 1994.

———. *Life and Lies of Bertolt Brecht*. London: Flamingo, 1995.

Gasbarra, Felix. In *Die Welt am Abend* (Berlin newspaper), January 1928. Quoted by Erwin Piscator, in *Das politische Theater*, 190–191.

Gibson, Walter S. *Bruegel*. New York and Toronto: Oxford UP, 1977.

Godzich, Wlad. "Correcting Kant: Bakhtin and Intercultural Interactions." *Boundary 2* 18 (Spring 1991): 4-17.

———. "Foreword: The Further Possibility of Knowledge." In *Heterologies: Discourse on the Other*, by Michel de Certeau, vii–xii. Translated by Brian Massumi. Minneapolis: U of Minnesota P, 1986.

Goertz, ed. *Erwin Piscator in Selbstzeugnissen und Bilddokumenten*. Reinbek, 1994.

Goffman, Erving. *Frame Analysis*. Harmondsworth, England: Penguin, 1974.

Grene, David. "Introduction." In *The Oresteia by Aeschylus*. Translated by Grene and Wendy Doniger O'Flaherty. Chicago and London: U of Chicago P, 1989.

Grimmelshausen, Hans Jacob Christoffel von. *Courage, the Adventuress*. Translated by Hans Speier. Princeton, N.J.: Princeton UP, 1964.

———. *Die Landstörzerin Courasche* (1670). Munich: Wilhelm Goldmann, 1969.

Grosz, George. *Ein kleines Ja und ein großes Nein* [A small yes and a large no]. Reinbek bei Hamburg: Rowohlt, 1955.

Guthrie, Tyrone. "Foreword," in Henrik Ibsen's *Peer Gynt*. Translated by Norman Ginsbury. London: Hammond, 1946.

Hall, T. E. *The Hidden Dimension*. New York: Doubleday, 1959.

———. *The Silent Language*. New York: Doubleday, 1966.

Hašek, Jaroslav. *Die Abenteuer des braven Soldaten Schwejk*. Dramatization by Max Brod and Hans Reimann. Vienna: Zsolnay, 1967. Herbert Knust attributes this version to the Piscator Collective, specifically Brecht, Piscator, Felix Gasbarra, and George Grosz.

———. *The Good Soldier Svejk*. Translated by Cecil Parrott. London: Heinemann, 1973.

Hegel, Georg Wilhelm Friedrich. *The Philosophy of History* (1837). Translated by F. Sibree. New York: Dow, 1965.

———. *Reason in History*. Translated by Robert S. Hartman. Indianapolis: Bobbs-Merrill, 1953.

Herzfelde, Wieland. "Dada-Show" (Summer 1918). In *Der Weg Nach Unten* (The way downward), by Franz Jung, 1242. Neuwied: Berlin-West, 1977.

Hintze, Joachim. *Das Raumproblem im modernen deutschen Drama und Theater* [The problem of space in modern German drama and theater]. Marburg: N.G. Elvert, 1969.

Huder, Walter. Founding Director of the Erwin-Piscator-Center. Interviews in Berlin, June 1985.

———, ed., with Hannelore Ritscher and Ilse Brauer, comps. Catalogue for the exhibition *Erwin Piscator 1893–1966*. Berlin: Akademie der Künste, 1971. English version published in 1979.

———, ed., with Ritscher, and Brauer, comps. *Theater in Exile*. Catalogue, Akademie der Künste, 1973.

Ibsen, Henrik. *Peer Gynt*. In *The Collected Works of Henrik Ibsen*. Translated by William and Charles Archer. London: Heinemann, 1906.

———. *Peer Gynt*. Copenhagen: Gyldendalske Boghandels Forlag, 1891

———. *Peer Gynt*. Translated by Rolf Fjelde. Second edition. Minneapolis: U of Minnesota P, 1980.

———. *Peer Gynt.* Translated by Norman Ginsbury. London: Hammond, 1946.

———. *Peer Gynt.* Translated into French by François Regnault. Lyon-Villeurbanne: Théâtre National Populaire, 1981.

Ingarden, Roman. "The Functions of Language in the Theatre." In his *The Literary Work of Art.* Evanston: Northwestern UP.

Innes, C. D. *Piscator's Political Theatre.* London: Cambridge UP, 1972.

Issacharoff, Michael. "Space and Reference in Drama." *Poetics Today* 2 (Spring 1981): 212–224.

Jacobs, Monty. "Pallenberg auf Rollen. 'Schwejk' auf der Piscator-Bühne" [Pallenberg on rollers. Schwejk on the Piscator-Bühne]. *Die Vossische Zeitung,* January 24, 1928. In the Erwin-Piscator-Center, Berlin. Also quoted in part in *Theater für die Republik 1917–1933 im Spiegel der Kritik,* edited by Günter Rühle.

Johnston, Brian. *Towards the Third Empire.* Minneapolis: U of Minnesota P, 1980.

Jung, Franz. *Der Weg Nach Unten* [The way downward]. Neuwied: Berlin-West, 1977.

Kant, Immanuel. "The Critique of Pure Reason" (1781). In *The Enduring Questions: Main Problems of Philosophy.* Fifth edition. Edited by Melvin Rader and Jerry Hill, 230–242. New York: Holt, Rinehart and Winston, 1991.

Kiernander, Adrian. *Ariane Mnouchkine and the Théâtre du Soleil.* Cambridge: Cambridge UP, 1993.

Knust, Herbert, ed. *Materialien zu Bertolt Brechts "Schweyk im zweiten Weltkrieg."* Frankfurt am Main: Surkamp, 1974. Includes a summary of the first script by Max Brod and Hans Reimann, the 1928 playscript and resume of the production of *Die Abenteuer des braven Soldaten Schwejk* developed by the Piscator Collective, as well as production photos, an essay by Piscator, reproductions of George Grosz's prints, Piscator's and Brecht's plans for a film of *Schwejk,* Brecht's 1943 typescript of *Schweyk im zweiten Weltkrieg,* and Brecht's editorial markings in his personal copy of Hašek's novel.

Kowzan, Tadeusz. "The Sign in the Theatre." *Diogenes* 61 (1968): 52–80.

Kowsar, Mohammad. "Althusser on Theatre." *Theatre Journal* 35 (December 1983): 461–474.

Kristeva, Julia. *Proust and the Sense of Time.* Translated by Stephen Bann. New York: Columbia UP, 1993.

———. "The True-Real." In *The Kristeva Reader.* Edited by Toril Moi, 214–237. N.Y.: Columbia UP, 1988.

Kroll, Jack. "Blood and Bones of Tragedy," *Newsweek,* October 5, 1992 51.

Landau, Tina. Symposium on her production of Charles Mee's *The Trojan Women a Love Story*. University of Washington in Seattle, April 1, 1996.

Lauretis, Teresa de. *Alice Doesn't: Feminism, Semiotics, Cinema*. Bloomington: Indiana UP, 1984.

———. *Technologies of Gender: Essays on Theory, Film, and Fiction*. Bloomington: Indiana UP, 1987.

Lennox, Sara. "Women in Brecht's Work." *New German Critique* 14 (1978): 83–97.

Lenz, Jacob Michael Reinhold. *Der Hofmeister: oder Vortheile der Privaterziehung. Eine Komödie* (The tutor: or Advantages of a private education. A comedy; Leipzig, 1774). Frankfurt am Main: Stroemfeld/Roter Stern, 1986.

———. *The Tutor. The Soldiers*. Translated by William E. Yuill. Chicago and London: U of Chicago P, 1972.

Ley-Piscator, Maria. *The Piscator Experiment*. New York: Heineman, 1967.

Loraux, Nicole. *Tragic Ways of Killing a Woman*. Translated by Anthony Forster. Cambridge, Ma., and London: Harvard UP, 1987.

Lyon, James K. *Bertolt Brecht in America*. Princeton, N.J.: Princeton UP, 1980.

Lukács, Georg. "*L'Education sentimentale* and the problem of time in the novel" and "Retrospective examination of the problem of time in the novels of abstract realism." In his *The Theory of the Novel*. Translated by Anna Bostock. Cambridge, Ma.: M.I.T P, 1971.

Mangolte, Babette, cinematographer and editor. *Lenz*. Film, copyright 1987.

Mansfield, Richard. *The Richard Mansfield Acting Version of Peer Gynt by Henrik Ibsen*. Based on William and Charles Archer's translation. Chicago: Reilly and Britton, 1906.

Marx, Karl. "The Buying and Selling of Labor Power." In his *Capital*. Chicago: Charles H. Kerr, 1912.

———. *The Eighteenth Brumaire of Louis Bonaparte* (1851). In *The Marx-Engels Reader*. Edited and translated by Robert C. Tucker, 594–619. New York: Norton, 1979.

———. *Manifesto of the Communist Party*. In *The Marx-Engels Reader*, 469–500.

McFarlane, James W., ed. *The Oxford Ibsen*. Vol. 3 of 8 volumes. New York: Oxford UP, 1972.

———. "Revaluations of Ibsen." In *Discussions of Henrik Ibsen*. Edited by McFarlane. Boston: D.C. Heath, 1962.

Mee, Charles Jr. *The Trojan Women a Love Story*. In his *History Plays*, 150–250. Baltimore and London: Johns Hopkins UP, 1998.

Merleau-Ponty, Maurice. *Phénoménologie de la perception*. Paris: Gallimard, 1976.

Meyer, Michael. *Ibsen: A Biography.* Garden City, N.Y.: Doubleday, 1971.

Miller, Judith. "Theatre Review: *Peer Gynt.*" On Patrice Chéreau's production at Villeurbanne-Lyon. *Theatre Journal* 3 (March 1982): 107–109.

Mnouchkine, Ariane. "Écorchement et Catharsis" [Flaying and catharsis]. In *LE CORPS EN JEU.* Edited by Odette Aslan, 296. Paris: CNRS Éditions, 1993.

———. Interview with Adrian Kiernander. In his *Ariane Mnouchkine and the Théâtre du Soleil.* Cambridge: Cambridge UP, 1993.

———. Interview with Eberhard Sprenge. *Theater Heute* 6 (June 1991): 9.

———. "The Space of Tragedy." Interview with Alfred Simon. In *Collaborative Theatre: The Théâtre du Soleil, a Sourcebook.* Edited by David Williams, 186–194. London and New York: Routledge, 1999.

Moses, Montrose J. "Richard Mansfield and Peer Gynt." *The Times Magazine,* New York, February 1907, 312–313.

Mukařovsky, Jan. *Structure, Sign, and Function.* Translated and edited by John Burbank and Peter Steiner. New Haven and London: Yale UP, 1978.

Nightingale, Benedict. "Epic Rewoven in Human Terms." *Life and Times* (London), July 20, 1992.

The Other Brecht/Der andere Brecht. Brecht Yearbook 17. Edited by Marc Silberman, Antony Tatlow, Renate Voris, and Carl Weber; guest co-editors Hans-Thies Lehmann and Renate Voris. Madison, WI.: International Brecht Society, 1992.

Patterson, Michael. "Brecht's Legacy." In *The Cambridge Companion to Brecht.* Edited by Peter Thomson and Glendyr Sacks, 273–287. Cambridge and New York: Cambridge UP, 1994.

———. *Peter Stein, Germany's Leading Theatre Director.* Cambridge and New York: Cambridge UP, 1982.

———. *The Revolution in German Theatre 1900–1933.* London: Routledge, 1981.

Pavis, Patrice. *Dictionnaire du Théâtre.* Paris: Messidor/Éditions Sociales, 1987.

———. *Languages of the Stage: Essays in the Semiology of Theatre.* New York: Performance Arts Journal Publications, 1982.

———. "Production et réception au théâtre: la concrétisation du texte dramatique et spectaculaire." [Production and reception in theater: the concretization of the dramatic and performance text.] *Revue des Sciences Humaines* 60 (1983): 51–88.

———. "La réception du texte dramatique et spectaculaire: les processus de fictionalisation et d'idéologisation" [The reception of the dramatic and performance text: the process of fictionalization and ideologization]. *Versus.* (March–August 1985): 69–94.

————. *Theatre at the Crossroads of Culture*. London and New York: Routledge, 1992.

————, ed. *The Intercultural Performance Reader*. London and New York: Routledge, 1996.

"Peer Gynt." Review of Richard Mansfield's production. *The Dial* (Chicago), November 16, 1908, 309–311.

Peer Gynt: Ein Schauspiel Aus Dem Neunzehnjahrhundert [Peer Gynt: A play from the nineteenth century]. Schaubühne am Hallischen Ufer, Berlin, 1971. Director: Peter Stein; scenographer: Karl Ernst Herrmann.

Piscator Collective. "*Schwejk — The Good Soldier:* from the novel by Jaroslav Hašek. As revised and staged by Erwin Piscator." Typescript in the Erwin-Piscator-Center. Translator unknown. Herbert Knust attributes the stage adaptation to Brecht, Piscator, Felix Gasbarra, and George Grosz.

Piscator, Erwin. "An Account of our Work 1929" [translation of "Rechenschaft (1)"]. In *Erwin Piscator: Political Theatre, 1920–1966*. London Arts Council, 1971. Exhibition by the Akademie der Künste, East Berlin.

————. "Piscator über den Dadaismus" [Piscator on Dadaism]. Recorded October 6, 1959 in Dillenburg. Erwin-Piscator-Center, Akademie der Künste, West Berlin.

————. *Das Politische Theater*. Berlin: Adelbert Schultz, 1929.

————. *The Political Theatre*. Translated, edited, and with introductions by Hugh Rorrison. London: Avon, 1978.

————. "Rechenschaft (1)" An account of the work of the Piscator-Bühne in Berlin, lecture at the former Berlin "Herrenhaus" March 25, 1929. In *Erwin Piscator: Schriften 2. Aufsätze, Reden, Gespräche,* 51–52. Berlin: Henschelverlag Kunst und Gesellschaft, 1968.

————. "Wie unterscheidet sich das Epische bei Brecht — bei mir?" [How does the epic differ between Brecht's work and mine?]. Diary 15, 1955 or 1956. In the Erwin-Piscator-Center, Berlin. Cited in translation by John Willet, in *The Theatre of Erwin Piscator: Fifty Years of Politics in the Theatre,* 187. London: Eyre Methuen, 1978.

Postlewait, Thomas. "The Sacred and the Secular: Reflections on the Writing of Renaissance Theatre History." *Assaph* C 12 (1997): 1–32.

Quinn, Michael L. *The Semiotic Stage: The Prague School Theorists*. New York: Peter Lang, 1995.

Reddick, John. *Georg Büchner: The Shattered Whole*. Oxford: Clarendon P/ Oxford UP, 1994.

Reinelt, Janelle. *After Brecht: British Epic Theatre*. Ann Arbor: U of Michigan P, 1995.

————. "Rethinking Brecht: Deconstruction, Feminism, and the Politics of Form." In *Essays on Brecht/Versuche über Brecht: The Brecht Yearbook* 15. Edited by Marc Silberman, John Fuegi, Renate Voris, and Carl Weber, 99–110. College Park, Md.: International Brecht Society, 1990.

Revolution 1989: Whither Brecht?/ Brecht wohin?. Brecht Yearbook 16. Edited by Marc Silberman, Antony Tatlow, Renata Voris, and Carl Weber. Madison, WI.: International Brecht Society, 1991.

Rich, Frank. "Taking the Stage to Some of Its Extremes." Review of Mnouchkine's *Les Atrides, The New York Times,* October 6, 1992, B1 and B4.

Rockwell, John. "Behind the Masks of a Moralist." Review of *Les Atrides. New York Times,* September 27, 1991, 1 and 5.

Rorrison, Hugh. *Erwin Piscator: Politics on the Stage in the Weimar Republic.* Introduction, 50 slides with commentary. Cambridge, U.K. and Alexandria, VA: Chadwyck-Healey, 1987.

————. "Introduction" to chapter "Epic Satire: *The Adventures of the Good Soldier Schwejk.*" In Piscator's *The Political Theatre,* translated and edited by Rorrison, 250–251.

————. "Democratic Production Process in Practice on 'Peer Gynt.'" *Theatre Quarterly* 13 (February–April 1974).

Rouse, John. "Brecht and the Question of the Audience." In *The Brecht Yearbook* 15: *Essays on Brecht/ Versuche über Brecht.* Edited by Marc Silberman, John Fuegi, Renate Voris, and Carl Weber, 111–123. College Park, Md.: International Brecht Society, 1990.

————. *Brecht and the West German Theatre.* Ann Arbor: UMI Research P, 1989.

Rozik, Eli. "Plot Analysis and Speech Act Theory." In *Signs of Humanity/ L'homme et ses signes.* Vol. 2. Edited by Michel Balat and Janice Deledalle-Rhodes, 1183–1191. Berlin: Mouton de Gruyter, 1992.

————. "Theatrical Speech Acts: a theater semiotics approach." *Kodikas/Code* 12, no. 1/2 (1989): 41–55.

Rühle, Günther. *Theater für die Republik 1917–1933 im Spiegel der Kritik.* 2 volumes. Frankfurt am Main: S. Fischer, 1967. Invaluable collection of reviews for every major production in Germany during the Weimar Republic.

————. "Was an uns ist noch Peer?" [What in us is still Peer?] *Theater Heute* 13 (1971): 29.

Rülicke-Weiler, Käthe. "Brecht and Weigel at the Berliner Ensemble." *New Theatre Quarterly* 7 (February 1991): 3–19.

Said, Edward. *Orientalism.* New York: Vintage, 1979.

Salter, Denis. "Hand Eye Mind Soul: Théâtre du Soleil's *Les Atrides.*" *Theatre* 1 (1993): 59–65.

Sartre, Jean-Paul. "Myth and Reality in Theatre." In *Sartre on Theatre*. Edited by Michel Contat and Michel Rybalka, translated by Frank Jellinek, 135–157. New York: Pantheon, 1976.

———. "Théâtre épique et théâtre dramatique." In his *Un Théâtre de situations*. Paris: Gallimard, 1973.

Scott, Virginia. "Context and Interpretation: Two Experiences of *Les Atrides.*" Paper at the Mid-America Theater Conference, Minneapolis, March 12, 1994.

Silberman, Marc, ed. *drive b: Brecht 100. Theater der Zeit/ Brecht Yearbook*. Collection of essays, in German and English. Madison and Berlin: International Brecht Society/ Berliner Ensemble, 1998.

———. "The Politics of Representation: Brecht and the Media." *Theatre Journal* 39 (issue "Distancing Brecht") (December 1987): 446–460.

———. "A Postmodernized Brecht?" *Theatre Journal* 45 (issue "German Theatre after the F/Wall.") (March 1993): 1–20.

Singleton, Brian. "Receiving *Les Atrides* Productively: Intercultural Signs as Intertexts." *Theatre Research International* 22 (1997): 19–23.

Smith, Iris. "Brecht and the Mothers of Epic Theatre." *Theatre Journal* 43 (December 1991): 491–505.

Spivak, Gayatri Chakravorty. "Can the Subaltern Speak?" In *Marxism and the Interpretation of Culture*. Edited by C. Nelson and L. Grossberg, 271–313. Urbana and Chicago: U of Illinois P, 1988.

Stein, Peter. Interview with Bernard Dort. In *Travail théâtral* (1972): 34–35.

———. Interview with Eberhard Sprenge. *Theater Heute* 12 (1971): 10.

Stockenström, Göran. "Charles XII as Historical Drama." In *Strindberg's Dramaturgy*, edited by Stockenström, 41–55. Minneapolis: U of Minnesota P, 1988.

Stuart, Jan. "A French Innovator Brings a Mega-Theatre Event to New York." *Fanfare*, September 27, 1992, 1-3.

Strindberg, August. *Queen Christina, Charles XII, Gustav III*. Translated by Walter Johnson. Seattle: U of Washington P, 1955.

Tatlow, Antony. "Analysis and Countertransference" In *The Other Brecht I/Der andere Brecht I: Brecht Yearbook* 17, eds. Hans-Thies Lehmann and Renate Voris, 125–133. Madison, WI.: International Brecht Society, 1992.

———. *The Mask of Evil: Brecht's Response to the Poetry, Theatre and Thought of China and Japan*. Bern: Peter Lang, 1977.

Taxidou, Olga. "Crude Thinking: John Fuegi and Recent Brecht Criticism." *New Theatre Quarterly* 11 (November 1995): 381–384.

Theatre Journal 39. Issue "Distancing Brecht." (December 1987).

Theatre Journal 4. Issue "German Theatre after the F/Wall." (March 1993).

Théâtre populaire. Journal of theater studies published 1949–1960. Essays on Brecht, epic theater, and the Berliner Ensemble appeared in this journal, until 1954 almost solely by Bernard Dort, then, after the Berliner Ensemble's first visit to Paris in 1954, also by Roland Barthes.

Thomas, Natalie. "Les Costumes et les Maquillages" [Costumes and makeup]. *Théâtre Aujourd'hui 1: La Tragédie Grecque. Les Atrides au Théâtre du Soleil*. Paris: CNDP, 1992, 30–34.

Tuan, Yi-Fu. *Space and Place: The Perspective of Experience*. Minneapolis: U of Minnesota P, 1977.

——. *Topophilia*. Minneapolis: U of Minnesota P, 1974.

Ubersfeld, Anne. *Lire le Théâtre* [Reading the theater]. Paris: Éditions sociales, 1982.

——. *L'Objet théâtral* [The theatrical object]. Paris: CNDP, 1978.

——. "The Space of *Phèdre*." *Poetics Today* 2 (Spring 1981): 201–210.

Ubersfeld, Anne, with Georges Banu. *L'Éspace théâtral* [The theatrical space]. Paris: CNDP, 1978.

Weber, Carl. "Brecht as Director" (1967). In *The Director in a Changing Theatre*. Edited by J. Robert Wills. Palo Alto, Ca.: Mayfield, 1976.

Weber, Samuel. *Mass Mediauras. Form, Technics, Media*. Edited by Alan Cholodenko. Stanford: Stanford UP, 1996.

——. "Taking Place: Towards a Theater of Dislocation." *Enclitic* (Fall 1985): 124–143.

Werkstatt Bertolt Brecht / The Brecht Workshop. Guide to Brecht's films. Edited by Bruno Fischli and Angelika Gutsche, English translations by Robert W. Rice. In German and English. Munich: Goethe Institute, 1997.

White, Hayden. *Tropics of Discourse*. Baltimore: Johns Hopkins UP, 1978.

Willet, John. *The Theatre of Erwin Piscator: Fifty Years of Politics in the Theatre*. London: Eyre Methuen, 1978.

Williams, David, ed. *Collaborative Theatre: The Théâtre du Soleil, a Sourcebook*. Translations by Eric Prenowitz and David Williams. London and New York: Routledge, 1999.

Winer, Linda. In "The Splendid Pageantry of Greek Tragedy," *New York Newsday*, October 6, 1991,

Wright, Elisabeth. *Postmodern Brecht*. London and New York: Routledge, 1989.

Yeats, William Butler. "The Gyres," 1936, and "The Second Coming," 1921. *The Collected Poems of W. B. Yeats.* New York: Macmillan, 1956, 291 and 184–185.

Index